Praise for

Aromatic Alchemy – Recipes for Transformation

❖ *Soothe your soul with 'recipes for transformation' from Ixchel Leigh's book,* Aromatic Alchemy. *The book shows you how to use alchemy, aromatherapy and vibrational medicine to heal your life.* (YOU Magazine UK)

— **Josephine Fairley,** author of *Organic Beauty,*
The Ultimate Natural Beauty Book, and many more.
Co-Founder of The Perfume Society, London, UK

❖ *Ixchel is a visionary in her own rite, having explored and mastered the subtle chemistry of perfumery for over forty years. And in her book,* Aromatic Alchemy, *she brings to us the magical world of vibrational aromatherapy. She takes perfumery beyond the pleasure of scent, and helps us to understand the powerful alchemy of the plant kingdom. An inspiration to all who enjoy essential oils and for those who want to deepen their intentional use, to create their own magic.*

— **Tara Grodjesk,** Founder and President, Tara Spa Therapy,
VP Earthlite-Spa Wellness Products;
Co-Founder, Green Spa Network (GSN)

❖ *If you have this book, you don't need any other!* Aromatic Alchemy *is a gift for all of us searching for the passion in our life. So we don't get lost along the way, Ixchel Leigh has provided an incredible and thorough map for us to follow. Experience the heart that comes through the pages of* Aromatic Alchemy *and begin your journey.*

— **Julie Shaw,** Julie Shaw Jewelry Designs, artist,
and Reiki Master, Cocoa, Florida USA

❖ *I can only recommend this book,* Aromatic Alchemy, *as an enjoyable experience that offers ideas about transformation and in the process makes for a practical, sensible, sensuous encounter. This book—and the tools suggested—has the capacity to attune with you and vibrate with you and make life that little bit better.*

— **Jan Kusmirek,** Medical Herbalist and
founder of Fragrant Earth, Glastonbury, UK

❖ Aromatic Alchemy *is a book that honors, ignites, and brings understanding to the mystery of alchemy. It demonstrates practical ways to learn about aromatherapy and provides guidelines for self-study. A wonderful source that celebrated and honors life.*

— **Angeles Arrien,** PhD., Cultural Anthropologist,
author of *The Four Fold Way, Signs of Life,* and *The Nine Muses*

❖ *Finally—an understandable book about aromatherapy, the subject that everyone is talking about.* Aromatic Alchemy *gives a comprehensive overview which ties aromatherapy to the wider world of metaphysics, as well as having details that a more serious student would be seeking.*

— **Shelley von Strunckel,** Internationally published astrologer
and consultant, London, UK

❖ *A beautifully-written, insightful, and thought-provoking look at the power of essential oils to heal, uplift and help us achieve our goals in life. Ixchel takes us on a journey of scent, intuition and the power of nature to gracefully shift our lives and achieve our fullest and most beautiful potential.*

— **Zhena Muzyka,** Author, Life by the Cup,
Success Coach and Founder of Club Magic Hour

❖ *Ixchel has been a friend and occasional collaborator for many, many years. She brings an insightful calm and spiritual wisdom to aromatherapy, which manifests in her remarkable talent for working 'magic' with essential oil blends.*

— **Robert Tisserand,** *Essential Oil Safety*-2nd Edition,
expert in aromatherapy and essential oil research

AROMATIC ALCHEMY

Recipes for Transformation

Ixchel Leigh

Second Edition
Revised and Updated

and introducing
AlcheMystical Parfumerie

PARK PLACE PUBLICATIONS
Pacific Grove, California

Aromatic Alchemy
Recipes For Transformation

by Ixchel Leigh
Second Edition, Revised and Updated 2020

ISBN 978-1-943887-83-5 softcover
ISBN 978-1-94887-84-2 casebound

Published by Park Place Publications, Pacific Grove, California

Library of Congress Control Number: 2019920413

Note to the reader: This book is intended as an informational guide. The recipes,
remedies, approaches, and techniques described herein are meant to supplement,
and not to be a substitute for professional medical care or treatment. They should
not be used to treat serious ailments without prior consultation with a qualified
healthcare professional.

Additional copies of this book may be ordered from indie bookstores,
and on-line booksellers. For further information and book signing events with
Ixchel Leigh visit: AromaticAlchemyBook.com

Dedicated to

Nature ... with all of Her gifts
And to Humanity ... may we grow evermore in wisdom.

If you would have the message of the Gods to direct your life, look for that which repeats, again and again; for this is the message given you by the Gods, the karmic lesson you must learn for this incarnation. It comes again and again until you have made it part of your soul and your enduring spirit. Flower and even fruit are only the beginning. In the seed lies the life and the future ... and what I am lies hidden, as the rose lies hidden within the seed.

– Marion Zimmer Bradley,
The Mists of Avalon

Twenty years from now you will be more disappointed by the things that you didn't do than by the ones you did do. So throw off the bowlines. Sail away from the safe harbor. Catch the trade winds in your sails. Explore. Dream. Discover.

– Mark Twain

... The mere self or mere I—a self that does not inherently exist—goes from one lifetime to another. Also, even though consciousness is closely related with matter, consciousness is an entity of mere luminosity and knowing and thus cannot be produced from matter (it) must be produced in dependence upon a former moment of mere luminosity and knowing. Therefore, the continuum of consciousness also has no beginning and no end ....

– Fourteenth Dalai Lama,
Kindness, Clarity and Insight

Table of Contents

Acknowledgements

*All inspiration is accompanied
by the ability to fulfill itself.* (Unknown)

It was a hot summer night that woke me from a hard-to-attain sleep.

Wide awake …. What is this? Was that a dream? Is it close to time to get up already?

I hadn't fallen asleep 'til very late, my mind circling around the rewrites for this book. My hand looked for the phone beside my bed. *12:45 am! It's only 12:45 in the morning?*

"Get up!" I obeyed the voice, which was not in the room with me.

"Write it down. The story. It's for the opening of the new edition of AA."

"Help me to remember," I said as I closed my eyes and took some deep breaths…

* * *

We were all in a large room. Everyone. Large. Small. Young. Old. I said, "Let's play a game. See those marbles you all are holding in your hands? Whoever gets the most marbles into the sunken hole in the center of the room, will get to kiss the one they love again. On your mark, get set, go!"

The cacophony in the room from all those marbles clanging into each other began, and it was deafening even in my sleep. My Granny looked at me sitting behind her. Her old wrinkled hands were shriveled, small, and crippled with arthritis, but her eyes glowed with a twinkle. She winked an eye at me. I started rolling the pile of marbles in front of me to her, as fast as her little hand could pick them up. She turned around facing the hole in the ground. That's all she could see. Her whole focus was on the target. She swirled (it looked like a swirl, Granny style) facing me again for the next marble.

I darted it to her. One after the other, rapid-fire. Again, Granny repeated her swift firing, her concentration solidly on the mark. The marbles kept shooting from everyone towards the central hole. And from me to Granny, I could see her intention was fixed in her head and intense. Nothing would dissuade her from her focus, and it took every ounce of her strength and attention for her frail body to get the most marbles in that pit.

"DONE!!! Last marble in." I yelled so quickly and loudly, my voice surprised even me, and the room went stoned-silent in disbelief. "Granny got the most marbles in the hole. Sixty-five of them. One for each year of her marriage to her boyfriend."

My Granny rose up to her full four-feet-six-inches. She brushed off her apron and swiped the silver lock of hair that fell from her normally immaculate swooshed back hairdo. "I'm not going to miss one opportunity to kiss that beautiful boy of mine." She said as she walked towards her husband, who was still her boyfriend in her heart.

* * *

PASSION! While this actual story was a dream, somewhere out there I know it's true for someone's Granny. However, it was inspired by both my grandmother, and her daughter, my mother. "Live life with passion" is what I inherited from them. As long as there is breath in you, find something to inspire you and go for it! Focus. Intention. Attention. Life's challenges come and go. But find within you something to feel passionately about and send that marble towards it with all you have in you.

* * *

Divine Source – I have come again to find the balance of both my spirit and my physical in this life. You are guide and teacher, loving and accepting. The Great Mystery of all Creation, thank you, I am in Gratitude.

My beloved husband, David, who consults with writers on writer's block and wrote a book, *The Blocked Writer's Book of the Dead*. Silently and with abundance patience, you watched me for a few years, at a time when my creative writing had halted after major surgery for cancer. You never criticized, or tried to give me your expert advice (while others paid you for it). I am healthy and thriving now, and back with a sweet vengeance. Thank you dearest husband, my eternal friend and lover, for always believing in me, for truly seeing me for all that I am, and for *only* encouraging me to follow my dreams and my passions. You are my manifested dream and my love passion.

My treasured son, Adam, you bring me forever love and delight. And to Melissa, your wife, you are a precious happiness for me, whom I call daughter.

My daughters shared from David: Meehan and Alison, I am joyous to call you my daughters and to know you as women. And to granddaughter Millie, I treasure watching you grow.

My sisters by blood: Joni, Laurie, and Cara ... we deeply and lovingly share blood and history, which is more-and-more important to me everyday.

To Carol Corio, you once again stepped up and edited this Second Edition. You are invaluable to me and to *Vibrational AromaTherapy*. We work magically together, weaving each of our left-brains and our right-brains, to perfect the format.

To Patricia Hamilton, my publisher: thank you for producing a book whose beautiful interior is modern and scented (it feels like it).

To Kristen Ruth Smith: you executed an exquisitely magical book cover, which makes my mouth water with delight.

To Zhena Muzyka: you champion my writing and encourage me

to continue my sensuous literary prose, and as a result, I am inspired to write. And thank you for showing me how to write my website from scratch and what branding looks like in the 21st Century!

To my loved other daughters and sisters by choice: some of you, we have shared moments together, and others we have grown together for years. You may live where I'm living now (Ojai, California) or in one of the other cities or countries I've visited or lived in. I talk to you in real-time or in spirit-time. Each of you … know that often I see something in the clouds, or when a bird visits, and a smile lights my visage with sweet thoughts of you. Keep dreaming your dreams.

To my grandmother Evelyn and mother Patricia … I learn from your actions, always finding something to dream towards.

To my father Richard, an original sensitive, who followed his heart with his family and his brain with his detective work … I am both sides of you.

To all those who are guided to this book, I share a part of me with you. Know that each one of you holds a unique place in the world, which is honored. In honoring yourself, you invite others to honor you, and our world changes.

I am in gratitude for the profoundness of all of Nature, where I find deep serenity and mystical inspiration.

> "That which is a mystery
> shall no longer be so,
> and that which has been veiled
> will now be revealed;
> that which has been withdrawn
> will emerge into the light,
> and all men shall see
> and together they shall rejoice."
> **– Alice Bailey, *The Rays and the Initiations***

Dance Your Dream

Whatever you can do, or dream you can, begin it.
Boldness has genius, power and magic in it. Begin it now.
– Goethe

Dreams carry us forward in life. At eighteen, I wanted to become a high fashion model in Paris. At twenty I did! Yet I changed my focus at least three times before discovering my Essence Self and my true heart's desire in my forties. And each time it took courage to pursue my new dreams.

Years ago, I was invited to speak to a graduating group of high school students who were about to step out into the world to express their individuality. "What makes your heart sing?" I asked. Many responded with "I don't know." Then I asked, "What are you going to do after graduation?" Most responded that they had no idea. As some of the youth were telling me what their plans were, I sensed that I was actually listening to their parent's words. Not often do I hear a young person's own voice. Often, our direction is designed by our parent's wishes (or another adult's) plans or goals for us.

When there is little *passion* behind a chosen direction, this is a good clue that your soul is not guiding you in this decision. Possibly, many of you have accepted this: You are expected to do work in the world, which you *do not* enjoy, because that is just what you do to support yourself. This is an accepted lifestyle. Or continuing doing work that was once fun and challenging (yet is no longer) is "just what you are supposed to do." I feel that by following someone else's idea of what you should do, often leads to an increase of stress and disease. I'm not stating this as fact. Nor do I ask you to blindly accept my observation. I have asked this question of myself (and of those close to me, friends and loved ones) and I ask you: What makes your heart sing? What do you love to do?

Most of us want intimacy in at least one relationship in our life, yet few really allow ourselves to be so *vulnerable* as to truly *feel intimate with another*. Intimacy opens you up to being vulnerable. You must bear your soul, your heart, your heart's joy, your disappointments, and your desires when you are truly intimate. Answering this question honestly can make you feel very vulnerable. You *must* be extremely intimate with yourself, and it begins by being honest. What truly are *your* dreams? After you try this intimate cloak on in the privacy of a personal moment with yourself ("moment" is figurative here for it can take years to answer this question), it will be easier to allow someone else to see you in your most vulnerable, open, honest, and intimate Essence Self.

Live what brings you joy. If what you are doing doesn't bring joy, then possibly it's time to consider another path, option, or choice? Life is too fleeting to not feel the singing and joy of your heart. I am eternally grateful for finding the courage to pursue my passions. So be brave. Step up. Dance your Dream! Isabela Burani says, "When we take TIME to dream, we discover the many windows to our SOUL."

– Ixchel Leigh
Ojai, California 2020

Foreword

by Jan Kusmirek

Alchemy is a word that reeks of history, of magic, of the secret, of the illicit, of the beginning of science. It evokes the images of mathematics, secret codes and the transformation or transmutation of base metal to gold. The word provokes ideas of mystery, of sacred union, secret societies and hidden meanings. Much of this is a misconception and indeed much of the mystery surrounding alchemy was to do with trade protectionism rather than something deep and unavailable.

For example, most people have heard of Nostradamus as a prophet and seer and the mysterious doctor of alchemy. Few people realise that outside of his sensational prophecies and verses that he wrote some very down to earth and practical things, perhaps we could say the real alchemy. His books cover such matters as preparing Benzoin oil, making body moisturisers, making aromatic soaps, darkening and lightening hair, tooth powder, making jams, preserves, sweets and scented waters.

These practical matters seem a far cry from alchemy yet all were made with attention to detail and a resonance to his universal truth of the five elements. Perhaps today he would be described as an esoteric man or healer and that is how I would describe Ixchel Leigh, whom I have known for many years.

As a lover of essential oils, I have long subscribed to the view of vital energies that suffuses or drives all living things. It is obvious to anyone that one essential oil is not the same as another and that chemical analysis does not deal in the perceptions of the soul that the nose discovers in every nuance of fragrance. To every action there is a reaction, a principle of physics and alchemy.

We live in a multi-dimensional world, both seen and unseen, yet perceived. As a multi-dimensionalist, it was Ixchel Leigh who first introduced me to the marrying of one substance to another to reinforce activity with the object of transformation rather than a simple chemical change. I must admit it was with a great deal of scepticism when I first received one of her massage oils containing a gemstone. I cannot say that the oil transformed my life! I can say that it set me thinking and I therefore commend to you this book as one to open your mind to perhaps a different way of thinking, one that is possibly more akin to our ancestors than to modern day rational, linear or mechanistic thought.

The use of essential oils in recent years for psychotherapeutic work or for the promotion of health and wellbeing has been loosely termed aromatherapy. Aromatherapy means different things to different people. There is a move afoot to make the term more scientific by the application of chemical analysis. That is if you know what it is made of, you know what it will do, a simple mechanistic and rationalist approach.

Alchemy, however inconvenient, formed the basis of modern day science. It may be that such mediaeval scientists had a different way of expressing themselves yet fundamentally they were establishing a methodology to produce an end result. They may have seen the world as made of earth, wind, fire, and water yet perhaps unlike mechanistic science today they also accepted a fifth element – something ethereal that was neither solid nor gas, yet could be both and which formed a link between heaven and earth. This fifth element gave its name to essential oils, more correctly called quintessential oils. They exist in a liquid state and could only be appreciated in a gaseous or evaporated state through their aroma. This unto itself harked back to the oldest ideas of our ancestors whereby the gods were appeased by the magic smoke of incense or perfume (*par fumum*). In Judeo Christian theology, prayers of the righteous are carried to God by such fragrant smoke.

Such ideas rested upon the concept of vibration, now enshrined in modern physics, each element, each molecule, vibrates to a tune which should be harmonic. Such ideas are as old as Plato and beyond. It is to such ideas that Ixchel Leigh has subscribed since her entry into aromatherapy. It was she who promoted the idea of colour and gem being united with fragrance in aroma. Latterly, she developed a system of what she calls *Vibrational Aroma Therapy by Ixchel™*, one that is in the true spirit of alchemy and transformation. At *Fragrant Earth*, we had long subscribed to the view that essential oils were affected by conscious intent and throughout Ixchel's work this aspect or feature comes very much to the fore. Providing a set of *Tools for Transformation* has been useful to many people.

At first glance, such things may seem naive or out of place and not at all right for mainline scientific thought. Such views are naive unto themselves. Symbolism is a unique human experience and our emotional or other cells are affected by the vibration of colour or visual form or pattern or by the sensation of touch and so on. The vibration of sound moves most of us and few are untouched by the vibration of aroma that reaches our emotions at hidden depths. So it is that something essentially simple can provide transformation.

Ixchel Leigh has always stressed the need for purity and working as near to nature as is possible. In today's world, nature is seen as a resource and provides diminishing returns. The alchemists of old knew that – the time of day, method of harvest, even the phase of moon could affect the health aspect or vibration of a plant. Today we are just on the edge of beginning to understand that these were not old wives tales of no value, yet may prove to be significant beyond our expectations.

Ixchel is a receiver of information, a communicant. What we put on or into our bodies or receive through our senses can therefore act upon us at very deep levels. This is the point of the exercises and ideas put forward within this work. It implies that one cannot simply substitute a synthetic substance for a natural substance or to translate one essential oil or herbal extract from one part of the world, industrialise it and expect it to work as well as something simply grown or wild crafted from its natural habitat.

One could almost say that the alchemist shrouded in mystery was the opposite to the shaman or druid working in the wild wood, yet they had a lot in common, of the understanding of doing things properly, of respect for nature. This respect may have manifested itself in tradition or in ceremony, which in our fast food society we treat as of no consequence. Looked at from the point of view of vibration or attunement or harmony, doing things in certain ways or with the right consciousness begins to make more sense.

Ixchel Leigh encourages people to work at the etheric physical interface, without prejudice or misconception, encouraging individual approaches, treatments, transformations, and transmutations. Certainly the system put together is a work of art, of skill in the traditional sense, a work of alchemy, a work of magic yet subscribing to principles, which are innate within us all, encouraging us to a state of balance and wellbeing. It is a world of experience rather than of dry academia and delightfully the work does not pretend to be more than it is.

One of the problems that I see with past alchemy and those who apply alchemy to essential oils today is the confusion brought about by trying to look important rather than by being practical. In alchemy, transformation came about in a multi-fold process and often the goal of the transformation got and gets lost in the theory. This work teaches the use of simple tools, everyday materials to reach ones personal point of balance.

I can only recommend this book, *Aromatic Alchemy*, as an enjoyable experience that may be transforming and in the process makes for a practical, sensible, sensuous encounter. This book – and the tools suggested – has the capacity to attune with you and vibrate with you and make life that little bit better.

* * *

—Jan Kusmirek is known internationally for his work with natural plant materials and aromatics. He trained in medical herbalism, naturopathy, nutrition, and aromatherapy. An early pioneer in aromatherapy, he writes and lectures globally. He founded the companies, Fragrant Earth and Fragrant Studies, located in Glastonbury, England. The companies are entirely naturopathic in approach and philosophy, working with the vital energies of plant material in order to supply all that nature has intended. They are suppliers of the highest quality raw materials, essential oils and products, all meeting the standards and needs of therapists worldwide.

P. Elder '85

PART ONE

Transmute, Transform, Transcend

To dare is to lose one's footing momentarily.
To not dare is to lose oneself.
– Soren Kierkegaard

Chapter 1

The Energetics of Metamorphosis

*Insanity is doing the same thing over and over again
and expecting a different result.*
– Albert Einstein

Many people speak about "transcending the body" and "transforming the spirit." There is much confusion about these concepts and about the words transmute, transform, and transcend.

- ❖ Transmute – to change or alter appearance, especially to a higher form
- ❖ Transform – to change form from one to another on a deep cellular level
- ❖ Transcend – to go beyond limitation

Many see the physical body as a limitation. For me, the body is the vehicle through which I am blessed to experience all of my senses, to – touch, taste, smell, hear, see, and feel. I consider it a blessing and an honor to be able to experience these. We humans, as multi-dimensional beings, are here on the Earth Mother to transform and transmute the body by using what is available to us. We transcend any limitation we might feel, and we become all that we can be! For our transformation, we can use the gifts or talents given to us at birth, as well as the many gifts that Nature provides.

Creating Sacred Space – Beauty Spaces

In my *atelier* (creative studio), as well as in my home, car, and office space, I have created many beauty spaces. A beauty space is a special place where I have put things that remind me of the beauty of life: of my beauty, of the sacredness of all life, and of the beauty in Nature and all around me. These beauty spaces are also called altars. Each of these beauty spaces has a different theme. One of my beauty spaces is all white (with shells, rocks, feathers and little boxes) reminding me of my unity with Divine Source.

Another is for my family, with photos and memorabilia. And another beauty space has natural tobacco, a feathered fan, pictures and fetishes of birds and animals that hold particular meaning for me. Even my desk, where I write at the computer, has its designated corner of beauty! I encourage you to try this for yourselves. Beauty spaces are a distinct reminder of the sacredness of every aspect of our lives.

A Spiritual Path and Net-working

What is a spiritual path? It has nothing to do with a particular religion. It is an inner feeling and commitment ... you acknowledge that there is a spiritual force, a Divine Source guiding you. This also means that you are doing your best to make choices that honor you. Everyday you are doing something that reminds you that you are moving closer towards being the essence of who you really are, and you are holding the vision of your dreams.

When we acknowledge to ourselves that we are on a spiritual path, we eventually search for others of like-mind and heart. Net-working means to connect with others of who share with you a common connection. My vision is that all those individuals on a spiritual path are as light beams. Our "light beams" are sent out around the world. When we meet another person and share a connection, we connect for whatever short or long a time period.

Picture our Earth Mother with all of these light beams criss-crossing around her. As these connecting and crossing light beams increase, they begin to form a net, thus ... net-working! The net of light holds the world safe through any darkness. This concept follows the hundredth monkey theory ... when one or more are gathered with the same thought, that thought is expanded to others. Scientists have discovered that when one monkey learned something new (for example to use a new tool) that other monkeys (even those not directly in the same study, yet possibly across the world) began to use the tool in the same way. Somehow, through osmosis, they just knew how to use the tool too.

We live in an exciting age, often fluctuating between joy and uncertainty. Balancing dreams with reality is more important than ever in the twenty-first century. It appears to be a lesson for all of humanity. Our creativity, resourcefulness, imagination, and inspiration must be enlivened for us to become all that we can be. As individuals, we owe it to ourselves to try to effect these changes. Our world will change only when the individual does.

A Larger Perspective

We cannot attempt our personal transformation without taking into consideration the larger perspective, Gaia, the Earth Mother. For the past several hundred years, humans have generally thought of the earth as here solely for their needs – mere dirt, a tireless sphere to call home, with endless and inexhaustible resources. Indigenous peoples and ancient cultures have generally remembered their connection to the Divine. They remembered their close relationship to the Earth Mother as Sustainer of Life, the Mother who nurtures all beings: humans, animals, fish, birds, minerals, plants, and the great bodies of water.

It is time to heal not only us, yet in doing so heal all. It is time to heal the Earth Mother. It is time to remember the importance of walking gently on the Earth Mother, respecting her and using only what we absolutely need. It is time to pay attention to preserving her resources and eliminating pollution and waste. With great influence as inhabitants on the Earth Mother, we effect change for all as we heal our bodies and transform our spirit.

I close this chapter offering my vision: May each step you take in your life hold promise. May you trust yourself. May you feel joy when you are in Nature. May you love deeply.

Chapter 2

Alchemy and Physics

... the key of all good things, the Art of Art, the Science of Sciences.

– Bonus of Ferrara, 14th Century, *On Alchemy*

The web of relationships and their inter-connectedness is the essence of all Life. To understand this natural phenomenon and try to perfect it has been the focus of all humanity since time immemorial. *Everything is related* – whether it is called by a name that refers to a form of science (whose purpose is to describe, observe, identify, investigate, experiment, or theorize on an explanation of nature) or humankind's need to discover their purpose for being (which takes many forms and many different philosophies).

The word *metaphysics* is derived from the Greek language, *meta ka physika*. When literally translated, it means *after the things of nature*. The term was first used in Hellenistic Greece to classify the philosopher Aristotle's volumes of writing. Based on Aristotle's writings, the original meaning of metaphysics meant "after the physics" or after the physical world. Modern day metaphysics recognizes that there is a world beyond what can be perceived on the physical plane, that all is composed of energy, and that every individual has both a physical and a non-physical body. Metaphysics today acknowledges the unseen realities of our universe.

The Philosophy of Alchemy and Physics

The philosophical alchemist and the philosophical physicist might ask the same questions: What is the secret of all creation? What is life force made of? The philosophy of alchemy and of physics, find relationship to each other:

❖ *Alchemy* : The study of related and unrelated materials and how they interact and connect together with the intention of bringing about changes that creates a more perfected form and with aspirations of seeking knowledge of creation and universal order.

❖ *Physics* : The study of related and unrelated materials, matter and energy, and how they interact and are connected together, with a purpose to discover the true laws of nature in order to create a more perfected form and with aspirations of seeking knowledge of natural phenomena.

The Origins of Alchemy

There are many different ideas about the word alchemy and its derivation. It is likely derived from the Arabic *al kimia*. It may also have connections to the Greek word *chyma*, the fusing and casting of metal and to the Egyptian word *chem*, signifying black.

Alchemy, whether in ancient Eastern or Western civilizations, has always been focused on the gathering and seeking of knowledge about creation and universal laws, with a focus on transformation. Alchemy in the East found its primary preoccupation and focus through creating the elixir for longevity. By the twelfth century, most European countries had decided to study alchemy. However, by now its reputation varied from being worthy of being practiced by royalty to being looked upon as a pursuit only by charlatans.

Hermes Trismegistus is referred to as the patron saint of alchemy. Through dreams and visions, he brought forth to the Western world the concept of the alchemical process. Through his revelations, he was guided and instructed about the relationship between the body, spirit, and soul as they relate to the elements and the numerous aspects of alchemy and symbolism. The great body of his collected works on alchemy is often referred to as *The Hermetic Work*, which was found in an ancient text, called the Kybalion.

The Hermetic Work includes the seven Hermetic Principles (or

Laws). Looked upon as truths by those who feel aligned to the principles of alchemy, everything in the Universe abides by these Laws.

The Hermetic Principles

1. Principle of Mentalism – All is mind; the universe is absolute thought.
2. Principle of Correspondence – As above, so below; as below, so above.
3. Principle of Vibration – Nothing rests; everything moves and vibrates.
4. Principle of Polarity – Everything is dual; like and unlike are the same.
5. Principle of Rhythm – Everything flows, out and in, everything has tides; all things rise and fall.
6. Principle of Cause and Effect – Every cause has its effect; every effect has its cause; Chance is yet a name for Law not recognized.
7. Principle of Gender – Gender is in everything; everything has its masculine and feminine principle; gender manifests on all planes.

The Alchemist and the Alchemical Purpose

The purpose of alchemy is to raise the vibration of the original substance, or *prima materia*, into its most perfected form. Alchemy can really be looked upon as a metaphor for transformation or as a symbol for the powerful transmutation that can occur when you *focus your intention.*

One could describe the purpose of alchemy and the pursuit of transformation in the same way as the following quote from Arthur Cotterell in *A Dictionary of World Mythology*:

"Eskimo art reflects the absence of the notion of creation. There is no real equivalent of our words 'create' or 'make.' The closest term means 'to work on;' it is a restrained kind of activity, like the aim of the Eskimo carver of ivory to release the characteristic form of the piece in hand."

To the ancients the underlying foundation of alchemy was to produce the *Philosopher's Stone*, the Elixir or Tincture. Once this Elixir was produced, it was the substance that was credited with having the ability to turn base metals into gold. The transmutation into gold signaled the mark of success; however, *the power was in the Elixir itself*, which was the transmuting agent. The Elixir, as the agent of transformation, also held the *secret* of transformation both for the physical and spiritual realms. A. E. Waite, author of *The Hermetic Museum*, refers to the Elixir as, "the perfect essence of all the elements, the indestructible body which no element can injure, the quintessence ... the most precious of all treasures."

Puffers, Initiates, and Adepts

The Puffer Alchemist is one who is "full of hot air." The Puffer might say that the purpose of alchemy is to raise the vibration of a base metal in order to turn it into gold. Yet the idea of turning metal into gold is *only* the very basic concept of the purpose of alchemy. This makes intellectual sense, for humans value gold more than lead. Gold has a higher vibration than base metals; if it didn't, it would be no more valuable than lead! Puffers see this as the *only* goal of alchemy and use *only* their intellect in their attempt to discover the secret of the transmutation of metal into gold.

The Initiate Alchemist is an alchemist who is in the beginning of their quest for understanding alchemy as in its totality of forms, the art of transformation. Initiates, as seekers, will find themselves on a new path of discovery looking beyond just the transmutation of metal into gold, to Nature and to the natural world for other signs and direction about the transformation process. They use and trust their intuition as a guide, and they observe and use the many Gifts from Nature and the natural world that are presented to them along their path.

The Adept Alchemist is an alchemist who understands that the true work in alchemy is the *art of transformation*. The Adept knows that the work of the alchemist is to invite succeeding changes in the *prima materia*, the original substance, bringing about a transformation to its perfected form. In the metaphor that alchemy truly is, the *prima materia*, also refers to each human being.

Each of us has an inner quest to perfect our individual nature – to be all that we possibly can be. What is this *prima materia* as it relates to you? The totality of all of the essence of you – Body, Heart, Spirit, Mind, and Soul. Perfecting all of you, the *prima materia*, involves physical, psychological, and spiritual work. Therefore, alchemy is as much to do with self-mastery as it is the mastery of the physical laws of Nature. Neither can be achieved without patience, observation, and devotion. The *art* of the Alchemist is the assistance given to activate a process that transforms the *prima materia* into the gold. Gold is the symbol of the perfected form, or the perfected self, your Essence Self.

Transformation with Alchemy

Everything must be in harmony for the process of alchemy to work. The *prima materia*, YOU, must hold the intention. You must be ready and willing to make the changes, to want transformation for yourself. In order to effect change, you need to gather all your tools. The tools you will need are whatever resonates with your sensibilities and whatever assists you in igniting the flame for your personal growth (transformation). You have many options to choose from in this book!

You as the *prima materia* are also the Alchemist. The entire process of alchemy is the education itself: recognizing the potential hindrances that obstruct your path, the epiphanies, and the ah-ha's.

Discovering your individuation, exploring how best to express the essence of whom you are in the world and realizing that you are an important part of the whole of humanity. Remembering your connection to the *whole of the universe* is an important part of the alchemical process.

This requires us to live consciously. Living consciously requires each one of us to feel our connection to everything around us – to all humans, to all of Nature, and to a Divine Source. The entire purpose of transformational alchemy, however many steps it takes, is similar to the unfolding of the creation of the world, which the alchemist is both the creator of the transformation and the witness watching the transmutation.

Alchemy is not merely a physical process, nor solely a spiritual one; it is the combination of both. It is our potential to be all what we can be. Your path is full of possibilities.

Ouroboros

The dragon is very symbolic in alchemy. In ancient texts, you will see a dragon biting its tail called *ouroboros*. The *ouroboros* represents the cyclical nature of both life and the work in alchemy. It is also a reminder that each of us already possesses exactly what we hope to achieve. In different words, on some other level of reality, our hopes, dreams, and desires are already a reality. We just need to match our current perceptions with this other level of reality, by focusing our intentions and attentions on our hopes, dreams, and desires.

The Sacred Marriage

Also in ancient texts you will see drawings of a double-headed dragon breathing fire upon the sun and moon which represent the male and female energies (archetypes or principles). They are called opposites and create a polarity. One of the key processes in alchemy is to unite these opposites. We cannot have the sun without the moon, nor male without female. Within our own personalities, our own male and female energies must be united (married) for us to be whole.

The Buddha said, "Essence without dualism is nonabiding. Know that all things are like this." This quote means that everything has its opposite, its other half, or its polarity. In alchemy, the uniting of the male and female energy is often depicted as the union of King and Queen and referred to as the Sacred Marriage. The integration of the polarity of opposites, the "marriage" of the masculine and feminine energies, is the Sacred Marriage. This union must take place within each one of us before we can truly be whole.

Adapted from a medieval sketch depicting the Sacred Marriage – The unity of opposites: Moon/Sun, Queen/King, Female/Male.

It might help to think of these opposites more as complementary to each other, for indeed they do truly create a balance with one another. We cannot use only our intuitive instincts (feminine archetypical energy) or only our intellectual capabilities (masculine archetypical energy). When the integration of the masculine and feminine energies takes place from within *first*, we are less likely to look for our own completion in a relationship with another person.

Does this sound familiar … 'our own completion in a relationship with another person.' Most of us have looked for something in another relationship, which we felt was missing in us. When we feel complete within ourselves, we do not look for another person to rescue us in *any* way. This means that we do not look for someone else to take care of us or provide something for us because we feel inadequate or incapable of providing it for ourselves. Coming from the perspective of feeling the wholeness within us, *all* of our relationships can experience more joy, with less feelings of anxiousness and insecurity.

In Egypt, there is a name for the energetic combination of the feminine and the masculine, the *Mystic* and *Vitality*, the Moon and the Sun; it is *Uttati*, which means seeing with both eyes. The feminine energy (left eye), associated with the Moon, relates to being, intuition, and mysticism. The masculine energy (right eye), associated with the Sun, relates to doing, the intellect, and vitality. When you *see with both eyes* – you have a balanced perspective of what you are viewing.

The process of integration of the opposites within us can sometimes feel like a war; at other times, it feels cohesive. Just as in marriage between two people, first there is bliss, followed by some reality check when we say, the honeymoon is over, and then an opportunity for the harmonizing of both energies occurs. The harmonizing of these energies is referred to in alchemy as the resurrection. Our essence, our Soul, is still the foundation of who we are and remains so throughout any transmutation or harmonizing.

Resurrection

In alchemy, the resurrection is described as having a luminous iridescence, called *The Peacock's Tail* (which is also seen as the child of the union of the two in the Sacred Marriage). For the transformation to be complete in its totality, the new self (the resurrected child) must be nurtured to grow into the Essence Self. Birth, death, resurrection – these are common terms in alchemy. They are not merely terms, yet rather metaphors and indications of the metamorphosis that we experience during our transmutation process, on our way towards transformation. Once we have re-newed ourselves, our new self needs further nurturing to continue our growth process. The new self grows and learns anew the *totality* of its individuation. This is the beginning of the first stage of *total transformation*, which leads ultimately to the Essence Self.

White Rose Red Rose

In this first stage, the new self needs nurturing in order for the female energy within the new self to find its identity and expression. Called The White Rose (or female tincture), it has the capacity to transmute metals into silver and is equated with the moon. The White Rose aspect of the new self is nurtured even more – with intention and attention – and evolves into the transmuted male self, which produces the gold-giving elixir (male tincture), The Red Rose. In alchemy, this process is called *the reddening*. The Red Rose, corresponding to the sun, is considered the substance that has the capacity to transmute metals into gold.

The finale is the synthesis of the complete male and female within the new self, which produces *complete transformation* and becomes the Essence Self. The White Rose and The Red Rose produce transformation – the Essence Self.

According to Irving Berlin: "There is an element of truth in every idea that lasts long enough to be called corny." Alchemy has been referred to as corny, or as a pursuit only by charlatans. But dreams know no boundaries. For every new path that is embarked upon, expect the unexpected. Whatever the path: easy, flowing, challenging, enlightening, transforming … dream, your dream, with courage, trust and faith … it has worked for me!

Chapter 3

Awaken Your Intuition

Connecting to our intuition unites us with both our soul and the soul of the Universe, Divine Spirit.

– Sonia Choquette, The Wise Child

Intuition. The word conjures up doubt and fear for many people. Doubt that this gift is not accessible for them; fear that it is! For what do you do with it when your intuition proves itself right? Awakening your intuition can be life enriching. Sonia Choquette, Ph.D., has authored several books on how to get in touch more deeply with your intuitive guidance. In her book, *The Wise Child,* she offers us this about 'connecting to our intuition': "It takes away our fearful sense of isolation and inadequacy. It replaces fear with a sense of spiritual direction and safety. The world becomes friendly, non-adversarial, and welcoming. Life becomes joyful, amusing, generous, and abundant. This is the divine plan. The intuitive life is one of confidence, inner peace, and creative expression. What better gift to ourselves and our children?"

Awakening Your Inner Guidance

In *The Intuitive Way: A Guide to Living from Inner Wisdom,* by Penney Peirce says, "It is only through deep connectedness and a personal, physical resonance with life that we know what is real and true for us, that we derive our sense of direction. Lose your body's live connection to the world, and intuition and creativity stop."

If you easily access your inner guidance, your intuition … congratulations. Our culture does not easily encourage you to listen and pay attention to your inner intuitive voice. My father, who was aware of his intuitive gifts as a child, was told by his mother when growing-up, that this wasn't acceptable; he needed to ignore it; it wasn't right. As an adult, he went into police work and became a detective. I once asked him, "In your detective work, you must be able to use your intuition?" He responded with, "NO! It's about deductive reasoning, not intuition." I always felt a little sad about that. I love detective work and I use both (although not professionally).

It's important to remember, if you are comfortable with your intuitive skills, try not to feel superior to others who are not as comfortable yet as you are. Or you can be likened to an intuitive tyrant: someone who invalidates others or tunes them out because they feel superior. We all have the gift of intuition, access it in different ways and at different times, and receive different information. Certainly, no two of us receive the exact same information intuitively at the same time. Even within ourselves, what may feel right one day, may not the next. What is important to remember? Keep an open-mind!

His Holiness the Dalai Lama says: "People take different roads seeking fulfillment and happiness. Just because they're not on your road doesn't mean they've gotten lost."

Three Steps to Accessing

The first step: Access your intuition and awaken it. Intuition is a gift given to all of us. Our soul is an amazing guide. Intuitive information awakens from Divine Source and is directed to our soul. The second step: Trust the intuitive guidance you received. The third step: Listen and take action.

❖ Access and Awaken your intuition
❖ Trust your intuitive guidance
❖ Listen and Take action

The more you utilize your intuition, the easier it becomes to access and trust it. If you don't act upon some of your intuitive information, how will you know if it is true? And if you use it and it is incorrect ...

don't give up! Try again! The more that you listen to it and respond to your intuitive insights, the more you will feel the subtle nuances of information and trust its accuracy.

Developing Your Intuitive Skills

Developing your intuitive skills demands that you are in-tune with your body and its feelings or signals. Being intuitive asks of you that you *know* quickly and respond accordingly. Victor Beasley, who has a doctorate in psychology and is the author of a book called *Intuition by Design* says, "Intuition and intellect belong to a single continuum of perception within consciousness. Like a right leg and a left leg, they are two necessary aspects of a single reality .... The situation is teacher."

How can you access your inner guidance? Try this simple game with yourself the next time you are in a building that has a group of elevators:

Stand by the elevators. Close your eyes. Take a deep breath. Ask yourself, "Which elevator will come to this floor next?" Then open your eyes and slowly walk closer to that particular elevator. Were you right?

When I play this with my inner guidance, other factors come into consideration. If I feel calm and centered (not in a rush or obsessed with many other thoughts) 90% of the time I will intuit the correct elevator. When I'm feeling stressed or anxious, I'm usually wrong! This tells me that accessing intuition and awakening to its delights comes easier when I feel in a more calm, grounded state of being and take the time to try to *feel* the correct answer for me. When you first try to tap into your inner guidance (intuition), do so when you are not trying to also juggle ten thousand other things at the same time! You will be much more successful if you can focus your intention.

Your intuition is your best friend. It can guide you through uncertainties. Test this out in fun and safe ways. Gradually your trust will grow. With trust, your intuition becomes stronger.

Determining and Assessing

We are all gifted with *intuition* ... no one has been left out! *Trusting* your intuition, *listening* to it, and *acting* on it takes time to develop. While you are developing your personal trust in this way of receiving information and testing your intuitive skills in your daily life, you have available to you some tools that have been created to assist this process.

Dowsing with a pendulum or kinesiology can help you find answers to your simplified questions.

Dowsing – Determining with a Pendulum

A pendulum can answer simple questions that have a YES or NO answer. It is easy to use if you *trust* the answers are coming from your own subconscious mind or that of the collective superconscious. The collective superconscious is like a pool of knowledge (from a higher energy source) that is available to anyone who wants to tap into it.

Dowsing is the process of using a pendulum, or other similar divining rod or tool, to determine answers to questions. Professional dowsers have been called upon for years to find where to drill for water. There are numerous books on dowsing and pendulum use. You will find pendulums in some health food stores and most metaphysical shops and bookstores. Choose one that you find attractive. Before you buy it, hold the pendulum by the smaller, non-pointed end, just in front of your body and ask the following question. Holding your hand *very still*, say "Does this pendulum suit me?" Wait ... be patient ... it will slowly begin to move back-and-forth or spin in a circular direction. What does this mean?

When using a pendulum, first determine what type of swing means a YES or NO answer. Commonly, a circular direction means YES and a back-and-forth direction means NO. However, everyone who uses a pendulum receives a slightly different set of directions.

When you get your first pendulum, initially ask if it suits you, as mentioned above. Next, ask the pendulum "Show me a YES answer," and watch to see the direction of the pendulum's swing. Then ask the pendulum "Show me a NO answer," and again watch to see the direction of the pendulum's swing. Experiment and you will find your way, your comfortable place with dowsing.

Kinesiology – A Tool for Assessing

Kinesiology is defined in Webster's Collegiate Dictionary (United States) as "the study of the principles of mechanics and anatomy in relation to human movement." Applied kinesiology (commonly known as muscle testing) can be a valuable tool for helping to determine answers to simple questions (as above, YES and NO). Muscle testing is a way of self-testing or health practitioner testing an individual in order to assess any imbalances in the body.

You can also easily self-test if a food, herb, supplement, medicine, essential oil, etc. is appropriate for you, by using kinesiology. Before you actually do the muscle testing, it is important to test for the strength response (for a YES answer) or the weak response (for a NO answer). There are many ways to effectively do muscle testing. Here are three different methods of testing for a YES or NO answer to a pre-determined question:

❖ Place the item in question, or a piece of paper with the name of the item, or the query, on a table in front of you or in your lap. Form a "C" shape with each index finger from each hand. Your index finger is the "pointing finger," the finger next to your thumb. Hook your two index fingers from both hands together. Ask the question, "Show me strength." Then steadily try to pull the fingers apart. For the strength answer, the two fingers should feel strong and tight and not pull apart easily. Then ask the question, "Show me weakness" and do the same thing. Even though you try to hold the hooked connection when asking for the weakness answer, the finger will pull apart fairly easily, almost as though they lost their power and strength and are now weak. Imagine asking this question, "Is this dessert good for me right now?" If you get a strength response, it signifies that the answer is strong, positive, or a YES. If you get the weak response as the answer to the same question, it signifies that the answer is weak, negative, or a NO.

❖ Connect the tip of the index (pointing) finger to the tip of the thumb of the left hand and make a circle. Make a "C" shape with your right hand, move it closer to the circle on your left hand and inter-connect the two together. You should now have two inter-connecting circles formed by the index fingers and thumbs of each hand. Now, ask: "Show me strength." Holding the finger and thumb connection on each hand as strong as you can, try to pull the two circles apart. If the strength of the connection remains firm, this shows you strength, affirmation, or an answer of YES. Now ask: "Show me weakness." If one of your circles becomes weak, gives way, and separates from the circle of the other hand, this signifies weakness and indicates a NO answer to your question.

❖ This method can also be done if there is a friend, facilitator, or other practitioner to assist the person who is asking the question. We refer to the person asking the question as the "client" and the friend who is facilitating, or helping to determine the answer as the "facilitator." First, do this exercise and determine a YES or NO answer through the strength or weakness of the response of the arm before you ask any specific question. The client holds their left hand (if they are right-handed) over their heart. Then hold out their right arm at shoulder height. Now, the facilitator takes their right hand and places it on the left-shoulder (if the client is right-handed) of the client. The facilitator puts their left hand on the extended arm of the client and gently and firmly presses down on the extended arm. The facilitator will now ask the questions, looking for a YES and a NO answer, as discussed above. In answer to the question "Show me strength," the arm of the person being tested holds strong for a YES answer even with firm downward pressure from the facilitator. In answer to the question "Show me weakness," the person being tested will not be able to hold up the arm for a NO answer; in fact, with less pressure applied, it still falls down from the outstretched position. Now you are ready to ask your question or questions.

Of course, it is also extremely important *how you phrase the question.* In the reverse phraseology, if you asked the question in a negative light, such as "Is this dessert *not good* for me at this time?" A strength response to this question means that you *should NOT eat the dessert!*

If you are not sure about doing assessing techniques (pendulum, dowsing, muscle testing), I recommend that you seek further study. When beginning, it is highly recommended that you study in a live class. It helps you to get a true feeling for how to use kinesiology. There are many other ways of muscle testing with kinesiology. The response from each method, weak or strong, gives you your answers.

PART TWO

Nature's Gifts

Listen within yourself and
look into the infinitude of space and time.
There can be heard the songs of the constellations,
the voices of the numbers, and the harmonies of the spheres."

– Hermes Trismegistus, 2000 B.C.

Divine Gifts for All –
Nature's Vibrational Medicines

In understanding the gifts that Nature offers, we are asked first to look to Nature as a part of us, not separate from us. Native American cultures, as do most indigenous cultures, have a respect for the Earth Mother that many Western cultures lack. Chief Seattle expresses it eloquently:

"This we know … the earth does not belong to man, man belongs to the earth. All things are connected, like blood which connects one family. Whatever befalls the earth befalls the children of the earth. Man did not weave the web of life – he is merely a strand in it. Whatever he does to the web, he does to himself."

In many Native American cultures, a medicine is a stimulus found in Nature that directly influences the activity of a living organism or a part of that organism. Using this philosophy, a medicine or remedy refers to anything that can have a positive effect on your wellbeing. All of Nature holds a vibrational energy that can positively affect humans. Exactly what we need is found in Nature, whether it is sustenance, medicine, or remedy. It is up to us to discover the many wonders of Nature.

The spark of all creation is often referred to as the masculine creative force, the Divine Life Essence: God, Creator, Infinite Source, Divine, and Great Spirit, etc. Nature refers to anything that is found or grows (has not been created in a laboratory by humans) on the Earth Mother. Nature Herself is the driving force of the elements and the elemental kingdoms. She is a great force, both a creator and a destroyer.

In Joseph Rael's book *Being & Vibration*, he recounts a story that was one of the last teachings told to him by his Tiwa (Native American) grandfather. His grandfather said:

"Pay attention!"

Joseph Rael continues to say, "I didn't understand what he meant. I know now he was saying that the key to life is sensitivity and that only through developing the capacity of sensitivity to everything will we hear the real message."

Nature's Vibrational Medicines

Nature's Vibrational Medicines include many different stimuli found indigenously in Nature. Through their individual essence and energy, they have the ability to effect change. In the book by Richard Gerber, MD, titled *Vibrational Medicine*, Dr. Larry Dossey (who is also the author of *Space, Time and Medicine*) says, "Anyone who is aware of the recent trends in medicine will realize that modern physicians – like the physicists before them – have begun to deal with finer and finer forms of energy both in the diagnosis and treatment of human illness. This trend can only continue. It is sure to bring with it the recognition of increasingly subtle expressions of our minds and bodies, which will require correspondingly subtler approaches in therapy."

Also in Gerber's book, Kenneth R. Pelletier Ph.D., from the University of San Francisco School of Medicine adds, "Twenty-first century health care will be based upon subtle energy principles and interventions involving the mind, body, environmental, and spiritual dimensions."

Some of these vibrational medicines include: essential oils, colors, shapes, gemstones, minerals, sound, the elements, the directions, numbers, and myths. Remember some of the stories and myths that we heard in school about ancient gods and goddesses? These gods and goddesses had the power to control and affect Nature and humans. Because of this, their stories, or the myths that surround them, can also be considered as vibrational medicines. Nature's Vibrational Medicines have a close synergistic healing relationship to humans and to our physical, emotional, and spiritual patterning and overall wellbeing.

Chapter 4

Essential Oils – Vibrational AromaTherapy

Thyme is essential,
Basil and Lavender too.
Rose for the heart,
Calming with Chamomile Blue.
Essential Oils for body and mind,
Ever is the Spirit
Enhanced with their kind.
– Ixchel Leigh, 1986

Essential oils are part of Nature's Vibrational Medicines. Vibrational means "of vibration." Vibration is energy that reverberates outwards from Original Creation. It is an emanation, aura, spirit, or energy that infuses, vitalizes, and instinctively can be sensed or experienced. Everything has a vibrational energy, since everything is created from original Divine Source. Vibrational energy exists in the subtle realms; it can be felt and sometimes seen. Some people see auras around humans, plants, or animals, and what they are seeing is the vibration.

"The eyes are man's pathways, the nose his understanding."
– Abbess Hildegard of Bingen, 12th century

It is not recommended to apply pure (undiluted) essential oils directly on the skin, but only apply when blended into a carrier oil or lotion. Applied to the skin, the essential oils immediately are absorbed into the bloodstream. They almost have an innate intelligence to travel through the bloodstream to the specific areas of the body where their particular potentials for providing wellbeing can take place.

Nature's Vibrational Medicines can create the arena to encourage and enhance transformation of your vital forces as a whole person. You are like a chalice, a cuplike blossom full of potential, with a deep well of possibilities. Transformation means to change form, from one form to another on a deep cellular level. *Vibrational Aroma Therapy* is a tool to aid in this transformation of personal growth and change.

Vibrational AromaTherapy by Ixchel™

I conceived *Vibrational Aroma Therapy* through visions and channeled information in 1990. It was legally trademarked with the United States Patent and Trademark Office in 1998 (applied for in 1996) as: *Vibrational Aroma Therapy by Ixchel™*. The system uses a multi-faceted modality for the purpose of igniting a flame for wellbeing. It utilizes our subtle energy system, affecting our deeper emotions, spirit and psyche on an unconscious level. Using essential oils, gemstones, colors (etc. Nature's Vibrational Medicines), it can encourage changes to our conscious thought patterns, thereby positively influencing our life's direction.

At the time when I applied for the status to trademark Vibrational Aromatherapy, I was told: you cannot trademark these two words because they are both generic terms; you can only trademark if you add your name, or a logo to the words. Thus, it became: *Vibrational Aroma Therapy by Ixchel™*.

Today, the words "vibrational aromatherapy" are often used to describe a form of subtle aromatherapy, of using essential oils to influence the subtle energy systems (less dense system than our physical body) such as the chakras and auras.

Vibrationally-conscious Essential Oils

Therapeutic-grade and vibrationally-conscious essential oils are the backbone of my *Vibrational Aroma Therapy by Ixchel™*. The term *vibrationally-conscious essential oils* was created by Carol Corio.

Carol has been instrumental in assisting me to bring my concepts to the world. She has offered her enthusiasm and support from the moment I first explained my concepts to her, when it was just in its infancy many, many moons ago. To this day, Carol gives hours of her time, ideas, creative input, and skills towards editing: the original *Aromatic Alchemy – Recipe for Transformation* (published in 2001); the textbook: *Vibrational AromaTherapy Manual* (her company, *Quality of Life Associates,* first published in 1997); and this Updated Edition of *Aromatic Alchemy* (2020). Whether I feel exuberant or discouraged, Carol heartfully lends a tireless ear. Thank you Carol!

A vibrationally-conscious essential oil refers to the *focused intent* of all who are involved in bringing the essential oil to you. Everyone involved creates an exchange of energy that a pure essential oil carries in its cellular memory: the farmers and distillers who grow the plants, the individuals who extract their essences, and the sellers who bring the essences to market. All are responsible for their focused intentions. Are they doing this just for the profit? Or do they feel a connection to the land and a special sense of satisfaction and purpose in what they are doing?

Vibrationally-conscious also extends to the conscious, focused intentions of the individual or healing arts practitioner, who is using the essential oils and preparing a product. Synergies, blends, products, or preparations created for wellbeing with conscious and focused intent, carry alchemical properties that have subtle, emotional, spiritual, and psychological benefits on deeper levels. As a multi-faceted modality, *Vibrational AromaTherapy* can lead us into a deeper more conscious understanding of healing and wellbeing.

When you purchase essential oils, look for a company who recognizes quality. Ideally, you want the company to have a relationship with the kind of farmers, distillers, and distributors who share the same philosophy. This way you can be assured that you are using a pure, vibrationally-conscious essential oil!

ChakraSynergy for *Vibrational AromaTherapy*

A ChakraSynergy is a composition of pure, therapeutic-grade, vibrationally-conscious essential oils, composed with focused intention by me (Ixchel Leigh) to coordinate with each of the seven chakras and two auras (for the nine ChakraAuras). For over twenty years they have been used in their pure essential oil form (no carrier) as a ChakraSynergy, by health practitioners and individuals for healing and wellness. In further chapters, you will see how you can use these and create similar formulas.

ChakraSynergy Elixirs for *Vibrational AromaTherapy*

In 2018, I created a new format using the basic compositions from the nine ChakraSynergies. A ChakraSynergy Elixir, uses the ChakraSynergy formula and is blended into organic jojoba and organic sunflower oil, creating a user-friendly product for any individual (untrained in aromatherapy or professional).

Focused Sessions

A focused session is special healing time set aside for bringing balance and wellbeing to the body, mind, and spirit. You can simply meditate or pray, or use a particular modality of energy work you are comfortable with, to encourage balance within. Energy balancing can return you to your ideal state of wellbeing. This ideal state produces endorphins that make you feel happier and with a greater sense of joy. When you feel joy, you are in your naturally intended state of being and this creates harmony in your life.

Healing arts practitioners who provide treatments such as: massage, acupuncture, acupressure, energy work, polarity, Reiki, and Therapeutic Touch can also use *Vibrational AromaTherapy by IxchelTM*. Their focus is to help restore inner balance and wellbeing. It helps to create a homeostasis in the body, mind, and spirit. Samuel Hahnemann, the originator of homeopathy, states, "In the state of health the spirit-like vital force animating the material organism reigns in supreme sovereignty. It maintains the sensations and activities of all parts of the living organism in a harmony that obliges wonderment."

Sometimes healing can be aided through the innate healing present in our hands. I'm sure you've heard, "the healing touch of a mother." Healing does not occur because someone forces his or her will upon another. True healing occurs when an individual desiring healing (consciously or with open mind) unlocks her (or his) heart and allows the healing energy to enter.

Using *Vibrational AromaTherapy by Ixchel*™
Case Study

The following is a case study, recorded by a massage therapist, and communicated to me in 1997:

"Jennifer B. was told as a child that she could never be an artist because artists don't ever really make enough money to support themselves, let alone a family. Jennifer then chose a career path of working as an administrator in business. She was constantly stressed and unhappy. Eventually, the stress took its toll on her body. She looked much older than her actual years, experienced digestive disorders, and smoked heavily. Jennifer sought out the help of a massage therapist who also had studied the principles of *Vibrational AromaTherapy by IxchelTM*. The therapist gave her weekly massages using essential oils added to her massage lotion and using the principles she had studied with Ixchel.

Within a few weeks, Jennifer felt compelled to begin taking some art and design classes. Two years later, Jennifer left her administrative job and opened a store where she offered the public a place to paint pottery. Jennifer put some of her artistically painted pottery creations on display in her store, and began selling them to her customers too. She combined her previous skills as a business administrator to run her successful business and she used her artistic talents to successfully support herself financially! One day Jennifer realized that she had regained a youthful vigor, stopped smoking, and had time to pursue another of her interests – hiking in the mountains."

Jennifer is an example of the benefits of working with the energy systems, in her case through using the principles of *Vibrational AromaTherapy by Ixchel™*. For Jennifer, it affected her on the subtle levels, then filtered down into affecting her physical body and her emotions. She was able to make changes in her life that positively reverberated deeply within her.

Rituals and Sacred Spaces

Vibrational AromaTherapy by Ixchel™ can be employed to scent a room or to create a feeling of *sacred space*. It can enhance intimate gatherings and be enjoyed for rituals. A sacred ritual is merely a focused act that brings beauty and a sense of peacefulness into your life – honoring life's sacredness. Prayer and meditation are examples of sacred ritual.

Compare with Traditional Aromatherapy

I want to briefly share here the principles of Traditional Aromatherapy for you, in case you do not know. Aromatherapy is the art and science of using therapeutic-grade, pure essential oils from botanicals to enhance, encourage, and balance wellbeing. Traditional Aromatherapy is primarily used for wellbeing and healing of the physical body, mind, emotions, and psyche. It focuses on the biochemical information of essential oils, yet it has its roots in cultures of old. Alexandra Avery, an herbalist, esthetician, and author of the book *Aromatherapy and You, A Guide to Natural Skin Care*, says:

"The art of Aromatherapy is not new to the world. The use of plants and their oils has been used to heal and beautify the body for over a thousand years. Whether ingested, absorbed through the skin, or simply inhaled, plant aromas are known to have an effect on the body, mind, and emotions. Today, the study of aromas has been elevated to a science which employs the balancing and beautifying properties of pure herbal and floral essences to enhance the condition of the skin, body, hair, mind, and indeed, the environment. For centuries, Aromatherapy has been a part of Ayurvedic medicine. This is an Indian system, which focuses on restoring the balance within the body, thereby promoting a healthful state of being. Since its first recorded use some 5,000 years ago, Ayurvedic medicine has been incorporating the healing powers of essential oils in candles, incense and massage oils."

Vibrational AromaTherapy by Ixchel™

Chakra Aura	Body Part	Key Word	Shape	Color	Stone	Goddess	Sound
#1	Base of Spine	Courage	Sphere	Deep Red	Garnet	Heket	*aah aah*
#2	Sacral	Create	Obelisk	Orange	Carnelian	Freya	*F-oh aah ee M-eh ee eh*
#3	Solar Plexus	Manifest	Triangle	Yellow	Citrine	Romi Kumu	*eh eh*
#4	Heart	Joy	Spiral	Pink, Green, Lavender	Rose Quartz	Skekina	*aah*
#5	Throat	Truth	Star	Blue	Lapis Lazuli	Brigid	*oh*
#6	Third Eye	Vision	Pyramid	Indigo Turquoise	Turquoise	Egeria	*eh aah uu*
#7	Crown	Inspiration	Polygon	Violet	Amethyst	Padma	*eh*
#8	Etheric Body	Release	Square	Black	Onyx or Volcanic Lava	Pasowee	*eee oh eh*
#9	Astral Body	Knowing	Heart	White	Moonstone	Kuan Yin	*aah eee*

Chapter 5

Color – Healing Light

*Real beauty is a ray which emanates from the
holy of holies of the spirit,
and illuminates the body, as life comes from the depths of
the earth and gives color and scent to a flower.*
– Kahil Gibran, The Broken Wings

"Light is the shadow of God," said Plato. Color is the refraction of Light. It is a phenomenon of Light. The author Goethe writes in *Faust*, "We have our life in the colorful reflection." Color reflects the way we feel. Color can express the way we think. Color can lower our spirits or brighten our lives. Color is being used with more conscious awareness everywhere, in hospitals, doctor's offices, restaurants, and stores. Bright colors cheer us; drab colors dull us. Even the word *drab* sounds drab!

We have long used color in our language to express feelings: "black with rage," "green with envy," "feeling blue," and "seeing red." All of these phrases relate to actual changes that take place in the colors of our own aura or electro-magnetic field as we feel these emotions. When our emotions change, so does the color of our aura.

Many people can see the subtle colors called auras around living matter. Some can even see these auras around what modern science calls non-living matter such as rocks and minerals. Auras can be captured on film through a special process called Kirlian photography. Drs. S.D. and V.K. Kirlian were twentieth century Russian electricians who developed a process of photographing that exposed the object to ultraviolet light. Through electronic and ionic interactions caused by an applied electric field, different colors surrounding an object could be photographed.

Ancient manuscripts from China, India, and Egypt show that healer priests had a complete system of color science. Modern color healing, chromotherapy, can restore wellbeing and balance to the human body. The first known book on the therapeutic use of color was written in 1877 by Dr. S. Pancoast called *Blue and Red Light, or Light and It's Rays as Medicine*. Healing using color can be as simple as visualizing the color, or it can take place in many other forms. There are many ways of using color as a healing tool.

Color Tools for Healing

There are many color tools and variations of tools. Color is used as a means of restoring and maintaining health. Dr. Kate Baldwin presented a paper in 1926 to a clinical meeting of the Eye, Ear, Nose, and Throat Diseases of the Medical Society of the State of Pennsylvania. This meeting was held at the Medico-Chirurgical Hospital in Philadelphia on October 12. Dr. Baldwin (former Senior Surgeon at Women's Hospital in Philadelphia) at the time of her presentation held a very prestigious position (especially for a woman during this period of history). Here is a quote from an abstract of her paper, which was printed in the *Atlantic Medical Journal* in April 1927:

> "In the effort to obtain relief from suffering, many of the more simple ... potent measures have been overlooked while we have grasped at the obscure and complicated.
>
> "Sunlight is the basic source of all life and energy upon earth. Deprive plant or animal life of light, and it soon shows the lack and ceases to develop .... For centuries scientists have devoted untiring effort to discover means for the relief or cure of human ills and restoration of the normal functions.
>
> "In order that the whole body may function perfectly, each organ must be a hundred per cent perfect. When the spleen, the liver, or any other organ falls below normal, it simply means that the body laboratories have not provided the required materials with which to work, either because they are not functioning,

as a result of some disorder of the internal mechanism, or because they have not been provided with the necessary materials. Before the body can appropriate the required elements, they must be separated from the waste matter. Each element gives off a characteristic color wave.

"The prevailing color wave of hydrogen is red, and that of oxygen is blue, and each element in turn gives off its own special color wave. Sunlight, as it is received by the body, is split into prismatic colors and their combinations, as white light is split by passage through a prism. Everything on the red side of the spectrum is more or less stimulating, while the blue is sedative. There are many shades of each color, and each is produced by a little different wave length. Just as sound waves are tuned to each other and produce harmony or discords, so color waves may be tuned, and only so can they be depended on always to produce the same result ....

"If the body is sick it should be restored with the least possible effort. There is no more accurate or easier way than by giving the color representing the lacking elements, and the body will, through its radioactive forces, appropriate them and so restore the normal balance. Color is the simplest and most accurate therapeutic measure yet developed."

There are many therapies based on color. One, called *Spectro-Chrome*, was developed by Dinshah P. Ghadiali. Ghadiali was born in 1873 in Mumbai, India. His early adulthood saw him as an assistant to the professor of mathematics and science at a prominent college in India, where he was awarded prizes for proficiency in the English and Persian languages. He learned eight oriental and eight occidental languages, and he gave experimental demonstrations in chemistry and physics at seven institutions of learning. He was appointed Electrical Engineer of Patiala State in India. In 1896, Ghadiali made his first trip to the United States. There he met Thomas Edison,

Nikola Tesla, and other noted scientists. He lectured in the U.S. on radioactivity and x-rays. The New York Times newspaper termed him the "Parsee Edison." When he returned to India, he continued his research on color light therapy.

A turning point in Ghadiali's medical thinking came in 1897. A friend of his was dying from mucous colitis. She had been treated by her physician with the then accepted drugs, yet she remained close to death.

Having researched the use of color as a healing tool and read about its effectiveness in books (such as *The Principles of Light and Color* by Dr. Edwin D. Babbitt and *Blue and Red Light, or Light and Its Rays as Medicine* by Dr. Seth Pancoast), he was convinced that the only hope for her recovery lay in an unorthodox method. Ghadiali proceeded using the techniques developed by Dr. Babbit. The light from a kerosene lantern with a colored glass bottle used as a filter was shone on her body. Milk was placed in another bottle of the same color glass and exposed to sunlight. Later, she drank the milk. After one day's treatment, her urgent straining to eliminate, which occurred almost a hundred times a day, abated to a need to eliminate only ten times a day. After three days, she was able to get out of bed! This was the beginning; yet another twenty-three years would pass before Ghadiali developed his healing system called *Spectro-Chrome*. Ghadaili wrote the *Spectro-Chrome Metry Encyclopedia*, which details some physical body diseases and the recommended treatment techniques using color. Even today, this treatise is considered by some to be the authoritative information on Color Therapy.

You can very easily incorporate color as a healing tool into your life. A few methods or color healing tools are: colored silk or cotton squares of fabric, colored lights, colored waters, and foods. Color tools can be used in meditations that focus on healing and balancing.

The actual color you choose for your particular healing needs is determined by the focus of your meditation or healing session, or the areas that are out of balance within your energy field.

Colored Fabric

Each of us has had the experience of getting dressed and changing our clothes because something didn't feel right. Maybe it was the style, but possibly it was the color. Color affects us in our surroundings and when we wear it on our body. Each of the energy centers in the body (ChakraAura) also has a specific color associated with it. You can change your mood by changing the color of your garments.

In meditation or healing sessions (as in *Vibrational Aroma Therapy*) you can use scarves of different colors (silk or cotton recommended) to lay over the body during the session or meditation.

- ❖ 1st ChakraAura – Base – Physical Transformation
- ❖ **Red.** This fiery color enhances the body's energies and is grounding and centering. Helps to encourage stability, setting the foundation for balancing all the ChakraAuras.
- ❖ 2nd ChakraAura – Sacral – Creative Transformation
- ❖ **Orange.** Awakens your given talents and increasing creative and physical power. Initiates inspiration from the spiritual realms.
- ❖ 3rd ChakraAura – Solar Plexus – Transformation of Individual Will
- ❖ **Yellow.** Reduces stress, alleviates fear, and balances male and female polarities. Promotes a healthy Ego.
- ❖ 4th ChakraAura – Heart – Emotional Transformation
- ❖ **Green.** Strengthens the heart while aiding emotional and mental stability and balance. Enhances the expression of inner light and joy.
- ❖ 5th ChakraAura – Throat – Transformation of Expression

❖ **Blue.** Energizes the throat and allows expression of your true nature. Allows for conscious alignment to the intuitive and psychic aspects of your nature and your expression of them.

❖ 6th ChakraAura – Third Eye – Transformation of Intuition

❖ **Turquoise.** Aids in alignment of the mental and etheric bodies. Encourages attunement to the spiritual realms by assisting in opening to insight and intuition.

❖ 7th ChakraAura – Crown – Spiritual Transformation

❖ **Purple.** Is the physical representation for transformation. Helps to cut through illusion. Holds the energy of eternal peace.

Colored Lights

Colored lights and gels are also called chromotherapy. Painted light bulbs with heat resistant paint using the needed color. Colored gels are colored film (similar to see through paper yet a thin plastic) used in photography and the movie industries, they give a prescribed color filter. You may find them in photography stores. You can use any of these colored lights by shining a light through the colored gel onto your body at the specific area in need of healing or balancing.

Collect colored glass bottles, jars, or containers. Fill them with spring water or good well water. Do not use your city's water if there are added chemicals like chlorine or fluoride, as these chemicals may not support your healing process. Place the bottles in a window where they can be exposed to the sunlight. Alternately, you can use gemstones to energize your water. For example, if you need to infuse yourself with the quality of *red energy* (to boost your vitality) place a red stone in a clear glass or bottle of water. Set this in a window where there is sunlight, just as you would for the colored glass bottles. Leave the colored glass bottle or the clear glass with the colored stone in the sunlight for at least twenty-four hours before you drink it. When you need a specific dose of color to liven or calm your energy or healing needs, pour yourself a glass and drink it. Sante - Cheers to Your Health!

Foods with Healing Colors

Just as each food is a different color, each color can hold an energy that is more appropriate to ingest at different times of day or for specific health concerns. In selecting foods that influence you by their color, ask yourself some questions ....

"What type of energy am I looking for?"

"What supports my body and spirit right now?"

Generally, most people sleep at night and awake in the morning ready to direct their energy and attention for the day's job, or whatever occupies their daily activities. Just for fun, try choosing your foods according to their color and energy.

Choose foods that give you energy for your morning and into the early afternoon meals. For the late afternoon and evening meals, choose foods that have a more calming effect. The foods listed below are assorted according to color. Notice that each color also relates to one of the major chakras? Foods chosen from the 1st-3rd ChakraAuras are considered energizing and would be appropriate for morning to early afternoon meals. Foods chosen from 4th-7th ChakraAuras are considered calming and are more appropriate for the late afternoon and evening meals. From the list below (only a partial list of foods), you can choose your Color Foods. Try experimenting. *Bon Apetit* .... Good Eating!

- ❖ **Red – 1st ChakraAura:** red apples, beets, cherries, cranberries, strawberries, radishes, raspberries, red grapes, red meats (optional, due to body type and preference), red peppers, tomatoes and watermelon.

- ❖ **Orange – 2nd ChakraAura:** apricots, cantaloupes, carrots, mangoes, nectarines, oranges, persimmons, pumpkins, sweet potatoes and tangerines.

- ❖ **Yellow – 3rd ChakraAura:** bananas, corn, eggs, grapefruit, lemons, most vegetable oils except olive, papaya, peaches, pineapple, yellow peppers, yellow squashes and yams.

- ❖ **Green – 4th ChakraAura:** asparagus, artichokes, avocados, broccoli, cucumbers, green beans, green grapes, green peppers, honeydew melon, lettuce (all), okra, peas, spinach, sprouts, watercress and zucchini.

- ❖ **Blue – 5th ChakraAura:** blueberries, loganberries and blue plums.

- ❖ **Indigo – 6th ChakraAura:** choose from the Blue and Violet foods.

- ❖ **Violet – 7th ChakraAura:** blackberries, ollalieberries, eggplant, purple grapes and passion fruit.

The Effects of Color in Our Surroundings

We choose the colors that surround us in our homes and often our offices because they allow us to shift our moods: to feel energized, calmed, creative, and serene. Music can make us feel passionate, sad, or happy. Nature's minerals, stones, and crystals carry a vibrational energy. Created by Divine Source and Nature, the author George Eliot says,

"How very beautiful gems are! It is strange how deeply colors seem to penetrate one like a scent. I suppose that is the reason why gems are used as spiritual emblems in Revelations (The Bible). They look like fragments of heaven."

All things in the universe are made of vibration. Vibration is energy. Dan Campbell in his book *Edgar Cayce on the Power of Color, Stones and Crystals*, quotes Edgar Cayce (pronounced kay-cee) regarding the vibration of things:

"As these are but lights, but signs in thine experience, they are as but a candle that one stumbles not in the dark. But worship *not* the light of the candle; rather that to which it may guide thee in thy service. So, whether from vibrations of numbers, of metals, of stones, these are merely to become the necessary influences to make thee attune, one with the Creative Forces …. So, use them to attune self. How, ye ask? As ye apply, ye are given the next step …. And how may ye know? … They only attune self that the Christ Consciousness may give the message! Listen to no message of a stone, of a number, even of a star; for they are but servants of the Lord and Master of all-even as thou! (707-2)"

Our fascination and pleasure derived from stones continues today. Why else do we adorn ourselves with diamonds, rubies, and gold? In Dan Campbell's book (same as above) he continues with this thought:

"If the fugitive qualities of light and color puzzled ancient man, stones and gems were at least more substantial and dependable …. Unlike colors, he could still touch or hold them in his hand at night, even if he could not see them. No matter that he did not understand their origin; he felt an elemental connection, a primal urge, to have them near, if simply because they struck his fancy."

Vibrational AromaArt

Combining essential oils with color and gemstones can ignite the possibilities of transformation. The effects of color can be absorbed energetically and in a healing way by many different methods. A special friend of mine, Sharon Walker (deceased 2019), was a visionary artist. She created beautiful paintings that uplift the soul and spirit. She began using some of my essential oil synergies blended in with her oil paints. Sharon explains:

"As an artist, I have always sought to create balance and harmony through art. I feel that healing of the body and upliftment of the soul is to be found through color and sound. When I started painting with essential oils, a new dimension in support of this belief emerged. By mixing pure pigment with essential oils, a painting was created which allowed the viewer's frequency to be elevated merely by being in close proximity to a painting. Auric photography documented this elevation. We took aura photos before and after contact with the paintings and were amazed at the significant color changes in the individual's energy field when being in close proximity to these works of art. The applications for healing are limitless."

Chapter 6

Stones – Mineralogical Blossoms

*The magi, the wise men, the seers, the astrologers of the
ages gone by found much in the matter of gems that we
have nearly come to forgetting.*

– George Frederick Kunz, *The Curious Lore of Precious Stones*

"Crystals are the blossoms of the mineralogical portion of
the Earth," says Melody in the introduction to her book *Love is in
the Earth, a Kaleidoscope of Crystals*. Melody continues to say, "They
are the myraid fireworks of both creativity and individual universal
energies." Crystals and stones have been used in the religious
ceremonies of ancient cultures such as the Celtic, Mayans, Egyptian,
and Native American. In Native American cultures, they refer
to stones as "Stone People" or "Grandfathers" for they have been
here longer than us. Crystals have been revered for thousands and
thousands of years. The Christian Bible refers to crystals: "crystalline
walls," "pearly gates," and crystal stones used in the breastplate of
Aaron, the Hebrew High Priest (Exodus).

Edgar Cayce received information on the vibrational healing
aspects of color, stones, and crystals. In the book *Edgar Cayce on the
Power of Color, Stones & Crystals* by Dan Campbell, in one of Edgar
Cayce's recorded sessions:

"Each element, each stone, each variation of stone, has its own
atomic movement, held together by the units of energy that in the
universe are concentrated in that particular activity. Hence they
come under varied activities according to their color, vibration and
emanation. (531-3)"

The energies of crystals, stones, and minerals receive their energy
from a Higher Source, the Creator. The mineral kingdom can act as a

steppingstone for your spiritual growth. As gifts or "tools," minerals aid us in our transformational process. Each stone carries a different vibration or healing focus. One stone in particular functions as a balancing agent for all of the ChakraAuras: *clear crystal quartz*.

Again from Edgar Cayce (Dan Campbell's book, mentioned previously):

"… they work (minerals and stones) to stimulate healing influences in the body, temper our emotions, and improve our mental faculties, as well as raise our spiritual consciousness. The subtle forces emanating from them are not theirs. Colors and stones are merely channels for the greater forces permeating the universe. They are helpful tools to better our lives and steppingstones along the spiritual path. That is their purpose, and perhaps through them we can gain a deeper understanding of our own purpose by looking at their effects on us – keeping in mind that we can attain whatever we desire so long as the desire is in accord with that universal force of development, called-God. (1714-1)"

All of Nature's Vibrational Medicines act to help us in our transformation. They are all gifted with universal energy and vibration, just as you are. However, they do not replace our own work. You must put in your time and focused intention in order to help yourself.

Chapter 7

Shapes – Visual Stimuli

The soul never thinks without an image.
– Aristotle

Before infants learn to speak, they think in images. Humans need and desire to establish communication with others. Shapes can express our interest and attention to power, health, fertility, wealth, and to our environment. They have symbolized important events and issues in the lives of humans since we began walking on the Earth Mother. Often shapes have replaced the spoken word in the telling of history and stories.

Shapes and symbols stir a very deep emotional cord within us. They have hundreds of meanings and interpretations due to differing beliefs in different cultures. In different cultures, a circle can symbolize the sun, the moon, the universe, God, or a wheel. They have been divinized and deified in every human culture, and to many they have been called sacred. Many of today's religious symbols were taken from the matriarchal societies of 5,000 years ago, then re-worked into present day religions to suit the patriarchal system that has guided our world for the last 3,000 years. Shapes and symbols help us connect to our ancestors and they can open new insights.

Victor Beasley, author of *Intuition Quotient Cards*, a divination system employing shapes and sacred geometry as a way to access guidance, says "Sacred geometry is an ancient means for creating an altered state…. Everything that exists, vibrates, and where there's vibration, there's a pattern. These patterns imprint consciousness."

Angeles Arrien (anthropologist and author) says that she "has always been intrigued by the variety of ways that people of diverse cultures handle similar life experiences." After years of research into the origins of hundreds of symbols, she wrote a book titled *Signs of Life: The Five Universal Shapes and How to Use Them*. Her hypothesis is that, even within different cultures, different shapes are generally accepted with similar interpretations. Much can be told about your personality and innermost desires by the shapes or symbols you choose. In this same book, Ms. Arrien created her insightful *Preferential Shapes Test*, where she takes five universal shapes and uses them as "an effective tool that can be used to determine the connection between a person's preferences for certain shapes and the same person's inner, subjective states."

Carl Jung was a man with many interests: philosophy, psychology, and alchemy, to name a few. He carried the strong belief that symbols silently trigger a psychological reaction that can transform energy.

For Indians (Native Americans), images are a means of celebrating mystery and not a manner of explaining it.
– Jamake Highwater

Chapter 8

Numbers – It All Adds Up

*So teach us to number our days, that we may apply
our hearts unto wisdom.*
– Psalms, 10th Century B.C.

As was portrayed in the movie, *Contact* (1997), many scientists consider that when contact is made (and acknowledged!) with beings from other planets, our common language will be through numbers. Pythagoras, a Greek philosopher born around 590 B.C., called it "the Science of Numbers." His basic concepts became the foundation of what we call numerology. He and his followers (called Pythagoreans) are credited with developing some of the basic principles of mathematics and astronomy, the concept of the earth as a sphere, and the mystical significance of numbers (numerology) and metempsychosis (that patterns eternally reoccur).

Science agrees that the recurrence of numbers or patterns can be found in our universe. Dr. Juno Jordan spent over fifty years of her life devoted to research and counseling in the science of numbers. In her book, *Numerology-The Romance in Your Name*, she says "… numbers are symbols … They do not of themselves make things happen. Instead, they announce and broadcast the programs of thought, feeling, and action being enacted in human relations. When symbolizing a condition, circumstance, or activity, they state without equivocation the nature of the happening – its character, past, present and future. They are signposts to guide, protect and reward all who have the wisdom and foresight to observe and understand."

Edgar Cayce was born into a family without financial gifts, did not have the privilege of education, was a gifted psychic, and became known as the "Sleeping Prophet." Cayce was a devout

Christian and used his gifts to benefit others. Placing himself in a trance-like sleep, he would diagnose the illnesses of his clients, recommending cures and treatments. In some of his readings, he makes references to the effects of numbers. In reading #261-15, he states: "As related to individuals these each (individuals) vibrate to certain numbers according to their name, their birthdate .... Then when these (numbers) appear, they become either as strengths or as losses or as helps or as change ... they are rather as the signs, or the omens; and may be given as warnings ... in any manner that they may be constructive in the experience of the individual." In reading #311-3, he says, "In any influence, will ... a self, the ego, the I AM ... is the greater force to be dealt with ... as numbers do influence ... a knowledge of same certainly gives an individual a foresight into relationships ...."

Begin Your Personal Numerology

Your research into numerology begins with a look at your name. Each letter of the alphabet has a corresponding number. Add the numbers up for your name using one of the following charts:

1- A, J, S	6- F, O, X
2- B, K, T	7- G, P, Y
3- C, L, U	8- H, Q, Z
4- D, M, V	9- I, R
5- E, N, W	

A-B-C	D- E-F	G-H-I
J- K-L	M-N-O	P-Q-R
S-T-U	V-W-X	Y-Z
1-2-3	4-5-6	7-8-9

I've chosen to use the inspiring and wonderful Beyonce Knowles for all the examples of numerology in this book. I've chosen to use only her first name, Beyonce, because she is generally known by her first name only. Beyonce's Soul's Path number (based on her first name) is: 6

B - E - Y- O- N - C - E
2 - 5 - 7 - 6 - 5 - 3 - 5
= 33; 3+3 = 6

For you, use the name that you use in the world. For example: you might have a different professional name, with a different married name. You can do the numerology for both, or choose just one name.

Soul's Path Number

Keep adding the numbers until you reach a single primary number (1,2,3,4,5,6,7,8,9). By adding the sum of the individual numbers corresponding to each letter in your name you receive your Soul's Path Number. The Soul's Path Number signifies what your Soul came here to experience and do in your lifetime.

So for our example, Beyonce, her Soul's Path Number is "6." To discover clues to her soul's path and what the number "6" represents, go to the chapter for the 6th ChakraAura to read the information written about the number "6."

Go to the chapter which corresponds to your identified primary number. If you have changed your name, or are considering it, I recommend that you compare the different name options to see which one most resonates with your chosen directions or interests.

Destiny Number

By adding up the month, day, and year of your birthday, you will get another clue to YOU … your Destiny in this incarnation. Your Destiny Number, in this lifetime, refers to the energy around how you, the individual, express yourself in the world overall with insights into who you are becoming. Your Destiny Number is your current life's journey, what fate has brought your way, and who you are becoming.

If you have had a near-death experience, or know that your heart stopped and returned to beating again, you can also do the "Destiny" numerology for this date. Going through a near-death experience is like a re-birth and changes your "Destiny". You will go the the chapter which corresponds to your identified primary number.

Continuing to use Beyonce as an example, her birthdate is September 4, 1981. Adding up all of the numbers until there is the lowest primary number (single digit):

9/4/1981

Add: 9+4+1+9+8+1=32; 3+2=5

Her Destiny Number is a "5." Go to the chapter for the 5th ChakraAura to read the information written about the number "5."

Life's Work Number

If you add your Soul's Path Number with your Destiny Number, you will get yet another equation: Your Life's Work Number. This number is the combination of your Soul's Path and your Destiny and gives you insights into how you might express yourself in your work in the world.

With this new equation, you will find a guide to what your Life's Work is about. What are some of your challenges? Which forks in the roads do you take? Right? Left? You can't change your Destiny Number, it relates to your birthdate. You can change your name, so your Soul's Path Number can change. As a result of this, your Life's Work (Number) could also change! Remember this phrase was first mentioned in the Introduction to Part Two: "Pay attention"? *Pay attention* ! What are the choices you are making? How are they affecting you? Being aware of the choices and their effects is being *conscious.* Being *conscious,* entails accepting responsibility for your choices.

Again using our example for Beyonce, her Soul's Path Number is "6" and her Destiny Number is "5" ... so, 6+5=11; 1+1=2. Her Life's Work Number is a "2."

This Year for You?

Interested in finding out what the current year has in store for you? Take your birthdate: the day and the month, along with the current year, and find the number that it reduces to. This gives you your numerical energy for the current year.

For Beyonce: Her birth month (September) is a "9." Her birth date is "4." Add these numbers to the current year (the year this book published is 2020):

$$9+4+2+0+2+0=17; 1+7=8$$

The overall numerology for Beyonce for 2020 is an "8." You can look at the chart following for a quick over-view of the number "8."

A Quick Numbers Reference Guide

I've recommended that you refer to chapters in this book for a little more information on what the nine primary numbers mean. I've also created a simple chart for a quick guide:

Your Garden of Primary Numbers

#1 Beginnings   Planting the seeds in your garden.
#2 Cooperation   Your seeds take root and blossom.
#3 Enjoyment   Your seeds are sprouting.
#4 Practicality   Work in your garden; your seedlings grow stronger.
#5 Change   Your garden is growing profusely; changes daily.
#6 Responsibility   Tend to your garden as it begins to flower.
#7 Trust Inspiration The fruits of your labor appear in your garden.

#8 Achievement Celebrate! Your fruits are ripe and ready
                to harvest.
#9 Fulfillment   End of the growing season, clean out dead
                weeds.

Every nine years, you begin a new cycle in your life. Once you have completed a "9" year (based on your birth month, day, and current year), you will circle back around to a "1" year again. This means planting new seeds for a new cycle with a new set of goals and dreams.

Numbers used as Vibrational Medicines

When incorporating numbers with *Vibrational AromaTherapy*, you have several options:

❖ Once you have determined which ChakraAura is the focus for the session or meditation, refer to the description of that number in the corresponding Essence of Life Realm chapters (Part Four). Read the information, determine its appropriateness, and think about how it is suitable at this time with your chosen ChakraAura.

❖ If you are creating a VibrationalSynergy, add up the number of the date you are making the scented formula, or if for a special event, the event's date (like a wedding, birthday, solstice, equinox, etc.) Take the number to its primary number or lowest digit.

❖ You might decide to combine some numbers … for example: the person's birthday (day, month and year) with the date of the day you are creating the VibrationalSynergy. The final primary number is the numerological signature for the formula, as well as this number holds more information to share with the individual(s), which may hold more beneficial clues for aiding their path.

The combinations are obviously endless and limited only by your imagination! Only a few combinations have been listed here. You will create your own unique ways of using numbers vibrationally along with the ChakraAuras for consulting and in sessions. Numbers are yet another tool available to us for our profound growth or transformation.

Of course a professional person who works with numerology, will go into greater detail than the simplied versions here. For example: same numbers repeated as a double-digit (11, 33, 77, etc.) are considered to be Master Numbers. These carry deeper and more complicated information. If this is of interest to you, I encourage you to seek further research. You will find suggestions in "Resources" at the end of this book.

Chapter 9

Sound – Resonant Vibration

… when we sing words, their true meaning is revealed
directly to the soul through bodily vibration.
– Hildegard of Bingen

Forming a sound, letting it vibrate with deep resonance in your mouth, and allowing it to come forth sounding as a chant, sends out a healing message to our spirit. Not only does it resonate with our spirit, it also has the ability to be timeless and without boundaries. This way of forming sounds, also known as chanting, has been used by many cultures for thousands of years. Chanting, singing, and toning are called sounding. We make sounds as a form of prayer and of vocalizing a vibration that expresses gratitude. These sounds are healing to the human spirit. Their resonance can be felt in the body. We sing or chant to express emotions and feelings. Hildegard of Bingen, the seventeenth century mystic, poetically describes the essence and depth of emotion expressed through singing, in this song:

> *O Ecclesia, your eyes are like sapphire:*
> *your ears the mount of Bethel, your nose*
> *like a mountain of myrrh and incense, and*
> *your mouth is like the sound of many waters.*

Our Throat Chakra is the avenue of expression for sound. Through our throat, by using our voice, we can unite earth and sky. The first three ChakraAuras: the Base of Spine (1st), Sacral (2nd), and Solar Plexus (3rd), represent the energy of the Earth – physical stability and basis of our physical expression. The upper three ChakraAuras: the Throat (5th), Third Eye (6th), and Crown (7th) represent the energy of the Sky – evolution and spirit. In the middle is the Heart – 4th

ChakraAura – the bridge between the lower three and the upper three ChakraAuras. Our voice unites all of these through one avenue of expression.

When you begin to chant, sound, or tone, it is important to pay attention to your breath. When you breathe in, imagine your body being filled with inspiration from spirit, the sky, and the heavens. When you exhale, imagine your body expressing *all* of the Elements and Earth's Energies. So your in-breath is Sky energy and your out-breath is Earth energy.

Joseph Rael eloquently explains how deeply sounds affect us: "Sound vibration connects the mind, body, and spirit, and makes the physical body whole .... The vibratory essence of sound affects the inner walls of the nerves and the blood vessels. The inner walls of each cell resonate and the power of vibration (sound) affects not only the physical cell walls (yet) also the mental, emotional, or spiritual walls ...."

Sounding (chanting, singing, toning, or forming sounds) is performed *with intention*. Intention is what sets sounding apart from any other form of using your voice. It does not matter so much where you do this. What is important is that you *give voice*, express with your own voice, and express with sincere focused intention. Sounding comes from your Heart and the depths of your Soul. Through its focused intention, sounding then celebrates all life.

Preparing for Sounding

Preparing to chant, tone, or sound is simple, not much different than preparing for meditation. Sit or stand comfortably. Feel grounded in your space. Whether you sit or stand, take three deep breaths. Deeply inhale using the previous visualizations of:

In-breath ... breathe in Sky energy.
Out-breath ... feel the joy of the Earth energy.

If you are standing: feel your feet solidly on the ground, connect to the 1st ChakraAura – Base of Spine and with the Earth Mother. Reach your head skywards and feel yourself connecting to the 7th ChakraAura – Crown, and then reach your energy further to infinity.

If you are sitting: with flat feet on the ground and shoes off (if possible), feel your connection with the Earth Mother through your 1st ChakraAura – Base of Spine. Reach your head skywards and feel yourself connecting to the 7th ChakraAura – Crown, and then reach your energy further to infinity.

Do this for a few minutes, helping you to center yourself, to be present to the moment, before you begin sounding.

The Sounds Selected for Vibrational AromaTherapy

Each word chosen for the transformational Sounds for the ChakraAuras comes from the *Tiwa* language. I chose their language because it is in danger of being lost to the world! The Tiwa are Native Americans, pueblo people who live in the Southwestern United States. Puebloans live in stone or adobe (handmade earth brick) houses. Sometimes they are individual houses with flat roofs and sometimes they are built on rock cliffs, as the homes of the Ancient Ones (also known as Anasazi) of the Four Corners region (states of Arizona, Utah, Colorado and New Mexico meet) in the United States.

You can find more of the Tiwa language in Joseph Rael's book *Being and Vibration*. Joseph Rael is of Tiwa descent. His father's family is from the Picuris Pueblo near Santa Fe, New Mexico. His mother's family lives on the Southern Ute Reservation, near Durango in Southwestern Colorado.

Chanting the Sounds

Joseph Rael suggests that as you begin to chant each word, visualize a stepladder. Allow the word to climb up the ladder as you hold the vowel sounds in the empty space of the ladder. He suggests that it is important to *emphasize the vowel sounds* in each word as you chant the words.

- ❖ Take a deep in-breath … breathe in Sky energy.

- ❖ Slowly chant the word, visualizing going up a ladder. At the same time, slowly let your breath out. Hold the vowel sound in the word.

- ❖ When you have reached the top of the ladder and your breath is fully exhaled, feel the joy of the Earth Mother's energy.

- ❖ Repeat each of the chosen words for each of the ChakraAuras, three (3) times.

- ❖ Joseph Rael again says: "With chanting, the repeated sounds of the consonants direct the power of the vowels in such a way as to create an energy design. Vibration impacts the physical body, bounces back, and on its return, the original form has changed into a new form ….The vowels in any given word reveal the power of the word while the consonants conduct the power of that energy into a healing current and give it a physical, mental, emotional, or spiritual impulse …. The vibration of the vowel sounds enters at the breath level (Spirit) and then through the physical level (matter) and flows (movement) through the body. Thus we can visualize chanting as the essence of – or metaphor for – Spirit becoming form in movement through matter."

Chapter 10

Goddess Archetypes – Mystery of Being

The first function of a mythology –
myths and mythic rituals, sacred songs and ceremonial dances –
is to waken in the individual a sense of awe, wonder,
and participation in the inscrutable mystery of being.
– Joseph Campbell

Myths

What is myth? The word itself comes from the ancient Greek culture and language: *mythos* meaning fable, tale, talk, and speech. It evolved to describe the opposite of the words *logos* (logic) and *historia* (history). In our early years in school, we are generally taught that myths are complete fiction, fairy tales of sort. Yet I offer you this food for thought…there might be a little bit (or possibly even a lot) of truth in between the lines of fiction. There may be more truth to myths than what we have been led to understand. Whatever your personal beliefs, myths have survived from generation to generation, for thousands of years, and for good reason. Our word *history* developed from the words: *his, story.* Generally, history has been written by men. Today the English language has another word that many people are beginning to use: *herstory (her, story).* Myth is… another side of the story.

Archetypes

Carl G. Jung says, "Myth is always an account of a creation of one sort or another or something coming into being, and reveals the sacredness or the supernaturalness of their work." Jung observed the amazing similarities between myths, dreams, and symbols amongst civilizations that had no apparent connection with each other. This led him to consider the existence of a collective unconsciousness. Consequently, the repetition throughout different cultures of these apparent similar myths, have become known as *archetypes*.

Most of the world's myths are focused on how the world and humans were created; stories that answer some of life's questions or challenges; female energy and male energy and how they differ from one another; or generally answering some of life's mysteries.

During the development of *Vibrational AromaTherapy*, I was guided to focus primarily on Goddess Archetypes/Myths. Humanity has been in a cycle of unbalanced patriarchy, which needs an input of matriarchy now to balance the scales. Just Balance – we do not want to tip the scales, repeating an unbalanced cycle!

Matriarchal and Patriarchal Cultures

In the ancient Egyptain culture, we can track periods of time that were strongly influenced by either the feminine or the masculine, or even overlapping with both. While it is difficult to find verifiable historical data that tells of a period of time when females ruled the masses, many believe (or know) that it existed. And the females ruling were not always about love and light!

Egypt's Goddess Isis

Isis (pronounced eye-sis) is the Great Mother, Power of Renewal. She is both mother and teacher to the other gods and the rulers on the Earth Mother. Isis is the symbol of fertility and known as exuding love so strong that it can create new life out of old. On her head, Isis wears the Full Moon disc, seen cradled by the horns of Hathor, an even more ancient goddess. Hathor's horns represent a woman's fallopian tubes (representing of birth and creativity). Isis ensured the fertility of the land and was revered as the inventor of agriculture, ruler over miracles, a Seer, and a symbol of resurrection.

Isis resurrected her dead brother, husband, and lover: Osiris

Isis – Egyptian Goddess "Twice Wise"
Artist Gayle Marie

(more than once). She resurrected Osiris reviving him for the second time and conceived their son, Horus. It was believed that Isis could hold back even death for her followers. She proclaimed the ability to overcome fate, yet she was not beyond grief herself. Eventually Osiris was killed. Unable to resurrect him a third time, Isis wept. Her grief was so deep that one of her tears caused the Nile River to flood.

Isis's original name was Isis Panthea, meaning The All Goddess. However, Greeks in Egypt eventually altered her name to merely Isis meaning Universal Goddess, which carries a lesser degree of status. Some of the other names given to this Goddess were Lady of Life and Divine Physician. She was hailed as a powerful healer with the ability to cure body, mind, spirit, and soul. Isis represents all aspects of the feminine archetype. To Egyptains, Isis and Osiris symbolized the completeness of the feminine and masculine principles.

Egypt's God Osiris

Osiris (pronounced o-sye-rus) means Liberated Soul, and Ra. He represents *life eternal*. His-story predates that of Christ. He was worshipped from about 3,000 B.C. until the end of Egyptian history circa 400 A.D., totaling about 3,400+ years. Known by over 200 other names, he is symbolic of the sunrise, sunset, and resurrection. Osiris is symbolic of virility and the force of Nature that dies and is reborn.

The *Egyptian Book of the Dead* dates back to 2400 B.C.. It is primarily texts of funerary practices. In this book, Osiris was called: "King of Kings, God of Gods and Lord of Lords." In the same book, they also said, "As truly as Osiris lives, so truly shall his followers live; as truly as Osiris is not dead he shall die no more; as truly as Osiris is not annihilated he shall not be annihilated." The ancient Egyptian scriptures tell of his coming as being announced by three wise men. It was said of Osiris that he was Truth. When his flesh was devoured (in the form of communion cakes of wheat) that individual also became Truth.

Osiris was called *Un-nefer* or Savior and Good One. The *Osirian Mysteries* (1450 to 1400 B.C.) were taught in ancient Egypt in order for one to become like Osiris. They were words of power, keys to heaven, were concealed from initiates, and refered to as a great mystery. "Knowest thou the name of this door, and canst thou tell it? .... Pass on, for thou has knowledge, O Osiris." (From the *Osirian Mysteries*.) Eventually Osiris' popularity declined because his scriptures were too wordy, long, and complicated for the average mind.

Osiris was the brother, husband, and lover to Isis. They are seen as one of the divine couples. In Egyptian mythology, the first divine couple were Shu and Tefnut, both created by the primal god Atum. Next came Geb and Nut, the parents of Osiris, Isis, Seth, and Nephthys. The myth says that when Geb and Nut were forced to separate from their loving embrace, the god Geb's body became the hills and valleys of the Earth Mother, while the Goddess Nut, lifted unwillingly from her lover's body, became the heavens and the firmament.

Myths From Different Cultures

Deities, gods, and goddesses have been associated with the human psyche for thousands of years. Since time began, the same mysteries have provoked questions all over the Earth Mother. "Why are we here?" "Where did we come from?" "What is the purpose for living?" Every civilization has tried to find the answers to these mysteries and to allay their fears in the same way – through the worship of gods and goddesses. Why have we needed gods and goddesses?

In our contemporary cultures, most religions today are *monotheistic*, single-god oriented: God, Allah, and Yahweh. But it was very different when humanity began on this Earth Mother. The most ancient of cultures such as the Mesopotamian, Sumerian, and Hittite, were *polytheistic*, meaning that they maintain the existence of multiple gods and goddesses.

Osiris – Egyptian God "King of the Living"
Artist Gayle Marie

Since the most primitive cultures, humans have associated everything that exists in their physical world to what they observe and find in Nature. Spiritual identity that is ever present, yet unseen, was left to the *shamans*, or wise ones, to explain, appease, or conjure. These deities and spirits carried attributes from Nature and were always endowed with human qualities – they walk and talk; enjoy sexual pleasures; represent male or female archetypes; show anger, joy, sorrow, mischief, compassion, and so forth. Consequently, you will find deities with names such as Corn Maiden, Old Man of the Rocks, and Lady of the Sea. Whatever their name or their culture of origin, all of these deities, gods, and goddesses are perceived with one common denominator – they are immortal. Primary myths all center on the creation of everything in the universe. These are called Creation Myths.

Creation Myths abound in every culture since the beginning of time. One of the original Creation Myths is that of the Garden of Eden. In the Garden, there were two trees – the Tree of Knowledge and the Tree of Life. The couple that lived in the Garden was asked by God to choose one tree. The couple chose the Tree of Knowledge. A serpent inhabited this tree (in many cultures a serpent also represents knowledge) and seduced the couple. Choosing the Tree of Knowledge, the couple was evicted from the Garden for doing so, and left to live out their lives seeking Knowledge. The Garden was a state of immortality for the couple, accompanied by a type of innocent grace. It equaled for the couple living in bliss, yet without knowledge of the expansiveness of who we are. With their eviction from the Garden, the couple lost their immortality, and consequently all future humans became mortal. Cast out of the Garden of the Gods they (and all humanity henceforth) were relegated to a life where they would experience good and evil, while seeking Truth and Knowledge, trying to return to their original state of grace (and immortality).

The Goddess and Her Role Today

All dieties can transcend cultures and time. They embody the relevance of their stories. They are all-seeing, all-knowing, self-existent, and immortal. In Goddesses myths, their stories are filled with beauty, grace, magic, creation, and mystery, as well as anger and retribution. Everything is about balance. You will not find a one-sided story in myths. Balance is always found within the story. The benevolent Mother Goddess also has her counterpart in the Dark Goddess.

Stories of the Goddesses have been lost in today's Western cultures. There is much evidence that many ancient civilizations were primarily matriarchal. The Goddesses of ancient cultures were demonized after they were overthrown by later religions. Most (if not all) of the sanctified cathedrals in Europe are built on sites that were at one time held sacred to the earth-based religions of the Goddesses.

The magic, mystery, and power surrounding the Goddess are being reawakened in our consciousness. Her attraction today to so many brings a sense of balance to a world that has been primarily patriarchal for millennia. Her re-emergence again is not to take over or replace the patriarchal, yet to bring balance to it. Our history has seen both male dominated and female dominated cultures, and neither has worked. Both denied the wonders of the other's energy.

The role of the Goddess today is to bring back a sense of balance and honoring into our lives. To find a balance between what has been and how we must be, to go forward and thrive, and to create a better world for our future and our children's future.

Paving New Paradigms for Humanity

We need to pave a new road – one that honors ALL. There is only one race, the human race, with its myriad of cultures. The Goddess reminds us of the balance that is to be found within each individual. The Goddess is not making her comeback to repeat history or to usurp masculine energy. She is here again to remind us how to work *together* on this beautiful planet, to help us to re-member who we are, to help us to heal (thus making us whole again), and to heal Nature and all beings.

You will notice in this book I have chosen to capitalize the word "Goddess." I use this format throughout the book to show the importance of finding balance, and the Goddess holds an important key to this balance. When you see written "Goddess," this refers to a characteristic of collective conscious, a feminine archetype (energy), and the deities that embody this energy.

When you see written "god," this refers to a characteristic of collective conscious, a masculine archetype, and the deities that embody this energy. In this book "god" refers to the 'masculine archetype' deity. It is not used to lessen the importance of the masculine archetype (energy), for it is of equal importance in finding balance. Rather it is to desiginate a difference between this deity and "God," the Creator, Infinite Source, or Divine Source.

The following is quoted from a most beautiful book: *She, The Book of the GODDESS*, written by Nigel Suckling, with art by Linda and Roger Garland:

> "To many people mythology seems a pointless study, a crock of mistaken beliefs ... (with no) relevance to modern life. To some, the tales are simply quaint and exotic fantasies, beautiful or terrifying fairytales about people and places that have only ever existed in dreams ... these myths of goddesses from around the world still have much to say. Particularly in this age of global realignment between the genders. In the past such shifts of power and relationship were reflected in myths about conflict between the gods and goddesses. On some plane of the imagination similar dramas are probably being acted out now, though what shape they will take is tomorrow's surprise. Myths are the distilled wisdom of the cultures that give them birth .... The language they use is the language of poetry, dream and vision."

Myth as Vibrational Medicine

We are here in this life to know ourselves more, and in the process grow and transform. In Chapter 2 *Alchemy and Physics,* remember the discussion about the balance of seeing with both eyes: *Uttatti* ?

In Part Four, you will find a Goddess archetype and myth for each of the nine ChakraAuras. Their stories are about balance, seeing things in balance, and correcting what is out of balance in our own life. Each of these Goddess Myths relates to your overall wellbeing. Today, with increasing recognition of gender and sexual orientation diversity, finding balance within your own spirit of who you are and how you express yourself in the world, will increase your feelings of self worth and your sense of belonging to the human race. By allowing others their path choices and their individualized expression, you will establish a new world for all of humanity.

PART THREE

Energetic Gifts

"With them the Seed of Wisdom did I sow
And with my own hand labour'd it to grow:
And this was all the Harvest that I reap'd –
I came like Water, and like Wind I go."

– Rina Swentzell, Pueblo Indian scholar from Santa Clara

Chapter 11

Earth Energetics – Elements and Directions

This we know …
the earth does not belong to man, man belongs to the earth.
All things are connected, like blood which connects one family.
Whatever befalls the earth befalls the children of the earth.
Man did not weave the web of life – he is merely a strand in it.
Whatever he does to the web, he does to himself.
— Chief Seattle

In the last twenty years since this book was first published, we have see many changes on the Earth Mother. Growing up in Southern California I remember knowing what each season would hold. I knew we didn't have snow or tornados in the valleys below the mountains where I lived. I knew the familiar warmth of the sun as its heat kissed my skin when I played at the beach on summer days. Today's world is much different: destructive tornados surprise old-timers living in areas where tornados never visited; fire season lasts all year long in California now; unheard of temperatures above 115 farenheit blast many cities globally, not just the deserts of Sahara or Mojave. The Elements and Nature today are unpredictable. They are asking us to wake-up.

"The elements of our universe, from the greatest solar system to the smallest invisible particle, are held together in an intricate design of divine intelligence. The magnetic force that determines the pattern of the planet's movements around our sun is but one example. That same divine intelligence directs my own spirit, mind, body, and all of my experiences. Many of my life's events seem to have been orchestrated long ago to aid my spiritual growth, as evidenced by the seeming coincidences through which I encounter just the right person, opportunity, or message at just the right time. The awesome, all-knowing presence of God that created the universe created me, too, and continues to guide me each day."

– quoted from Silent Unity's *Daily Word*

The Elements

For as long as humanity has inhabited the Earth Mother, five basic Elements have supported us:

❖ Earth – the bodies that animate us are made up of all the elements.

❖ Water – our bodies require water to exist.

❖ Air – we could not exist without air in our lungs.

❖ Fire – the fire of the sun warms the Earth Mother, making her habitable.

❖ Aether – unseen life-force and essence in everything.

According to early humanity's thinking, The Elements are associated with the creative energies of the universe. When we lived in villages, or were nomadic, we knew the importance of our connection to The Elements. Our survival depended on it. But we lost most of those connections when we began urban living.

Today more people are waking up and feeling the need to re-connect with Nature in some way. More and more people are recognizing this consciously, feeling a sense of loss, yet maybe are unaware of exactly what that loss is. There is a very real universal need to bring back into our lives a deep reverence and connection with Nature.

Before the birth of Christ, the predominant belief was of the Creatrix (Goddess) as a Universal Mother, and also the Universal Creator. She is the one who has the power to bring into creation and form the Love from the Divine. Because of these beliefs from every corner of the globe, the primordial Mother Goddesses of ancient cultures are closely related to the basic four/five Elements. The Elements, as her creations, were highly regarded and honored. Every culture has their interpretation of the Elements.

In oriental cultures, the egret is a symbol of balance. Susan B. Otten says, "Egret possesses the knowledge to channel desire (fire) by using emotion (water) and intellect (air) in a constructive way (earth)." In India, the Hindu goddess Kali, is also known as *Knowledge-Itself*, *Life-in-this-World*, and *Supreme Divinity*. She is credited with the creation of the sounds of the Sanskrit letters, which she used to bring the universe into being. These Sanskrit sounds, considered to be of the primal essence of The Elements, were in turn used to create all of creation. Uniting all of these Elements was Kali's own spirit, *Ma*, which means both *intelligence* and *mother*. Here, in Sanskrit sounds, are four Elements: Earth-*La*, Water-*Va*, Air-*Ya*, and Fire-*Ra*.

Another philosophy of the Elements came from the Neolithic Age when people discovered that other than cannibalism, there were four ways to dispose of the dead: cremation (fire), burial (earth), sinking in water (water) and exposure to carrion birds (air). Death was looked at as the opposite of birth and a natural cycle – birth, life, and death. In many cultures, death is still considered a return to the Earth Mother, who brings forth all life on the earthly plane.

There are traditional esoteric circular symbols (thousands of years old), which depict the basic four Elements. They appear here, depicted from the lightest to the densest (weight) of the Element:

- ❖ The empty circle represents Fire, and shows that fire has no weight.
- ❖ The circle, with a solid dot inside a sphere, stands for Air.
- ❖ The circle, with the diameter line, symbolizes Water.
- ❖ The circle, with the four corners inside it, created by the

equidistant cross, signifies the Earth Mother. This symbol is also used by the Native Americans to represent the Earth Mother and is called a Medicine Wheel.

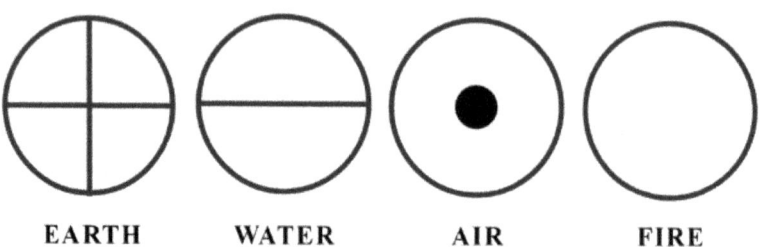

| EARTH | WATER | AIR | FIRE |

The Esoteric Symbols for the Elements

Western and Oriental Five Elements

Today, there are basically two schools of approach for the concept of the Elements – the Western and the Oriental. Numerous books have been written for each approach. Within each approach there are many different philosophies. For example, there are hundreds of different Native American Nations, and many have different interpretations of which elements, colors, and animals belong associated with each corner of the Medicine Wheel (a healing tool).

The Western philosophy's Five Elements are: Earth, Water, Air, Fire and Aether. (Some people omit Aether and focus on only four elements.) I prefer to incorporate all five of the elements, as it is closer to the concepts of alchemy and my concept of (what I call) the *AlkemicalElements*. Aether is The Element that binds the act of transformation and is the unseeable life force in everything. In alchemy it is called the *quinta essentia* (Latin).

The Oriental philosophy's Five Elements are: Earth, Wood, Water, Fire and Metal. You will find these in Chinese Medicine, acupuncture, and Feng Shui. If you are interested in more information about the Oriental approach to the Five Elements, Chinese Medicine, essential oils and acupressure, see Gabriel Mojay's wonderful and in-depth book, *Aromatherapy for Healing the Spirit.*

I have intentionally given you a brief overview of The Elements. It is intended to give the highlights and some history. Beyond what is in this chapter, and in upcoming chapters, you can go deeper based on your interests. If you are interested in further study, there are books listed in "Resources."

The Directions

The Directions for many indigenous cultures are considered cosmic intelligences. All ancient and present day cultures recognize four Directions – east, south, west, and north. Many cultures identify seven Directions – east, south, west, north, above, below, and center.

The Native Americans are one of the indigenous cultures who hold that these cosmic intelligences are a presence, which affects all living creatures, including the environment and the atmosphere of the Earth Mother. Kenneth Meadows says in *Where Eagles Fly*:

> "These Intelligences belong to a dimension which transcends physical and mental reality, and in generating movement they affect the nature of what is coming into manifestation. They are, therefore, far more than philosophical concepts, metaphysical principles, or religious beliefs. They are spiritual realities that actually regulate Nature and the Universe! In some cultures they were known as the Four Winds, because as Spirits, they could not be seen, yet like winds, their presence could be experienced through the effect they had on their surroundings."

Here is a list of the seven Directions and what they represent:

❖ **East** – New Beginnings, Illumination, and Wisdom

❖ **South** – Innocence, Faith, Growth, and Trust

❖ **West** – Endurance, Strength, and Dreams

❖ **North** – Eternity, Renewal, Purity, and Wisdom

❖ **Above** – Honors Father Sky, the Divine Presence

❖ **Below** – Honors Earth Mother, Giver of Abundance

❖ **Center** – Honors of Self

The AlkemicalElements

What are the *AlkemicalElements*? A terminology that I created decades ago, they are the true elements contained in each one of us that influence our life. The *AlkemicalElements* hold the mysterious promise of transformation for personal evolution. Look at the innate energies that are in each one of us – Body, Heart, Mind, Spirit, and Soul. Each one of these energies holds a very special essence, creating the delicate tapestry of who we are.

❖ The Body is as the Earth – rich, full of promise and nurturing, if we honor it.

❖ The Heart is as the Water – with the ability to soothe, purify, love and heal.

❖ The Mind is as the Air – innate intelligence, moving, fresh, seek with openness.

❖ The Spirit is as Fire – an intelligent essence with the ability to transmute.

❖ The Soul is as Aether – the *quinta essentia*, life force and essence of all.

When these *AlkemicalElements* (Body, Heart, Spirit, Mind, and Soul) are enlivened and transformed, then the *prima materia* (You) are embodying your full potential. What does this mean? You are living the kind of life you want. A life that all humans desire, one saturated with love, joy, and creativity and a life directed by a sense of purpose and relevance.

Five Elements, Directions and Their Energies

Earth (Western) – Earth (Oriental)

Earth Element is the heaviest of the Elements. If you mix it in a container with water, it will sink to the bottom. Earth relates to your physical body and the Earth herself. Stones represent the densest form of the Earth. The pinky (little) finger on your hand relates to the Element of Earth. The Earth provides sustenance and nourishment. All that we need to sustain our physical body is found here. The Earth feels stable beneath our feet (most of the time, no accounting for earthquakes)!

The basic nature of the Earth Element is fertile, moist, stabilizing, grounding, and nurturing. Earth Element is a receptive energy (archetype). The season associated with the Earth Element is autumn (harvest time). The Direction is West. It represents strength and endurance. The time of day represented is sunset. The *AlkemicalElement* of Earth is the Body.

Water (Western) – Water (Oriental)

Water Element is lighter than the Earth Element. Our bodies are between 70%-80% water. Our blood is mostly water. The Water Element is soothing and refreshing and relates to the energy of the Heart. Through the essence and energy of the Heart is the magic and ability to transform. The ring (next to pinky) finger relates to the Water Element. Most people enjoy bathing in the ocean, sea, river, lake, or being near water, and the effects of this enjoyment are much deeper than we realize.

The Water Element can bring up emotions in most people. It has the ability to disperse and dilute unwanted and negative energies. It assists us in being more fluid and resilient, which means less stuborn or resistant. Water Element is crucial to all. We cannot exist without it. When humans use water in Nature (river, ocean, lake, etc.), it has the ability to consciously (and unconsciously) wash away strong emotions (such as anger and rage). The Earth Mother has the ability to absorb these strong emotions and to transmute the disharmonies. Water allows for a mutable cleansing of the rage and for it to be dispersed, where it is safely absorbed by the Earth Mother and transformed to a calmer process.

The basic nature of the Water Element is flowing, purifying, soothing, loving, and healing. Water Element is receptive energy (archetype). The season associated with the Water Element is winter and the direction is North (frozen water is in suspension and nurtures in a time of darkness). Water represents renewal and purity. The time of day represented is midnight. The *AlkemicalElement* of Water is the Heart.

Air (Western) – Wood (Oriental)

Air Element when mixed with Water Element turns into bubbles and rises up. Air has the ability to penetrate every aspect of your being. The index (pointer) finger relates to the Element of Air. Air also feeds and supports Nature, which is all around you. Take a deep, deep, deep breath. Breath is Air. Prana, Chi, Qi (known in many cultures). Air is the sustainer of life. Air is our energy. Air can create powerful movement and carries the energy of your Mind and your intentions. Air Element represents the force of the intellect and the power of the Mind. You can either be present and focused with your mind or let your mind wander exploring a universe of subjects!

The basic nature of the Air Element is moving, fresh, and intelligent. Air Element is a projective energy. The season associated with the Air Element is spring (time of freshness) and the direction is East. It represents illumination and wisdom. The time of day is sunrise. The *AlkemicalElement* of Air is the Mind.

Fire (Western) – Fire (Oriental)

Fire Element rises up when it is mixed with Air Element. The Sun is the ultimate symbol of Fire. Heat and Passion are both fueled by Fire. Fire Element represents the vital heat in our body. Fire is both a creator and a destroyer. Fire carries the essence of the Spirit. Unlike any of the other Elements, Fire cannot exist without consuming something else. It has the ability to transform objects into other forms – light, heat, ash, and smoke. Therefore, to receive the benefits of Fire, it must be controlled, otherwise it destroys. Yet even out of the fires ashes, there are benefits. There is an ancient myth of the Phoenix, a bird symbolizing transformation, as it arises from the ashes. The middle finger relates to the Element of Fire.

The basic nature of the Fire Element is destructive, forceful, purifying, cleansing, and sexual. The Fire Element is a projective energy. The season associated with the Fire Element is summer (time of heat) and the direction is South. It represents growth and trust. The time of day is midday, the time of the full sun. The *AlkemicalElement* of Fire is the Spirit.

Aether (Western) – Metal (Oriental)

Aether (ether) is even lighter than Fire. The ancient Greeks hypothesized that the Element Aether was the matter of which the heavenly bodies and stars are made. They asserted that Aether existed only in the heavens. Our word *Aethereal* (ethereal) is derived from the word aether and its concepts. Aether holds the essence of the Soul. This fifth Element was so highly regarded that it became known as *quinta essentia* in ancient alchemy. The American Webster's Collegiate Dictionary describes aether as "a medium that in the undulatory theory of light permeates all space and transmits transverse waves."

The Aether Element is found in the void. It has the potential to manifest the other basic four Elements and to balance them all. Aether holds within it the promise of transmutation and transformation. The thumb relates to the Element of Aether. The basic nature of the Aether Element is both receptive and projective and can be associated with any time of day. All seasons are associated with the Aether Element and the direction is Center (Self). Joseph Rael calls this Center position of the circle on the Medicine Wheel, the position that "calls greatness into existence for its own personal unfolding or 'Caller of Highest Greatness.'" *AlkemicalElement* of Aether is the Soul.

The Elements and The Directions as Vibrational Medicines

The information above expresses how important all of these energies are in our lives. It is necessary that we don't ignore our body or our emotions. As a human being, many of us can get caught up in daily life and forget to take care of ourselves. Daily we go on our way, taking care of everything in our mind and on our lists. Then we fall into bed exhausted and possibly with a headache (or other ailment). 'Pay attention' to your body and your emotions for they are a barometer telling you what is out of balance.

There are many different theories (depending on the culture of origin) for how The Elements and The Directions may influence for us. As Vibrational Medicines, The Elements and The Directions can act as guides to help you identify where to focus your attention and where to direct your healing energy. (Please be responsible and consult a physician when needed.)

In the *Vibrational AromaTherapy* approach you will take into consideration the Elements and Directions, yet you will decide for yourself what feels appropriate for you. A particular ChakraAura can be associated with specific Elements or Directions (in many cultures and approaches). However, sometimes another element's energy may be needed to balance or heal a particular ChakraAura. Here is a detailed example of why I feel that assigning one Element to one ChakraAura is too limiting:

The 2nd ChakraAura – Sacral, by some cultures and approaches, is considered to be associated to the Water Element. The Sacral is the Creative Energy center. Creative Energy is probably the strongest energy that propels everyone of us to leave our *mark* on the world in some way, through our children, our work in the world, or by being who we are (in a positive way).

One of our biggest challenges as a human is to understand and use the creative gifts given to us as energy within us, both consciously and with wisdom. Located in the human body at the Sacral ChakraAura, if we liken the Creative Energy to a garden, we can see:

- ❖ The Fire Element can light the spark at this ChakraAura to begin growth, yet *too much* Fire and the energy can *burn you out*.

- ❖ The Earth Element provides the physical base and tangible foundation for the creative seeds to grow and become real, but too much earth and the fire is extinguished. The Air Element enters in with its conscious intent when using this ChakraAura wisely, but too much air fans the fire.

- ❖ The Water Element, in its intrinsic fluidity, seeks the earth to help ground, nourish, and form the foundation for the creative energies to grow. Balance is key.

- ❖ The Air Element helps to shift the seasons, bring in different growing conditions so that all the garden grows in balance.

The Medicine Wheel

A Medicine Wheel is a teaching and healing tool used by Native American cultures that incorporates the Directions. It can hold within it messages of balance, information for self-awareness, and deeper connections and attunement with the natural world. The drawing below is inspired by the Native American Medicine Wheel and depicts The Directions along with their energetic associations.

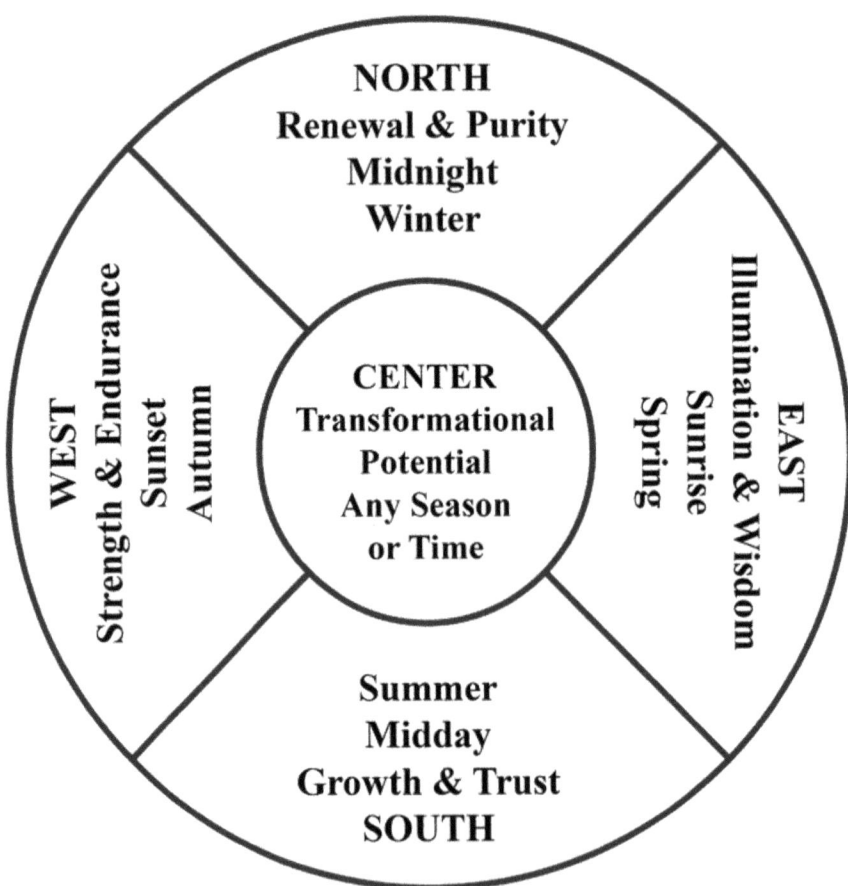

The Medicine Wheel

Chapter 12

Moon – Heavenly Guide

High in the sky, the Moon shines like a beacon in the night, guiding the wanderer and the seafarer on their way. As regularly as clockwork, her constantly changing face marks the passage of time for each and every thing that lives on the face of the Earth.
— Lori Reid, *Moon Magic*

Ancient Peoples and the Moon

The Moon is a sister to the Earth Mother and her influence upon this globe is undeniable. Indigenous and ancient people (some cultures today) organized their lives around the Moon's Phases. Dates for marriages and other important events were not set until the phases of the Moon were taken into consideration. In India today, most marriage dates are not set without first consulting to see where the moon and its phases are for the appointed date. The phrase – *once in a blue moon* – means the rare occurrence of two full moons in the same calendar month (Gregorian calendar). Hence, the term can also refer to an unusual event, one that doesn't happen very often. Normally, we will have a *blue moon* occurance once every 33 months.

It is well accepted by most present day cultures that the Moon affects the tides and waters on our great Earth Mother. As we humans are made up of between 70% and 80% water, the Moon Phases also affect us. Unusual and excessive events occur during full moons. Police departments internationally record that during the time of the Full Moon, there are more passionate crimes such as murders. Hospital records tell us that more babies are born during the Full Moons.

The Moon's influence on all of us is incredibly important. So, once again, I leave it to the discretion of you (the reader) to utilize this information in the most appropriate and suitable way you desire. Many communities around the world have celebrations, meditations, and/or prayers during the important phases of the Moon. Join one in your community, or begin your own gatherings!

Bathing in Moonlight
Artist Patricia Elder

The Eight Lunar Phases

There are eight different Lunar (Moon) phases. Each phase lasts for about three and a half days. The total time from the New Moon to the next New Moon (or Full Moon to the next Full Moon) is approximately 28 days. This constitutes a complete Lunar Cycle. Before the Gregorian Calendar (now in use in the world as a means of detailing time) many people calculated time by the Moon's phases, referring to its phases as the lunar calendar. Traditionally there are 13 sets of Lunar Phases in a given year.

How do the Moon Phases affect us? The following is a list of the eight different phases and the energies that surround us during those times.

1. **New Moon – the Dark Moon:** This phase is a time to initiate new projects and to plant seeds in all forms. It is the starting point. It is a symbol of the Mother, containment, and nurturance. Much drama, enthusiasm, and magnetism surround the New Moon. Keywords are new beginnings, growth, and ideas.

2. **Crescent Moon – First Crescent:** This phase represents assertiveness, adventurousness, and joyous curiosity. Experiencing transmutation and growth within your being is like the first sliver of light after the New Moon. It is as being reborn. There is an ability to overcome obstacles at this time. It is a time of moving towards expansiveness. Keywords are emergence, initiation, renewal, and transformation.

3. **First Quarter – First Half, Waxing Moon:** This phase is a time for rejuvenation and a time to learn how to direct activity. A challenging time, it is also a time of germination. It is a time to re-build. Possibly, it is a time to tear down the old in place of the new, which is more appropriate and up-to-date.

The Waxing Moon resembles a "D" shape and represents a moon that is developing or increasing in size. Keywords are positive, assertive, expressive, and strong-willed.

4. **Gibbous Moon – Almost Full:** This phase is the calm before the storm! It is also an important time to focus on helping others. The focus is positive contributions to the world. This energy can almost become obsessive because of the intensity to illuminate just around the corner. Moving towards the Soul's growth does not happen without some turmoil. Keywords are creative and expressive.

5. **Full Moon – Total Lumination:** This phase is a very intense time, with much spiritual energy and strong emotions flooding the Earth Mother. Quite often, it is a time of action before thought, fueled by irrationality. Sitting in mid-phase offers an adeptness to balance logic with instinct and practicality with creativity. The Full Moon is also the time of the lover, romance, and completion. Keywords are fulfillment, culmination, and endings.

6. **Disseminating Moon – Sharing:** This phase is a time for communication and teaching of ideas, thoughts, and feelings. Compassionate and philosophic, it is a time of reformation and a time to reap the rewards from past experiences. Such passion also demands the wisdom of timing and of not allowing the zeal to become pushy. Keywords are teaching communication and reformation.

7. **Last Quarter – Last Half, Waning to New Moon:** This phase is a time of the warrior personified, one who uses great passion in all of life's experiences. It is a time to gather thoughts, expand awareness, resolve problems, and organize. Don't dwell on the past … move forward. The Waning Moon

resembles a "C" shape and represents a moon that is getting smaller or contracting in size. Keywords are understanding, sympathy, maturity, and poise.

8. **Balsamic Moon – Last Sliver Before New Moon:** This phase represents letting go, transition, and building new foundations. It is a period of introspection and contemplation, to tie up loose ends, to journey inwards, and to prepare for new beginnings ahead. Deep metaphysical overtones and an openness to explore the mysteries of life are embodied before the New Moon. Keywords are intuition, mystical understanding, far-sightedness, and innate wisdom.

The Thirteen Full Moons

In most Native American languages, words that are capitalized are considered *holy or sacred*. As Jamie Sams heartfully says in her book, *The 13 Original Clan Mothers*, "In Native American culture, we see everything as being alive. Each living thing has a specific role as a teacher and family member. Everything on Earth (whether stone, tree, creature), above Earth (cloud, sun, moon), or human being is one of our relatives. We capitalize the names of each part of our Planetary Family because they represent the sacred living extensions of the Great Mystery who were placed here to help humankind evolve spiritually …."

Jamie Sams, is a member of the Wolf Clan Teaching Lodge. Her teachings focus on native feminine wisdom. The richness of the primarily oral traditions were passed on to her by two Kiowa Grandmothers – Cisi Laughing Crow and Berta Broken Bow – both said to be over 120 years old when Jamie was 22 years old. A wonderful book full of inspiration and feminine wisdoms. Jamie explains in her own words why she chose to share these teachings with others,

"I have chosen to open these teachings and my personal vision in order to share the map of healing I have received. These Medicine Stories and Traditions are my Give-away to human beings everywhere, so that we may continue to dream the dream, and to dance the Dance of Creation, bringing inner peace and, therefore, world peace."

A *Give-away*, a term used in many Native American tongues, is a gift that is given from your Heart; without expectation of something in return.

Each of the Full Moons has a special relationship, energy, and focus. I recommend Jamie's book highly as a resource for anyone who feels a close connection with this brightest planet in our sky. What I have outlined for you is my abbreviation (quoted from the eloquent detail of Jamie's book) of the focus for each of the Full Moons.

First, each full moon beginning in January is listed with its cycle in relation to our calendar (i.e. January's Moon – First Moon Cycle).

Second, it explains in the Kiowa tradition the Name of the Full Moon (i.e. *TALKS WITH RELATIONS – The Mother of Nature*).

Third, listed is what I refer to as the Moon's essential energy (ie: *How to LEARN THE TRUTH*). I wish to heartfully thank Jamie Sams for her open sharing of information so that we all "may continue to dream the dream" and grow in wisdom.

Jamie Sams' Yearly Full Moon Cycles

January's Moon – First Moon Cycle

TALKS WITH RELATIONS – The Mother of Nature
How to LEARN THE TRUTH

February's Moon – Second Moon Cycle

WISDOM KEEPER – The Protectress of Sacred Traditions
How to HONOR THE TRUTH

March's Moon – Third Moon Cycle

WEIGHS THE TRUTH – Keeper of Equality and the Guardian of Justice
How to ACCEPT THE TRUTH

April's Moon – Fourth Moon Cycle

LOOKS FAR WOMAN – The Seer/Oracle/Dreamer/Prophet
How to SEE THE TRUTH

May's Moon – Fifth Moon Cycle

LISTENING WOMAN – Mother of the Stillness & Inner Knowing
How to HEAR THE TRUTH

June's Moon – Sixth Moon Cycle

STORYTELLER – Guardian of the Medicine Stories
How to SPEAK THE TRUTH

July's Moon – Seventh Moon Cycle

LOVES ALL THINGS – Mother of Unconditional Love and All Acts of Pleasure
How to LOVE THE TRUTH

August's Moon – Eighth Moon Cycle

SHE WHO HEALS – Intuitive Healer/Midwife/Herbalist
How to SERVE THE TRUTH

September's Moon – Ninth Moon Cycle

SETTING SUN WOMAN – Keeper of Tomorrow's Dreams and Goals
How to LIVE THE TRUTH

October's Moon-Tenth Moon Cycle

WEAVES THE WEB-Mother of Creativity/the Muse/the Artist/the Creatress
How to WORK WITH TRUTH

November's Moon – Eleventh Moon Cycle

WALKS TALL WOMAN – Guardian of Leadership and
   Keeper of New Paths
How to WALK THE TRUTH

December's Moon – Twelfth Moon Cycle

GIVES PRAISE-The Mother of Thanksgiving and Keeper
   of Abundance
How to be GRATEFUL FOR THE TRUTH

Blue Moon of Transformation – Thirteenth Moon Cycle

BECOMES HER VISION – Guardian of Transformation
   and Transmutation
How to BE THE TRUTH

Other Off-Planet Influences

We are now living in the Aquarian Age. It's clear to see that everything is changing, and fast! I came of age in the late 1960's, and I remember singing the song and only imagining what it could possibly be like to live in "The Age of Aquarius." It was so far off to me at that point, that my mind couldn't rap around it. It indeed felt like some dream or play someone had concocted. Yet here it is! So I sought counsel from a dear friend in London, a renowned Astrologer and Spiritual Consultant, Shelley Von Strunckel:

> "The Aquarian Age isn't merely about a new cycle, it's about a profound shift, on our planet, and within our beings, individually and as a group. How to describe it? How would lasting, profound, peace smell? That's it."

Chapter 13

Energy Centers – ChakraAuras

It is not easy to find happiness in ourselves,
and it is impossible to find it elsewhere.
– Agnes Repplier

There are hundreds of energy centers in our body. Each energy center holds vital life forces and acts to transmit and assimilate energy and information to each of us. Our energy centers act as indicators to us of our state of wellbeing. The seven major energy centers recognized within the physical body are often referred to as *chakras*. The four primary energy centers outside of the body are often referred to as *auras*. In *Vibrational Aroma Therapy by Ixchel™*, all of the chakras and auras are referred to as: *ChakraAuras*.

The Chakras of the ChakraAuras

Chakra is a Sanskrit word meaning Wheel of Light. The formal and complete name for the chakra energy centers in the body is Kala Chakra. Kala Chakra means Wheel of Light and Time. The Tibetans refer to the chakras as Time Machines. They perceive that in time or through lifetimes, each one of us grows, changes, and transforms. To the Tibetans therefore, the major energy centers, chakras, or our Time Machines are producing Enlightened Beings. Chakras are centers of energy in the body. Energy flows through the body. Where energy collects, there is a chakra, which is like a vortex and whirling ball of energy. Those who are sensitive to energy can sometimes see the chakra as light. Other sensitives may feel the energy within each chakra. Everything consists of this life force energy; modern physicists have proved this. In Chinese Medicine this energy is called *Qi*, and in East Indian yogic tradition it is called *Prana*.

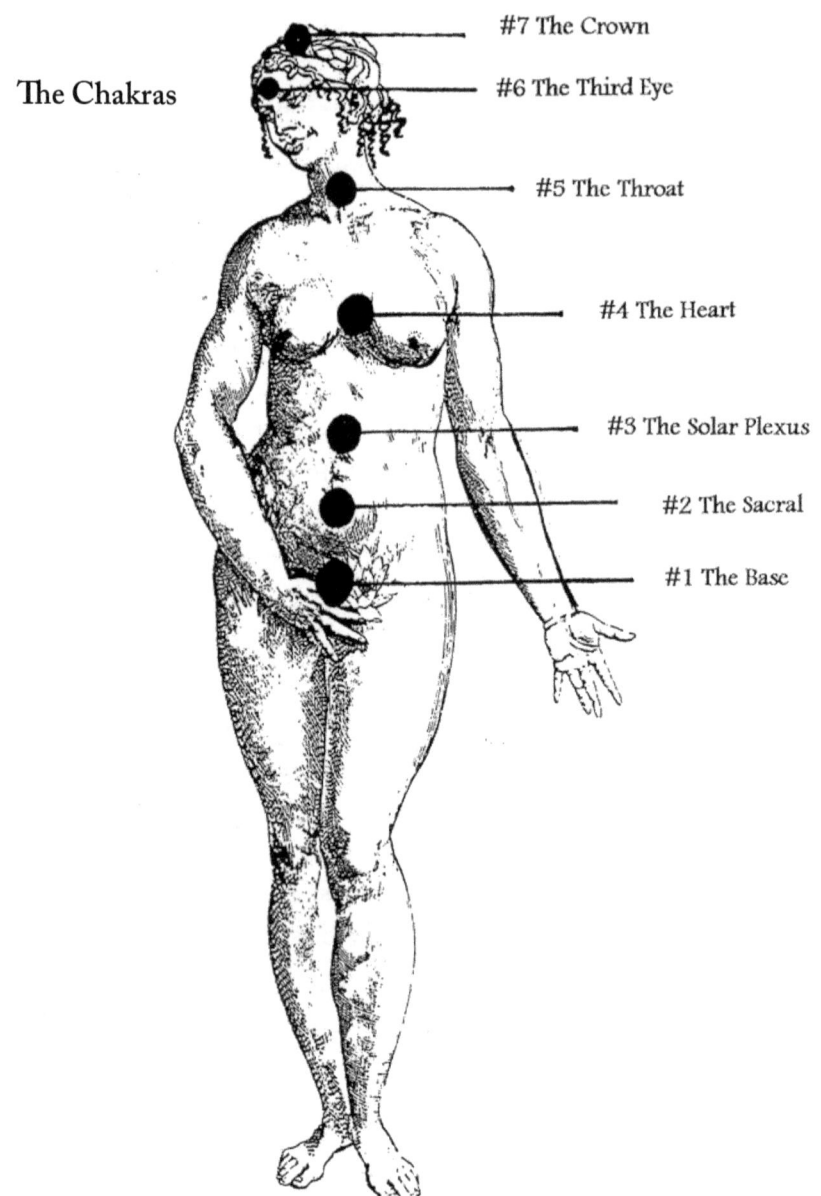

The Chakras

#7 The Crown

#6 The Third Eye

#5 The Throat

#4 The Heart

#3 The Solar Plexus

#2 The Sacral

#1 The Base

Chakra Woman
(Illustration adapted by Ixchel Leigh from out of print material texts and
were first published in the *Vibrational Aroma Therapy Manual*)

The seven major chakras of the Chakras in the body are:

- ❖ 1st Chakra – Base of Spine
- ❖ 2nd Chakra – Sacral
- ❖ 3rd Chakra – Solar Plexus
- ❖ 4th Chakra – Heart
- ❖ 5th Chakra – Throat
- ❖ 6th Chakra – Third Eye
- ❖ 7th Chakra – Crown

(See Chakra Woman illustration on opposite page)

The state of health of each chakra directly affects the physical body. Each major chakra is associated with important organs within the physical body, relating to the body's health and wellbeing. Healthy chakras are referred to as being clear and balanced. They help us to maintain our sense of harmony and clear direction in life. We are dependent on free flowing and unblocked energy through our bodies to remain healthy. When a chakra is blocked, clogged, or out of balance, it can affect our physical, emotional, mental, and spiritual state of wellbeing. Because every part of us consists of energy, our mental attitudes and emotions can also cause blockages of the energy.

If we are stressed, worried, unhappy, or live in doubt or fear, even a little bit, we can disturb the free flowing of this energy and our physical body eventually will carry this burden in the form of a disease, either physical, emotional, or mental. A change in our thought processes or a shift in our lifestyle can facilitate a balancing or healing in a particular chakra. As a result of the changes, we are then healing the energy center, creating a balanced flow of energy and truly creating transformation in our lives.

The chakras appear differently to those sensitive to seeing or feeling energy. Becoming sensitive to seeing or feeling energy can be developed. See the diagrams below to help you to visualize the difference between healthy and unhealthy ChakraAuras.

Healthy Chakras

Close your eyes. You are now going to visualize and imagine healthy, balanced chakras and auras. They appear round and full, like the full moon or a ball.

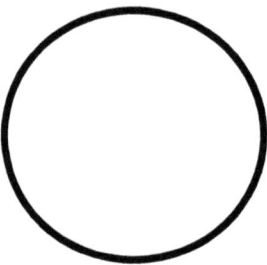

Unhealthy Chakras

Now close your eyes again. You are going to visualize and imagine what unhealthy, clogged, and out of balance chakras look like. They appear skinny or with broken edges.

The Auras of the ChakraAuras

Wellbeing begins not in the actual physical body, yet rather in what we would call our aura. The auras, or auric fields, are subtle energy fields that surround the body in many different layers. In *Vibrational AromaTherapy by Ixchel™*, we refer to two of the primary auras as ChakraAuras. The auric fields, closest to the physical body, following the contour of the physical body, is the Etheric Body. The second auric field extends from the Etheric Body, beyond the physical body and is called the Astral body. The auric fields are independent of each other, yet each can interact with each other. They act as filters for the physical body.

Healthy auric field colors or light are: clear, bright, and transparent. Before our physical body becomes out of balance, the dis-ease (disease) or disturbance enters our aura. The auras then become congested and depleted of their vital energy (which also supports the physical body) and their colors often appear muddied and darker. If this happens, we have the opportunity to clear the dis-ease before it reaches the physical body. If the auric fields are out of balance, you can feel low energy and a lack of vitality. By focusing on balancing the auras with conscious intention, you raise your vibratory rate and consequently your energy levels and vitality. If the dis-ease is not detected, cleared, and balanced in the subtle energy fields of the aura, the disease can then proceed to our physical body to get our attention!

The two primary auric fields of the ChakraAuras are:

❖ 8th ChakraAura, Etheric Body – 1st Auric Layer

❖ 9th ChakraAura, Astral Body – 2nd Auric Layer

(See Aura Man illustration on the following page.)

The Auras

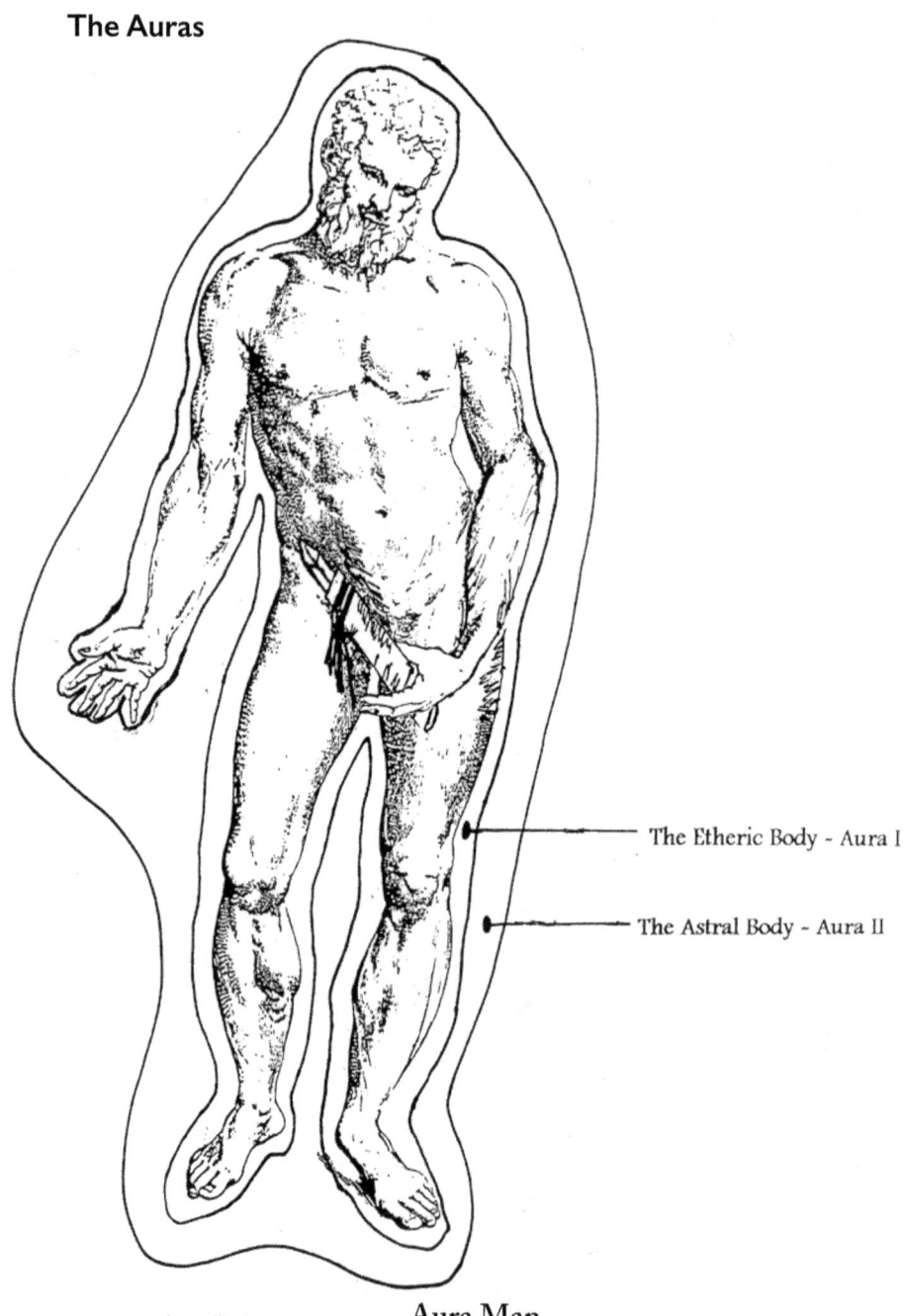

The Etheric Body - Aura I

The Astral Body - Aura II

Aura Man

Illustration adapted by Ixchel Leigh from out of print material texts and were first published in the *Vibrational Aroma Therapy Manual*.

Focus. Intention. Attention.

Once you define and state the focus of your intention, you are ready to bring attention to intention. Your intention needs to be supported by your attention. Imagine a clear pathway leading to your intention, one free of hindrances. Better yet ... *see your intention* as already a part of your life, rather than something that you are striving towards!

Clearing and balancing the ChakraAuras on the subtle level can lead toward transformation of the individual on all levels. What is your intention? Clearly define this intention before you begin. Focus your intention. For example, if your intention is to clear and balance a chakra or aura, you may want to *state* this verbally out loud, silently to yourself, or write it on paper. What feels most comfortable to you?

Balancing of the ChakraAura returns them to their ideal state of wellbeing. When all of the ChakraAuras are in balance, we feel happier and more in joy. When we feel joy, we are functioning on our natural path of harmony in our life. It helps to create a homeostasis in the body, mind, and spirit. Sometimes this takes place due to the natural healing capacity that is innately present in our hands and sometimes it is through focused loving intent. Healing does not occur because someone forces his or her will onto another individual. True healing occurs when the individual desiring it opens her or his heart and allows the healing change.

These concepts can be applied to many areas of life, not just your wellbeing and the balancing of your energy centers or ChakraAuras. Ponder this for a minute. How powerful is it to use these concepts in your personal or your professional life?

❖ Define your intention

❖ Focus on your intention

❖ Bring your attention to your intention

The Nine ChakraAuras and The Essence of Life Realms

The ChakraAuras (energy centers) and what they represent in relation to transformation are detailed further in this book (Part Four). Each chakra and aura has one word that also represents what that particular energy center is focused on. For example: the Base of the Spine is the 1st ChakraAura. Its *Essence of Life Realm* (word) is Courage. Courage is something that we can all relate to in some way. For some, it takes courage just to walk out of their home and go into the larger outside world. For others, courage may be giving the speech to their class, office, or the country! Where does courage fit into your life? Where in your life might you need courage right now? It takes Courage just to be human. We are here to grow in wisdom. And each of us is given our set of challenges along the way.

I have created an easy reference chart (on the next page) called: *Essence of Life Realm ChakraAura Transformation* chart. The list below explains the meanings of each category on the chart:

- ❖ **Essence of Life Realm**: The word relating to the ChakraAura that best describes the realm, or area of focus in your everyday life that is affected by the energy of the particular ChakraAura.

- ❖ **ChakraAura**: Each chakra and each aura has a number and the corresponding part of the body.

- ❖ **Transformation**: The area of your life where you will find personal growth when you focus on a particular ChakraAura for balancing, healing, or personal transformation.

Essence of Life Realms for Transformation

Essence	ChakraAura	Transformation
Courage	1st Base of Spine	Physical Transformation
Create	2nd Sacral	Creative Transformation
Manifest	3rd Solar Plexus	Transformation of Individual Will
Joy	4th Heart	Emotional Transformation
Truth	5th Throat	Transformation of Expression
Vision	6th Third Eye	Transformation for Intuition
Inspiration	7th Crown	Spiritual Transformation
Release	8th Etheric Body	Transforming Negativity
Knowing	9th Astral Body	Transforming to Universal Love

Determining Out-of-Balance

When ChakraAuras are in balance, each of us feels very specific personal and spiritual desires. When they are out of balance, we experience certain blockages that relate to personal and/or spiritual fears.

If you aren't gifted with seeing or feeling the ChakraAura's that are out of balance, you can use your intuition, or one of the assessing tools (dowsing, pendulum, kinesiology). Using a pendulum or dowsing rods (or through kinesiology ask the questions) to determine which ChakraAura is out of balance:

Hold the pendulum about 7 inches above the physical body at each ChakraAura and ask, "Does the 1st ChakraAura need balancing?" Do this all the way up the ChakraAuras of the body.

For the 8th-9th ChakraAuras, suggestions for positioning the pendulum:

- ❖ 8th ChakraAura/Etheric Body – Hold pendulum about 2 inches from top of head.
- ❖ 9th ChakraAura/Astral Body – Hold pendulum about 4 inches from top of head.

Now observe how the pendulum is swinging:

Are you getting a: S—L—O—W - S—W—I—N—G, on some of the ChakraAuras you are dowsing? This may be saying it is unclear as to whether or not it needs balancing.

Are you getting a: FAST and WIDE swing on? Usually, the quicker, faster, fuller, and wider swings of the pendulum are more definitive YES answers! Practice with this method will improve your ablility to determine the ChakraAura's balance at the moment. Follow your intuition and guidance.

If you receive a YES answer on more than one ChakraAura:

You will need to choose one ChakraAura to focus on (for each meditation or focused healing session). **Do not attempt to balance more than one chakra or aura at a time**! Yes we can get excited about returning our body to radiant health. However, too much at one time can trigger more challenges. So please pace yourself and know your body, mind, and emotions.

ChakraAura Tree for Transmuting Energy

If you prefer to use a diagram of the body (rather than the actual body present or live) I have included two diagrams in this book – *Chakra Woman* and *Aura Man*, they have all chakras or auras listed on the diagram.

Alternately, you can refer to another chart: *ChakraAura Tree for Transmuting Energy* (opposite page) that is also suitable to use to determine and assess (through intuition, dowsing, pendulum, or kinesiology), which ChakraAura is out of balance answers. In this chart:

"FEAR OF" = Out of Balance ChakraAura identifies the personal or spiritual issue holding you back.

"DESIRE FOR"= When ChakraAura is in Balance, you will probably have a Desire for something.

ChakraAura Tree for Transmuting Energy

Out of Balance ChakraAura = Personal & Spiritual FEAR OF:	Keyword ChakraAura	In Balance ChakraAura = Personal & Spiritual DESIRE FOR
Doubt. "What if I'm wrong." Mis-trust in humanity. Judging others.	**KNOWING** 9	Allowing other's their process for change without judgment. Universal love. Belief in a positive humanity.
Losing self-identity and security. Someone or something is in your way.	**RELEASE** 8	Creating a new paradigm for Being. Release from the "old" which inhibits transformation.
Separation. Sees the Divine as accusatory. Like a critical parent.	**INSPIRATION** 7	Union with Divine. Transcendence. Unconditional Love.
Mis-using psychic powers. Mis-trust of your intuition.	**VISION** 6	Trust. Psychic power. Mystical understanding.
Criticism. Punishment. Responsibility. Fear of being "unveiled."	**TRUTH** 5	Speaking and acting with integrity. Being a conduit for spiritual truth. Being free of convention.
Fear of giving of feelings and emotions. Feelings of anguish and jealousy.	**JOY** 4	Connectedness to Divine. Openheartedness. Joyfulness. Compassion for others.
Mis-using power. Losing control. Having no effect. Being incapable.	**MANIFEST** 3	Longing to influence. Taking action. Making a difference. Manifesting change.
Sexual contact. Touching. Expressing your capabilities. Transformative energy.	**CREATE** 2	Enjoying intimate contact. Wishing to express your innate gifts and talents.
Lack. Fear. Change. Depletion. Insecurity.	**COURAGE** 1	Abundance. Courage. Vitality. Security.

Energetics of the Body

In Chapters 14-22, you will be exploring the nine ChakraAuras, the Energetics of the Body. Each ChakraAura has a word (Courage, Create, Manifest, etc.) that describes the focus of the energy center, and its particular influence in your life. These influences (the words) are referred to as *Essence of Life Realms*. Thus you can discover in what area of your life, you might set your intention, focus your attention, to seek healing and balancing, in order to feel that you are fully your Essence Self.

Sometime the intention may be to heal, remove blockages in your way, or to ignite the flame of energy anew. I created a phrase to help you remember them. Beginning at your 1st ChakraAura – Base of Spine (#1 Courage) and moving upwards through your body towards the 7th ChakraAura – Crown (#7 Knowing), then beyond the physical body through into the first two auric layers, the 8th-9th ChakraAuras. As you say the phrase, visualize balancing each energy center and being accompanied by abundant, vibrant, radiant health and wellbeing:

I have the **COURAGE**

to **CREATE**

and **MANIFEST**

my **JOY**

and **TRUTH**,

through **VISION**

and **INSPIRATION**.

I **RELEASE**,

to have **KNOWING**,

In each chapter there is information on the particular ChakraAura, how it relates to your body, and what some of the physical symptoms or dis-eases can be when the ChakraAura is out of balance. Details are given for each of Nature's Gifts (Nature's Vibrational Medicines) that have their associations with each ChakraAura. Use them for meditations and focused healing sessions. You will also find associated for each energy center: the Myth and archetype, a special Meditation, and suggested Affirmations for each energy center.

Affirmations help to utilize energy, allowing you to focus your intention so you can more easily energize your attention. In other words, they open the door and allow for more concentrated penetration of your intentions. There are five Affirmations for each Essence of Life. If you are focusing on healing a particular area of your life, choose the Affirmation that feels the most appropriate to you.

Say the Affirmation when you awake (as you begin your day), during the day when you need an extra boost of energy and positiveness, and to end your day. Saying the Affirmation continues to affirm to your subconscious of your intentions (balancing or healing). There is even space at the end of each chapter for you to write your own affirmations or notes.

Creating with Conscious Intent

Creating with conscious intent means that you clearly define your goals and then consciously set forth to see them realized in your day-to-day life. Doing this causes you to listen more closely to your spoken words and to what you may wish for. Maybe you said something and then followed it quickly with, "I did not really mean that!" Being "conscious" means that you are aware that the spoken word is much more influential than you were taught. You do create your reality from your thoughts and your words! As overwhelming as this may seem, my experiences in my life have shown me the truth of this.

I suggest that you begin by really listening to your thoughts and words. Make a conscious effort to keep them in a positive light. For example, in a rash moment, don't wish a serious disease to befall the person who just cut you off at the street corner, while you're driving your car! These quick rages are easy to succumb to, yet add up to sending messages unconsciously that we (hopefully in truth) have no real intention of doing or desiring. At one time or another, we all have done this. However, it is time for changes. You can apply the concept of creating with conscious intent to all aspects of your life.

This concept is one of the important and basic principles of alchemy ... where you consciously set out to create something. You have a clear picture of what you want, and you take one step at a time to very determinedly create your goal. Did you know that upon his death Sir Isaac Newton had written over one million words on alchemy? The concepts of alchemy are not based on magic. There is really nothing magical about it! The steps are clearly defined. It is important to do every step, no skipping over the one you might find monotonous. Your intention is important.

I have always created my aromatherapy products with conscious intent, even before I designed the *Vibrational Aroma Therapy* system of energetic healing, based on each of the ChakraAuras. What does conscious intent actually mean? It means that first you decide what the intent or focus is to be and why you are creating it.

Your Focus and Intention Require Attention

First, determine what the intention is. What is the desire, intent, goal, or focus you are trying to achieve? For example, an individual came to me who was going to be displaying her unique jewelry at a trade show and wanted something "to attract buyers and to repel envy from others." So, my *conscious intent* and focus for her VibrationalSynergy, was for the purpose of attracting abundance and repelling jealousy and envy.

Second, my attention was needed in order to create an effective synergy for her. This is how I proceed in creating most *Vibrational Aromatherapy* products – I take a few deep breaths to center myself before I begin the blending process. After the breaths, I state my conscious intent and focus. Then I proceed with choosing the essential oils and any other carriers that may be involved in the end product. When I prepare an aromatherapy blend, product, or preparation using conscious intent or focus, I am truly creating one that has *alchemical properties*. Why? Because by definition, an alchemical product is one that has enhanced positive, therapeutic, and wellness qualities, created by the intention, and combined with the ingredients. Thus, the whole is greater than the individual parts. Alchemy has the power of transforming and transmuting combined items into something beyond their individual ingredients.

You can use this method of Focus, Intention, and Attention when you choose a particular chakra or aura for meditation, prayer, or a healing session. Just ask your inner guidance what is going to best support you right now, for this moment in your life, to assist you with support and in creating what you desire.

P. Elder '85

PART FOUR

Essence of Life Realms

Imagination is more important than knowledge.
I never came upon my discoveries
through the process of rational thinking.
– Albert Einstein

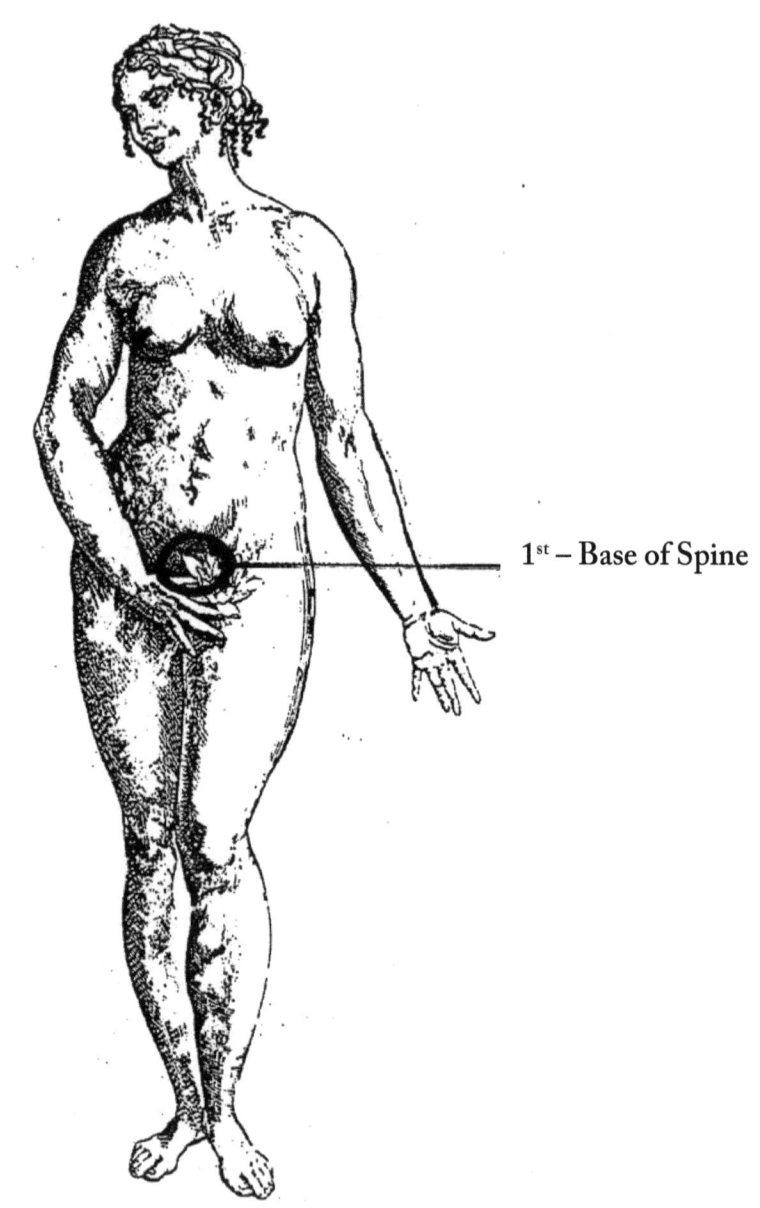

1st – Base of Spine

1st ChakraAura: Base of Spine – Physical Transformation

Chapter 14

COURAGE –

Physical Transformation

1st ChakraAura: Base of Spine

ChakraSynergy: Courage

Shape: Sphere

Color: Deep Red

Stone: Garnet

Number: One

Sound: aah aah

Goddess: Heket – Egyptian Goddess of Life

1st ChakraAura: Base of Spine

Located at the bottom of the spine (pubic bone area on front of body), this is the foundation for our roots on the Earth Mother. "As above, so below," an old adage originating from alchemy (and explained in more detail in *Alchemy and Physics*), the physical structure finds its solidity here. Here is the beginning of the support for the physical body, as well as its vitality and energy.

Energy begins at the 1st ChakraAura and runs up the body to vitalize the life form, then down the body again into the Earth Mother to connect the physical body to the Earth herself. Connecting with the Earth Mother is vital. She is traumatized right now. This trauma has been caused by the lack of concern, which we humans have shown over hundreds of years of neglect – inconsiderate attitudes that have abused and depleted the Earth Mother's resources.

This 1st ChakraAura, also called the Base of Spine, is associated with our physical body, its dense flesh and bones. The sciatic nerve, the largest in the body, is energized here. To understand more clearly how important the 1st ChakraAura is, we can liken our physical energy and physical body to a house. In building a house, if you have a sturdy, strong foundation, your physical structure can withstand more from the elements of nature … so too, with the 1st ChakraAura.

❖ constipation

❖ obesity

❖ spinal problems

❖ bulimia

❖ anorexia nervosa

❖ sciatica

ChakraSynergy #1: Courage

The ChakraSynergy for the 1ˢᵗ ChakraAura is named Courage. All of the essential oils in this formula help you to establish your physical energy, which is the foundation for all of the other ChakraAuras or energy centers. Courage is revitalizing, opens the way for health and healing, and helps you to maintain a sense of balance and control in your life. It is strengthening, energizing, grounding, and protective. It gives a strong base of understanding and encourages longevity through adversity. The primary essential oils in Courage are:

- ❖ Elemi (*Canarium luzonicum*)
- ❖ Lemon (*Citrus limon*)
- ❖ Patchouli (*Pogostemum cablin*)
- ❖ Tagetes (*Tagetes minuta*)
- ❖ Vetiver (*Vetiveria zizanoides*)

1ˢᵗ ChakraAura Shape: Sphere

The shape chosen to represent physical energy is the sphere. A symbol of equality, the sphere or circle is a primary shape and symbolizes protected space. Think of the physical body as a unit, part of the whole, yet capable of holding its own protected space. There is a Hindu quotation that says, "God is a circle whose circumference is nowhere and whose center is everywhere."

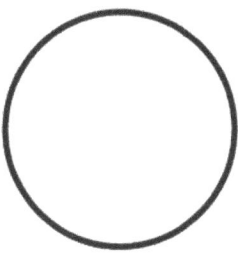

1st ChakraAura Color: Deep Red

Red is the color for the 1st ChakraAura. It is associated with the Earth Mother, and with vitality, strength, and courage. It is the color of power and determination. Red helps to give us that added boost when we feel low.

1st ChakraAura Stone: Garnet

Garnet is a crystal. A deep burnished red color. Gem quality, you can see clearly into its rich hue. Sometimes referred to as a stone for health, Garnet's job is to transmute negative energy into beneficial energy. Assisting you to make a commitment to yourself, to your foundations and stability, your creative and manifesting abilities are supported by the dynamism of Garnet.

Other stones for the 1st ChakraAura are: Red Jasper, Red Tiger Eye, Ruby, Red Coral, Hematite, Black Obsidian, and Black Tourmaline.

1st ChakraAura Number: ONE – Beginnings

The number ONE is about new beginnings. It is a time to plant the seeds of your garden. The 1st ChakraAura is about building foundations and this is the key focus for the number ONE. Your *garden* is what you intend to make grow. This could be a new life direction, or the current one that is taking on new directions. The number ONE can refer to the current year's directions, relationships, or whatever in your life feels like it is being newly formed. Patience is key. A garden does not grow overnight. It takes time for the seeds planted to germinate. This may take months or even more than a year.

The number ONE is also about leadership, taking initiative, originality, and determination. All of this will keep you busy … preparing the soil, so to speak. Focus on what is at hand. Nurture the seeds. Give them what they need to begin to grow in a healthy, balanced way. Be attentive to not being too domineering, selfish, or egotistical.

1ˢᵗ ChakraAura Sound: aah aah

The sound for the 1ˢᵗ ChakraAura is *aah aah* – Tiwa for buttocks. (Refer to Chapter 9 *Sound* before chanting this word.)

1ˢᵗ ChakraAura Goddess:
Heket – Egyptian Goddess of Life

Heket (pronounced Heh-ka-tay) is full and fertile. She is a healer and the Goddess as Wisdom Woman or Crone. She is the storyteller who carries the *herstory* (history) and therefore the foundation for the tribe. She is the *Great Wrinkled One* who ushers in maturity with wisdom. *Queen of the Crossroads* for mature living, she teaches that rarely is anything solely black and white … it is always subtly tinged in various shades of color. She is the original Earth Mother, a Wise Woman. She holds life's renewing and transforming energies. Sadness and depression can deter us from advancing in life, yet adversity can sometimes propel us forward and thus be the beginning for a bright future.

A triple goddess, Heket teaches about the three mysteries of Creation, Dissolution, and Immortality. Her heart is full with the sacred scarab beetle of fertility, a symbol of Life's renewing energies. Feelings of fear, despair, and defeat can rob you of hope and paralyze the ability to act. Yet the time of defeat can actually be a fertile time to sow the seeds and build the foundation for future success, just as the mythology of the phoenix that rises from the ashes of the funeral pyre with renewed strength.

1ˢᵗ ChakraAura Goddess
Heket – Egyptian Goddess of Life
Artist Patricia Elder

Meditation

To bring the energy of the Goddess Heket into your healing focus, use this meditation:

I feel deeply passionate about my desires
and I commit to their fulfillment.

Affirmations

I am the representation of Divine COURAGE.

I have the COURAGE to create my dreams.

I am now COURAGEOUS.

With COURAGE, I accomplish what I need.

I am in full realization of my COURAGE everyday.

Your Affirmations for COURAGE—*Write your personal affirmations here:*

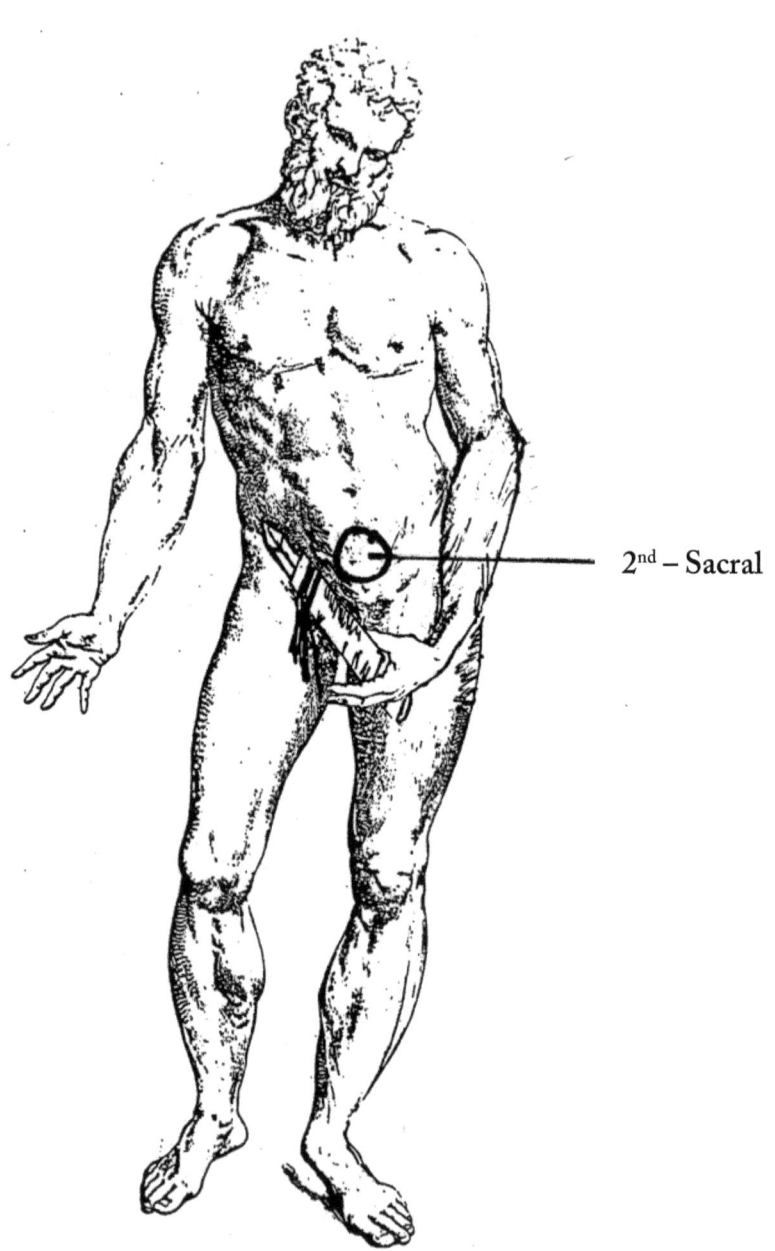

2nd – Sacral

2nd ChakraAura: Sacral – Creative Transformation

Chapter 15

CREATE –

Creative Transformation

2nd ChakraAura: Sacral

ChakraSynergy: Create

Shape: Obelisk

Color: Orange

Stone: Carnelian

Number: Two

Sound: Feminine: *oh aah ee*

        Masculine: *eh eee eh*

Goddess: Freya – Scandinavian

        Goddess of Creativity

2ⁿᵈ ChakraAura: Sacral

Located at the abdomen below the naval, the 2ⁿᵈ ChakraAura is known as the Sacral. It includes the physical organs of the gonads and the ovaries or testicles. All creativity, sexual desire, and emotional awakenings originate here. Passion, pleasure, reproduction, motivation, and manifestation are generated here.

The Sacral affects the liquids of the body: urination, circulation, reproduction, or diabetes can be indicated (also at #3 ChakraAura). Hundreds of generations have caused the repression of their creative urges, which if not repressed, encourage creativity and wholeness. It is important to also be discerning and to separate greed and pure desire from need.

Enliven your creative energy; it is the source of all life. Find what you truly love and feel your connection to the Divine or God, to all of Nature, and to the Earth Mother.

Some of the physical indications that the 2ⁿᵈ ChakraAura is out of balance are:

- ❖ kidney and bladder problems
- ❖ circulatory problems
- ❖ impotence
- ❖ frigidity
- ❖ diabetes

ChakraSynergy #2: Create

The ChakraSynergy for the 2ⁿᵈ ChakraAura is named Create. When using this synergy focus on the word Create. All of the essential oils in the formula support and relate to this energy center. Create helps to stir and enliven your creative energies, while balancing the emotions related to all forms of creativity. When balance exists, it helps you to begin healing from any dysfunctional sexual behavior or choices. Create helps to put sexual desires into perspective. It invites wealth, love, happiness, and health. Create also helps to quiet mental chatter and prepare for physical healing and spiritual connection to the Divine. The primary essential oils in Create are:

- ❖ Cardamon (*Elettarria cardamomum*)
- ❖ Dill (*Anethum graveolens*)
- ❖ Lavendin Grosso (*Lavandula x intermedia*)
- ❖ Marjoram, Sweet (*Origanum marjorana*)
- ❖ Sandalwood Mysore (*Santalum album*)

2nd ChakraAura Shape: Obelisk

An obelisk is like a tall column, pointed at the top. It comes from the Greek word *obelischos* meaning pointed pillar. In Egypt, obelisks symbolize creativity reaching upwards into the heavens (the home of spirit) and are also reflective of the male penis or lingam (a Sanskrit word). Ancient Egyptians maintained that the obelisk represented the erectness of the lingam of their earth god *Geb* (representing the grounded and the physical), as he lay on the Earth Mother trying to unite himself with *Nut* (representing the intuitive and spiritual), Goddess of the heavens.

2nd ChakraAura Color: Orange

Orange is the color for the 2nd ChakraAura. It is associated with life, happiness, independence, and resourcefulness. It is a color of decisiveness, adaptability, self-esteem, and self-assurance. Orange helps to stimulate laughter and playfulness.

2nd ChakraAura Stone: Carnelian

Carnelian is a mineral. The color is varying shades of orange, from a dusty to a brick color. It awakens ones given talents, increasing creative and physical power. It initiates inspiration from the spiritual realms. Helps you to stimulate your creative drive and physical verve. Supports the health of all the organs associated with the Sacral chakra.

Other stones for the 2nd ChakraAura are: Topaz, Amber, Obsidian Needle, Coral, and Agate.

2nd ChakraAura Number: TWO – Cooperation

The number TWO is about cooperation. It is time for patience while your seeds germinate. Yes ... more patience! The 2nd ChakraAura is about creativity. Creativity is the activity of creating. Whatever form the creativity takes is its expression. The expression of creativity is what is important! It does not have to be related to the arts. Each of us is unique, with special talents; yours might be math or computers or working with your hands in some way. Your attention may be to your family. Whatever it is, all creativity is about your particular seeds taking root and blossoming.

Creativity needs to be nurtured and well tended. This may be a time of studying and gathering more knowledge. It may also be a time to learn about working in partnership with others and paying attention to details. Stay focused and be careful not to be duplicitous or indecisive while you are in this germination time period. The number TWO is also about diplomacy, friendship, and kindness. Diplomacy means don't yell at the seeds, telling them they are lazy when they take their time to grow! Friendship means understanding and nurturing, and if weeds try to take over, be diligent about removing the obstacles. Kindness means knowing that everything has its own timing; you can't rush or push growth.

2ⁿᵈ ChakraAura Sound:

oh aah ee for the Feminine or eh ee eh for the Masculine

The feminine sound for the 2ⁿᵈ ChakraAura is *oh aah ee* – Tiwa for the ovaries. The masculine sound for the 2ⁿᵈ ChakraAura is *eh ee eh* – Tiwa for the testicles. (Refer to Chapter 9 *Sound* when chanting one of these words.)

2ⁿᵈ ChakraAura Goddess:

Freya – Scandinavian Goddess of Creativity

Freya (pronounced fray-ya) represents the spirit of fertility. Her absence from the Earth Mother during autumn and winter causes the leaves to descend from the trees and a blanket of snow to cover the land, worn as a cape of mourning. She is the essence of sexuality, beauty, tenderness, and nurturing. We have a day named after her, Friday, known as Freya's day and also as the day of Venus.

Her lucky number is thirteen, because it is the same number of the Moon's cycles and a woman's menstrual cycles in a year's time. She was widely revered by the country peoples of Europe for centuries after Christianity became the official religion over much of the world. As a result, the catholic authorities of Northern Europe chose to make her sacred day, Friday, a Catholic holy day when the people could eat only fish, a symbol of transformation and one of Freya's sacred animals! Her sacred number, thirteen, became a number to be avoided, especially when it fell on her sacred day, Friday! To her original devotees, this day would have been extra special, carrying much added magic.

Freya symbolizes endless creative energy. She is a goddess of beauty, love, joy, and pleasure. One of her nicknames was *The Large Wombed Earth*. Freya's principles are about right living, justice, honor, and peace. She inspired the arts and all poetry. Her motto is "Attract to me everything I wish to experience."

2nd ChakraAura Goddess
Freya – Scandinavian Goddess of Creativity
Artist Patricia Elder

Meditation

To bring the energy of the Goddess Freya into your healing focus, use this meditation:

I have the power to create for my life,
my deepest desires and dreams.

Affirmations

I CREATE and manifest my dreams.

I am packed with CREATIVITY.

I am the representation of Divine CREATION.

I am in full realization of my CREATIVE gifts.

Expressing my CREATIVE Self, I feel whole.

Your Affirmations for CREATING—*Write your personal affirmations here:*

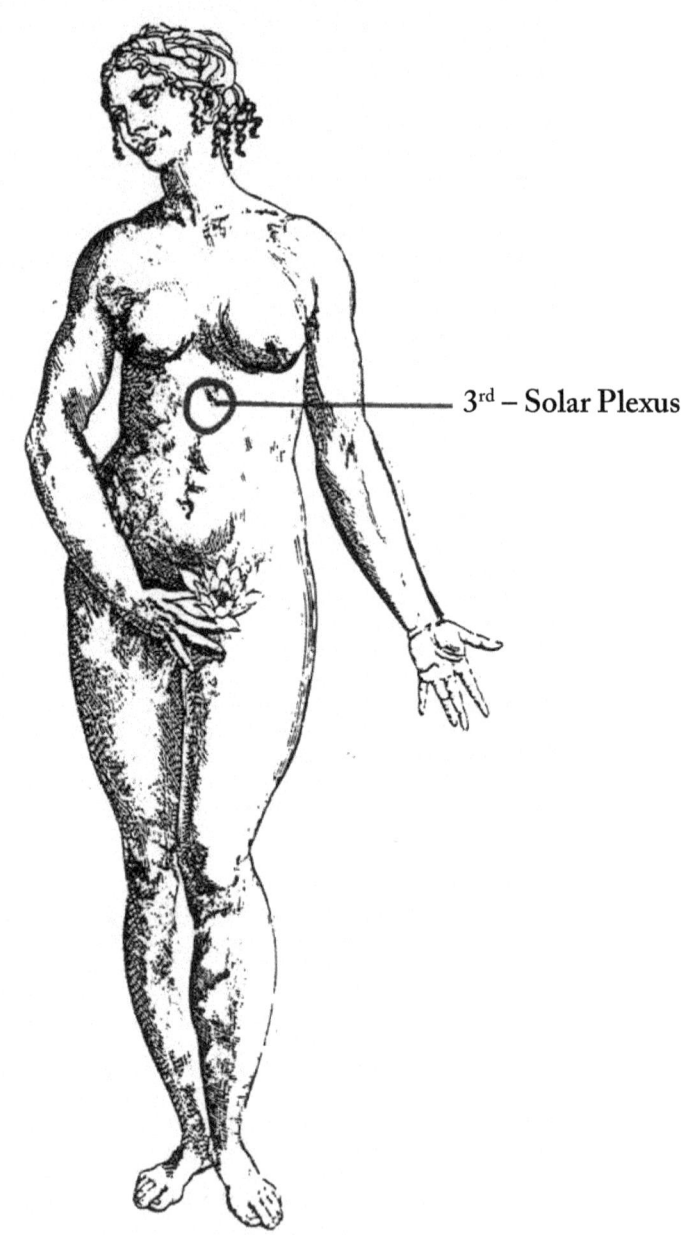

3rd – Solar Plexus

3rd ChakraAura: Solar Plexus –
Transformation of Individual Will

Chapter 16

MANIFEST –

Transformation of Individual Will

3rd ChakraAura: Solar Plexus

ChakraSynergy: Manifest

Shape: Triangle

Color: Yellow

Stone: Citrine

Number: Three

Sound: *eh-eh*

Goddess: Romi Kumu – Brazilian
      Goddess of Willpower

3rd ChakraAura: Solar Plexus

Located at the hollow found in the center of the bottom of the ribcage, the 3rd ChakraAura – Solar Plexus is the seat of will and control. The organs associated with the solar plexus are the pancreas and the stomach. The solar plexus regulates the metabolism of the physical body. This ChakraAura represents how we relate to the outer world from the level of our intellect and how we use power. Our Ego sits here; it ignites action and generates personal power. It is the center for empowering us with that *get up and go* take action energy. When stress and shock initially affect this area it can create a feeling of *fire* in your body … that burning feeling in your stomach.

Action requires taking responsibility for your actions. Learning to be strong and firm, with grace and balance, is important and necessary to health, harmony, and wellbeing.

The function of the pancreas is to secrete digestive enzymes and the hormones insulin and glucagon. (For other viewpoints on diabetes read: 2nd ChakraAura – Sacral or 4th ChakraAura – Heart.)

Some of the physical indications when the 3rd ChakraAura is out of balance are:

- ❖ digestive system disorders
- ❖ ulcers
- ❖ liver
- ❖ stomach
- ❖ pancreatic malfunctions
- ❖ hypo-glycemia
- ❖ sometimes diabetes

ChakraSynergy #3: Manifest

The ChakraSynergy for the 3rd ChakraAura is named Manifest. All of the essential oils in this synergy support the solar plexus, the center for our Will and the connecting point with Divine Will.

Manifest helps to reduce mental fatigue and effect positive change. It quiets the nerves and helps to balance and stabilize the pancreas and solar plexus. It allows you to hold your space through adversity. Manifest stimulates the conscious mind, sending it creative energy, and gives the ability to be gentle yet strong. The primary essential oils in Manifest are:

- ❖ Basil (*Ocimum basilicum*)
- ❖ Bay Leaf (*Pimenta racemosa*)
- ❖ Cassia (*Cinnamomum cassia*)
- ❖ Cistus (*Cistus ladaniferus*)
- ❖ Myrtle (*Myrtus communis*)

3rd ChakraAura Shape: Triangle

The shape chosen for the 3rd ChakraAura is a triangle. The triangle shape leads your eye upwards, as the upward moving fire burns. Since ancient times, the triangle has also been the symbol of the feminine principle. Called a *yoni* in Sanskrit, it is associated with the number three. In the matriarchal cultures of 5,000 years ago and to the Gnostic Christians, the holy trinity was the Virgin, Mother, and Crone, or the three aspects of Woman. Crone means Wisdom Woman. She represented the Wise-One, the Story-teller and the Creative-Intellect.

3rd ChakraAura Color: Yellow

Yellow is the color for the 3rd ChakraAura. It is associated with the Sun and with knowledge, optimism, and clarity. It is connected with the intellect, rationality, intelligence, concentration, clear thinking, and wisdom. Yellow helps to sharpen your Mind and remind you that you need to be able to love yourself before you can give love to others.

3rd ChakraAura Stone: Citrine

Citrine is a quartz mineral. The colors of Citrine vary from yellow to amber. It stimulates mental focus and endurance and encourages abundance and the maintenance of wealth (on all levels). Citrine gives positive influence to your pursuits, providing inspirational in problem solving and helping you to find resolutions. Citrine is said to aid digestion and digestive disorders. It reminds us that we are on the physical plane not just for ourselves, yet also to be an avenue of joy for others and, consequently, an important part of your personal growth. Someone else's growth is also reflected in both directions of our personal growth.

Other stones for the 3rd ChakraAura are: Topaz, Yellow Jasper, Gold Calcite, Pyrite, Petrified Wood, and Gold Tiger Eye.

3rd ChakraAura Number: THREE – Enjoyment

The number THREE is about joy. Adela Rogers St. Johns said, "Joy seems to me a step beyond happiness – happiness is a sort of atmosphere you can live in sometimes when you're lucky. Joy is a light that fills you with hope and faith and love." Oh, those seeds in your garden have begun to sprout! What joy fills your heart to see their little green beginnings. Roots are taking hold for your creative endeavors, time, and energy. Have a party and celebrate all that is coming to life. Continue with your creative energies … use your self-expression. Imagination, laughter, and joy are boundless. At the same time, recognize your limitations. Don't party so much that you forget to water your garden. Watch out for boredom caused by too much of one thing and forgetting the balance. THREE, don't forget to finish what you started. Be attentive to nurture the little greens! Expel the weeds. Since travel is an aspect of the possibilities of the number THREE, make arrangements for the garden to be looked after while you are away.

THREE is the Solar Plexus. This is about your Will and Ego and the balance of both in your life. Ego is healthy if it doesn't feel like it needs to control everything. "I don't have a problem with control, you do! I *like* controlling!!!" Your Will is expressed in the outside world; it is evident in your work in the world, whatever form it takes, yet try to find its balance.

3rd ChakraAura Sound: *eh eh*

The sound for the 3rd ChakraAura is *eh eh* – Tiwa for the liver. (Refer to Chapter 9 on *Sound* before you begin to chant this word.)

3rd ChakraAura Goddess:
Romi Kumu – Brazilian Goddess of Willpower

Romi Kumu (pronounced row-me kuma) is certain of her reason for being. Her home is the Brazilian rainforests. Her head is crowned with the same fire that lives in her eyes and finds expression in her voice. Romi Kumu's sacred animal is the tiger. Like the tiger, her fearless beauty declares a wild physical presence and her power demands honoring. Survival in the rainforests command a toughness that is without compassion for any weakness or threats from competitors. Romi Kumu is also considered a female shaman. She has the ability to focus her Will and to burn away thoughts of compromise and defeat. Her special flower is the passionflower, which symbolizes beauty without hesitation.

Romi Kumu reminds us that no one can stop us unless we let her or him. Only we can take control of our life. We must take full responsibility and not put blame on others for our circumstances. Feel your worth. Let nothing shake your faith in yourself. Respect others as well as yourself.

3rd ChakraAura Goddess
Romi Kumu – Brazilian Goddess of Willpower
Artist Patricia Elder

Meditation

To bring the energy of the Goddess Romi Kumu into your healing focus, use this meditation:

I have the willpower to overcome defeat,
and with grace, to manifest my deepest desires.

Affirmations

I am the MANIFESTATION of my dreams.

I MANIFEST my needs.

I am in full realization of my ability to MANIFEST.

I MANIFEST my joy.

I MANIFEST my Divine Essence.

Your Affirmations for MANIFESTING—*Write your personal affirmations here:*

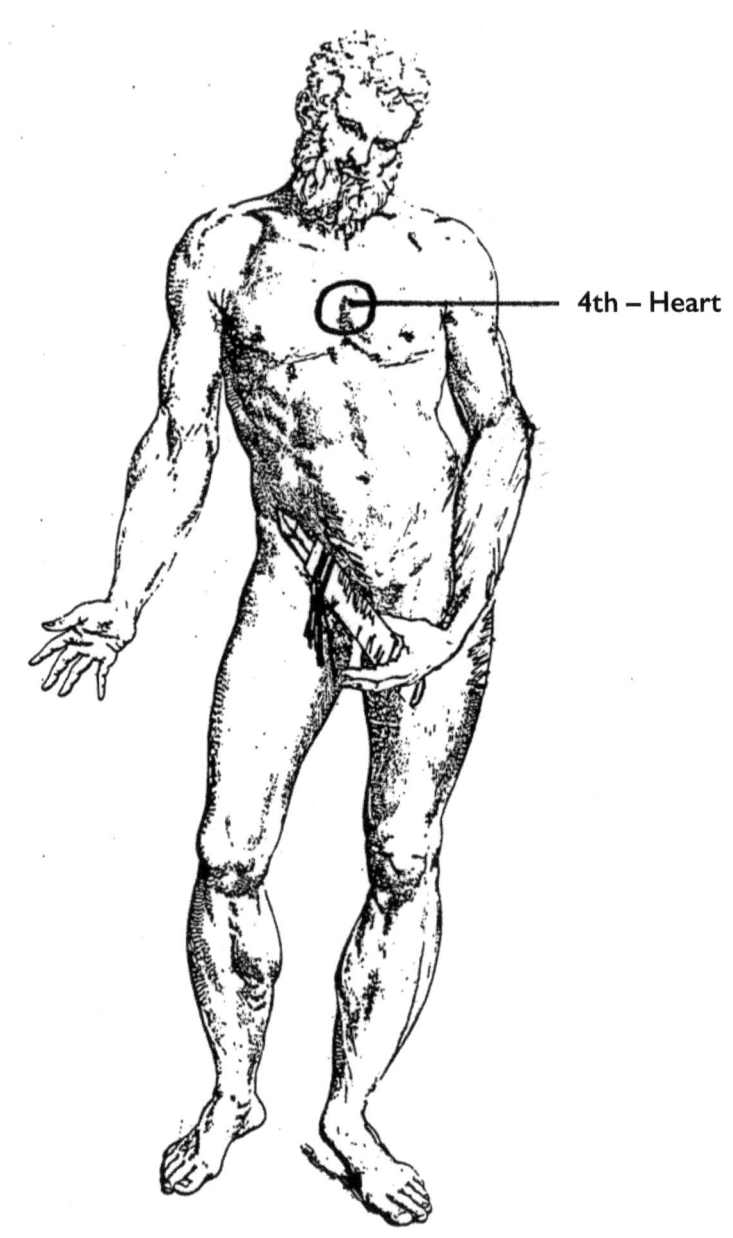

4th – Heart

4th ChakraAura: Heart – Emotional Transformation

Chapter 17

JOY –

Emotional Transformation

4th ChakraAura: Heart

ChakraSynergy: Joy

Shape: Spiral

Colors: Pink, Lavender, Green

Stone: Rose Quartz

Number: Four

Sound: aah

Goddess: Shekina – Babylonian
  Goddess of Universal Balance

4th ChakraAura: Heart

Located in the middle of the chest, the 4th ChakraAura is known as the Heart. It is associated with the thymus gland and the actual heart. The 4th ChakraAura is the seat of our connection with the emotion of love and compassion. God's love is felt at this ChakraAura as a force of energy that is without limitation, called unconditional love.

The 4th ChakraAura, considered the center of the body, is the bridge and the binding force for *all* other energies. The Heart is in a place of balance between the lower three ChakraAuras that represent your experience in the physical world and the upper three ChakraAuras that represent intuitive and spiritual expression. Balancing and harmonizing the emotions finds its greatest opportunities symbolically through this ChakraAura.

The Heart is concerned with equilibrium and relationships. *Love,* or a loved one, represents joy and sweetness in life. To feel love and to experience love, is the sweetest experience known to humankind. Without it, life is bitter, joyless, and lackluster. The loss of a loved one, or loss of the experience of love and joy, can mean the taking away of the sweetness in your life.

Diabetes is caused by a sugar (sweetness) imbalance. Diabetes is often diagnosed in an individual within a year after the loss of a loved one. The loss can be experienced as the result of a death, divorce, or even a traumatic separation. Some diabetes is rampant, almost epidemic level, within certain cultures, such as the Native American.

I would suggest a look into cultures who experience this with their people; most likely there has been a long history of denial of their expressed joy, as a result of oppression by others. *Regaining* your sense of joy for being who they are, *accepting* your cultural essence, and *expressing* joy (without tyranny from another) helps pave a new path to recovery when we see masses culturally who suffer with diabetes.

Some of the physical indications when the 4ᵗʰ ChakraAura is out of balance are:

- ❖ high or low blood pressure
- ❖ lung problems
- ❖ asthma
- ❖ heart conditions

ChakraSynergy #4: Joy

The ChakraSynergy created for the 4ᵗʰ ChakraAura is named Joy. All of the essential oils in this synergy assist the 4ᵗʰ ChakraAura. Love on the physical plane can grow towards a nurturing and reciprocal unconditional love, free of possession and control. When this is experienced, true joy is felt. The ChakraSynergy Joy, opens your energies to receiving love. It is harmonizing and balancing to the Soul. When you feel overwhelmed by life, Joy helps to dispel fear, regret, or grief and brings acceptance, understanding, and movement towards your heart's joy. The primary essential oils in Joy are:

- ❖ Bergamot (*Citrus aurantium, ssp bergamia*)
- ❖ Galbanum (*Ferula galbanifera*)
- ❖ Lavender, Alpine (High Altitude) (*Lavandula augustifolia*)
- ❖ Rose Otto (*Rosa x damascena*)
- ❖ Spikenard (*Nardostachys granduflorum*)

4ᵗʰ ChakraAura Shape: Spiral

The Spiral shape is a bridge, a teaching unto itself. The symbol of the Spiral can be seen in many cultures representing growth and evolution. In ancient times, the Spiral was perceived to be encoded with information. The Spiral represents the process of coming to the same point again and again and again, yet from a different perspective. A meaningful quote from an unknown source says, "The journey into self is non-ending; the journey outside self is non-ending. Both are equal and lead toward universal truth."

4th ChakraAura Colors: Pink, Lavender, and Green

Pink, Lavender and Green are the colors for the 4th ChakraAura. Pink is a gentle color, and the color of love and the heart. It brings in a sense of clarity and calmness. Lavender, pink with a drop of purple, adds spirituality to the qualities of Pink. Green is the color of hope, renewal, harmony, and balance.

4th ChakraAura Stone: Rose Quartz

Rose Quartz is a crystal mineral. Its colors range from very palest of pink, soft lavender, to a medium rich, pink tone. It instills a peaceful calm and soothes the heart in all matters. Loving and gentle, it inspires self-love, healing, and brings ease to relationships. It promotes receptivity to the beauty of Nature and the arts (music, art, written word). While seeking spiritual attunement Rose Quartz assists you to feel the power of love. It strengthens and activates the heart while aiding emotional and mental stability and balance. It reduces stress and helps alleviate despondency, enhancing your expression of inner light and joy.

Other stones for the 4th ChakraAura are: Lepidolite, Pink Calcite, Rhodochrosite, Rhodonite, Kunzite, Emerald, Watermelon Tourmaline, Peridot, Green Quartz, Malachite, Aventurine, Jade, Gaspyite, and Green Obsidian.

4th ChakraAura Number: FOUR – Practicality

FOUR is a number that reminds us that all Life is truly about balance. FOUR is a time for self-discipline and stability. Put the work into your garden; if you don't, the seedlings that are now green young plants and several inches tall may die. Come from your heart and be cheerful about the work, you reap the rewards later.

Be attentive not to become a workaholic. Yes, practical and logical has its place, yet don't get into a rut or you will be rigid and dull! Be spontaneous, at least occasionally! Remember to live, at least once in awhile, the *enjoyment* which was characterized by the previous number THREE.

FOUR as the Heart allows for the emotions to find their balance. Too much emotion is just as dysfunctional as none at all. Learn to find your stability in the boat on a stormy ocean, so that the ocean of Life doesn't throw you overboard!

4th ChakraAura Sound: *aah*

The sound for the 4th ChakraAura is *aah* – Tiwa for the heart. (Refer to Chapter 9 *Sound* before you chant this word.)

4th ChakraAura Goddess:
Shekina – Babylonian Goddess of Universal Balance

Shekina (pronounced she-kee-na) is the balance between Heart and Mind. She is both Wisdom and Erotic – full of emotion and the stirrings of love. Yet, to experience her wisdom, you must love with your emotions – emotions that are balanced with the wisdom of your Soul and your entire being. In the Kabbalah, the Jewish mystical writings, the word *daath* means insight accompanied by great feeling and also the knowledge that comes from the union of conscious and unconscious minds. A deeply erotic experience, *daath*, additionally refers to the union of God and His Bride, the Shekina.

Her name meaning the female presence of God, Shekina is the feminine aspect of God. Shekina is the female Soul of God, his feminine counterpart and his balance. She is said to have abandoned the Earth Mother when humankind became too evil and will return when we come to our senses and our greed and evil is eradicated.

4th ChakraAura Goddess
Shekina – Babylonian Goddess of Universal Balance
Artist Patricia Elder

Meditation

To bring the energy of the Goddess Shekina into your healing focus, use this meditation:

I come from my Heart, my Soul, and my entire being – pure, and with balanced emotions.

Affirmations

I am filled with JOY.

My JOY is expressed in truth.

I am in full realization of my JOY.

I am the Divine Essence of JOY.

I ENJOY my Life.

Your Affirmations for JOY—*Write your personal affirmations here:*

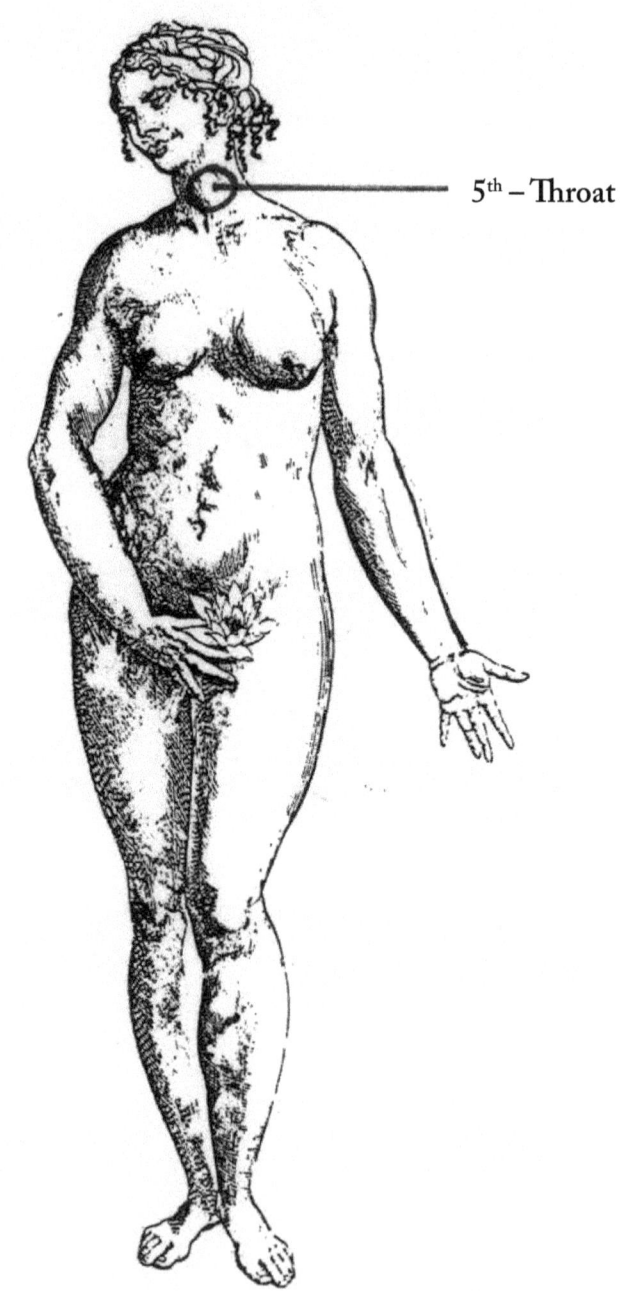

5th – Throat

5th ChakraAura: Throat – Transformation of Expression

Chapter 18

TRUTH –
Transformation of Expression

5th ChakraAura: Throat

ChakraSynergy: Truth

Shape: Star

Color: Blue

Stone: Lapis Lazuli

Number: Five

Sound: *oh*

Goddess: Brigid – Celtic Goddess
                    of Eloquence

5th ChakraAura: Throat

The 5th ChakraAura is the Throat. It is located at the center of the neck. Related organs are the throat and the thyroid gland. The Throat is the gateway of expression and communication and the center for expressing sound. Sending and receiving the vibration of sound opens up our connectedness to universal truths and energies.

The 5th ChakraAura is associated in our physical body with our neck, shoulders, arms, hands, and ears, all physical body parts involved with communication and expression. Whether receiving or transmitting information, communication and expression of any kind are crucial to making decisions that support us. The Throat is where the truth is felt and understood by the Heart and the creative impulses meet and are expressed. Problems in the throat, such as a sore throat or laryngitis, can mean conflict between the Heart and the Spirit. Are you communicating what is really in your heart? Are you following what your Spirit desires?

Some of the physical indications that the 5th ChakraAura is out of balance are:

- ❖ sore throat
- ❖ laryngitis
- ❖ pharyngitis
- ❖ earaches
- ❖ poor hearing

ChakraSynergy #5: Truth

The ChakraSynergy for the 5th ChakraAura is named Truth. All of the essential oils in this synergy support the 5th ChakraAura. Open communication and honestly expressing yourself is necessary, whether relating to loved ones or others. The timing of expression is very critical. It is important to assess a situation and clearly communicate with balanced heart and mind. Truth helps you to communicate without anger, ego, or animosity. It helps to clear any stuck emotions that may get in the way of expressing yourself. Truth enhances clear-sightedness so you can see the truth and be able to speak what you see. The primary essential oils in Truth are:

❖ Cananga (*Cananga odorata*)

❖ Chamomile, German (*Matricaria chamomilla*),

❖ Mugwort (*Artemesia vulgaris*)

❖ Tanacetum, Tansy (*Tanacetum annuum*)

❖ Thyme ct Linalool (*Thymus vulgaris)*

5th ChakraAura Shape: Star

The star is the most widely used and revered of esoteric symbols. It represents knowledge. The star reflects light, or knowledge, and radiates this knowledge outwards. The ancients thought of stars as living beings – unborn souls, heroes, heroines, and even angels. The usual image of a star is depicted with 5-points, which, in Western esoteric schools of philosophies, represents the five Elements – Earth, Water, Air, Fire, and Aether. Of course, real stars do not actually have points. The points are suggestive and give the impression of light radiating outwards.

5th ChakraAura Color: Blue

Blue is the color for the 5th ChakraAura. Blue signifies spaciousness, the skies, and the oceans. The blue sky above is where the planetary heavenly bodies reside. Blue is a color of harmony and understanding. Blue draws in inspiration from the universe and surrounds us with its healing energy.

5th ChakraAura Stone: Lapis Lazuli

Lapis Lazuli is a mineral and a gemstone. The color is a deep electrifying blue. It energizes the 5th ChakraAura, allowing expression of your true nature. It allows for conscious alignment and expression to the intuitive and psychic aspects of your nature. Held sacred for millennia, it is revered for being able to help you to gain the wisdom from the mysteries of the unknown, to be able to get in touch with esoteric ideas. It helps stimulate expression of wisdom and to balance how these wisdoms are shared with others (calmly not tyrannically). It balances feminine and masculine archetypes. Lapis has an affinity to promote wellness for the throat, thymus, and immune system.

Other stones for the Throat ChakraAura are: Indigo Tiger Eye, Sodalite, Blue Tourmaline, Aquamarine, Sapphire, Azurite and Celestite.

5th ChakraAura Number: FIVE – Change

Whoa ... look at the growth, you can hardly keep up with it! Your garden is growing profusely; everyday you can see changes. Listen to how your garden communicates with you. Being a good communicator begins with hearing and listening well. With the number FIVE, you learn the art of going with the flow; change is constant at this time. You learn to be versatile. Sensuality is also an aspect of FIVE.

Be watchful of becoming addicted to change and needing it for the excitement that it delivers. Pleasure seeking may also become *over* emphasized with the focus on FIVE.

The communications aspect of FIVE relates to the Throat Chakra, as the throat is the avenue for expression and communication.

5th ChakraAura Sound: *oh*

The sound for the 5th ChakraAura is *oh* – Tiwa for the throat. (Refer to Chapter 9 *Sound* before you begin to chant this word.)

5th ChakraAura Goddess:
Brigid – Celtic Goddess of Eloquence

Brigid (pronounced breed-ged) is a Muse and a Healer. She governs smithcraft, the martial arts, healing, and medicine, as well as poetry and inspiration. Brigid is the Goddess who inspires both the written word and communication. She is the great triple goddess of the Celtic realms of Europe. Some of her nicknames are *Fiery Arrow, Power* and *Renown.*

Devotion to Brigid was so deep among the peoples that the new religion of Christianity adopted her in order to subjugate her devotees. They changed the spelling of her name to Briget (meaning the human daughter of a Druid) and then claimed that St. Patrick baptized her. As the story continues, Briget took religious vows and was canonized after her death by her adoptive church, which then gave the saint an interesting list of attributes, all that coincidentally were *exactly* like those of the earlier Goddess Bridgid! Brigid's energy radiates outward, as does the star, with her light, energy, and wisdom.

"Every divine word came into existence by the thought of the heart and the commandment of the tongue." (Translated from an Egyptian stone known as *Stela 797,* by American Egyptologist James Henry Breasted, circa 1805.) Inscribed on another stone around the eighth century B.C., "When the eyes see, the ears hear, and the nose breathes, they report to the heart. It is the heart that brings forth every issue, and the tongue that repeats the thought of the heart .... thus were fashioned all the gods, from Atum on." (*Atum* is the Egyptian name for the Primal God.) This quote actually echoes a much more ancient text from about 2850 B.C. That text says that the original act of creation was a sort of speech and commandment of the tongue to repeat the heart's desires and thoughts and make them manifest.

5ᵗʰ ChakraAura Goddess
Brigid – Celtic Goddess of Eloquence
Artist Patricia Elder

Meditation

To bring the energy of the Goddess Brigid into your healing focus, use this meditation:

I Feel. I express my thoughts and feelings
in abundance and with balance.

Affirmations

I am the expression of my TRUTH.

I am living my TRUTH.

I know what is TRUTH to me.

With clarity and vision, I see the TRUTH.

I honor Divine TRUTH.

Your Affirmations for TRUTH—*Write your personal affirmations here:*

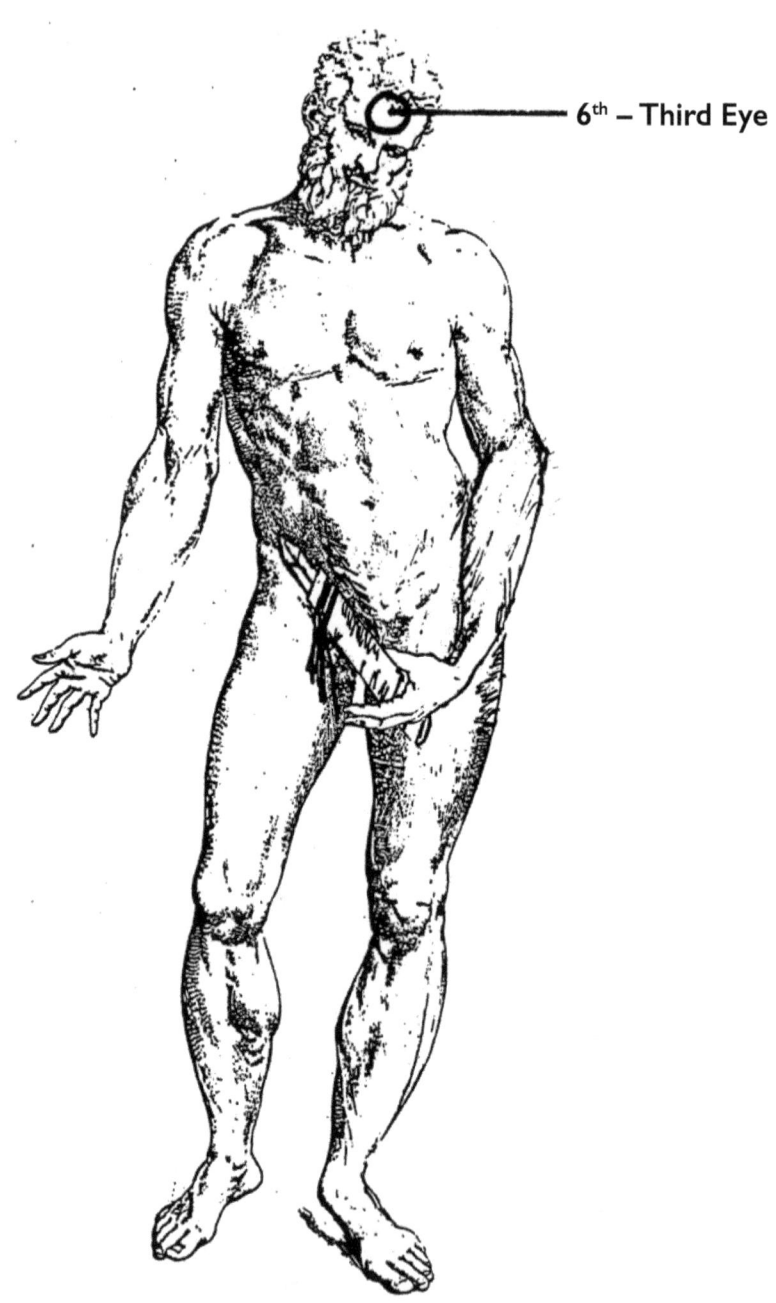

6th – Third Eye

6th ChakraAura: Third Eye – Transformation for Intuition

Chapter 19

VISION –

Transformation for Intuition

6th ChakraAura: Third Eye

ChakraSynergy: Vision

Shape: Pyramid

Color: Indigo, Turquoise

Stone: Turquoise

Number: Six

Sound: *eh aah uu*

Goddess: Egeria – Roman Goddess
of Wisdom

6ᵗʰ ChakraAura: Third Eye

The 6ᵗʰ ChakraAura is referred to as the Third Eye. It is located in the center of the forehead. In actuality, this energy body is also an energy vortex of visionary perception – the awakening of the energies of three ChakraAuras, one secondary and two major ChakraAuras. The Third Eye is symbolically the center of a triangle of three energy centers: the Base-of-the-Brain (pineal) that activates insight or the Mind's eye; the Brow (pituitary) that activates the intuitive; and the Crown (pituitary) that activates higher purpose.

The Third Eye represents insight and visionary perception and is depicted by a triangle with an eye in the middle. (*See diagram below.*) Have you ever had that feeling of *knowing* something on an innermost level? Most likely you have. Opening to your intuitive energy and then learning to trust the information you perceive is a major part of transformational growth. It is possible for a healing arts practitioner to assist you in energetically unclogging your Third Eye, allowing you to continue in your personal development.

Developing intuitive perceptions through your Third Eye happens naturally as you progress in your awareness and growth. Be wary of anyone who suggests they can "adjust" or "open" this energy center for you, being especially sensitive if this may be coming from her or his own need for manipulation and control.

Some physical indications that the 6ᵗʰ ChakraAura is out of balance are:

- ❖ eye problems
- ❖ near and far sightedness
- ❖ feelings of uncertainty
- ❖ confusion

ChakraSynergy #6: Vision

The ChakraSynergy created for the Third Eye is named Vision.

The Third Eye is where the power of Vision and Intuition are activated. It must be clear and finely tuned. Learn to listen to your inner knowing feelings and act on them. Follow your own sense of knowing and let others do the same! All of the essential oils in this synergy support the Third Eye. Vision aids in the protection of unwanted energies while opening the Third Eye. It opens new pathways, gives clear sight, encourages psychic dreams, and activates the right brain (the energetic place for intuition and creativity). Vision aids meditation and assists clairvoyance when used for unselfish purposes. The primary essential oils in Vision are:

- ❖ Carrot Seed (*Daucus carota*)
- ❖ Clary Sage (*Salvia sclarea*)
- ❖ Helichrysum (*Helichrysum italicum*)
- ❖ Juniper Berry (*Juniperus communis*)
- ❖ Palmarosa *(Cymbopogon martinii)*

6ᵗʰ ChakraAura Shape: Pyramid

The Pyramid symbolizes a unity of consciousness. It gathers energy from the Earth Mother and sends it upwards towards higher aspirations. Many variations of the Pyramid are found all over the world in Egypt, the Americas, and Mesopotamia. They were considered to be Mountains of Heaven where the deities and mortals met at the apex. In ancient Greece, the word *pyramid* meant a spirit, thought, symbol, or the idea of fire. Fire, you will recall from Chapter 11 *Earth's Energies*, is symbolic with energy. The Pyramid is representative here at the 6ᵗʰ ChakraAura of a striving to attain wisdom through insight.

6th ChakraAura Color: Indigo, Turquoise

The color chosen by most for the Third Eye is Indigo. In this work, I add turquoise. Indigo is the color of intuition, meditation, and mysticism. Turquoise is the color of expressing confidence, a rebuilder of energy, and a producer of favorable change. When you combine the two together, Indigo and Turquoise helps you (with confidence and grace) to listen to your intuition. It helps you to maintain your energy and focus your energy on intentional transmutation that leads you to profound transformation on all levels of your being.

6th ChakraAura Stone: Turquoise

Turquoise is a mineral. The colors vary from aqua, to dark turquoise-green, to a bright carribean blue. My preferred stone for the 6th ChakraAura because it has the ability to marry heaven (Sky Father) and earth (Earth Mother). It is a very spiritually focused stone with fervent healing abilities. While it strengthens all of the ChakrasAura, it particularly helps you to see and manifest the greatest of healing for the greatest good. During meditations, it helps you to connect with spiritual attunement and to ground it into your physical body.

Other stones for the 6th ChakraAura are: Amazonite, Azurite, Abalone (shell), Chrysocolla, Fluorite, and Blue Opal Displaced Petrified Wood (Indonesia).

6th ChakraAura Number: SIX – Responsibility

Your garden is beginning to flower now. It is time to enjoy the flowers. Focus on friends, family, home, or maybe even groups of people. Be attentive to all of your personal belongings and things, including relationships. This is a time of service; and it is also important to accept what seems like duties willingly. You've spent all this energy to make your garden grow. Now tend the flowers! Appreciate the beauty and harmony. Discover or re-establish partnerships. SIX is a domestic number. Great creativity is also to be found here if over indulgence and single mindedness does not take over. Don't fret the small stuff!

The balance, which was the focus of the number FOUR, is well understood by the number SIX. SIX is constantly seeking harmony. SIX is responsible and takes responsibility seriously. Yet SIX can be pushy and insist that others be just as responsible as they are themselves, so be watchful of this.

SIX is the numerical energy of the Third Eye. Be responsible for your visions. It is not always necessary to tell the world (or your partner, child, or friend), *everything* that you *see*. Learn the proper timing for harvesting and picking the flowers!

6th ChakraAura Sound: *eh aah uu*

The sound for the 6th ChakraAura is *eh aah uu* – Tiwa for the brow or forehead. (See Chapter 9 *Sound* before chanting this word.)

6th ChakraAura Goddess:
Egeria – Roman Goddess of Wisdom

Egeria (pronounced ee-gaer-e-a) is a semi-divine water nymph known for her wisdom and foresight. Egeria taught the correct rites for worship of the Earth Mother. The name Egeria is still used today in Italy as synonymous with that of women advisors. In Roman legend, she is the one who pronounced the first laws of the city. She is also the divine goddess of pregnancy. Pregnant women have worshipped her in order to help with easy delivery. As many other midwife-goddesses, Egeria is responsible for foretelling the future of the newborn child.

Egeria is the early Italian goddess of wisdom and foresight. As a human-woman, she married King Pompilius and became his supernatural advisor. She also governed the arts and sciences and was caretaker of all water springs and wells. Shekhinah Mountainwater, in her book *Ariadne's Thread*, says of Egeria, "Her waters are healing waters and full of inspiration, taking the seeker onward into peace and understanding. She heals through poetic insight, trance journeying, celestial music, and universal understanding."

6th ChakraAura Goddess
Egeria – Roman Goddess of Wisdom
Artist Gail Marie

Meditation

To bring the energy of the Goddess Egeria into your healing focus, use this meditation:

*I open to my inner wisdom and
to Divine purpose for myself,
for the Earth Mother,
and for all sentient Beings.*

Affirmations

I hold the VISION of my dreams within my heart.

I open to my intuition and my VISION.

I ENVISION a more joyful world.

With clarity and VISION, God's innate love is expressed through me.

I use my VISIONS wisely.

Your Affirmations for VISIONS—*Write your personal affirmations here:*

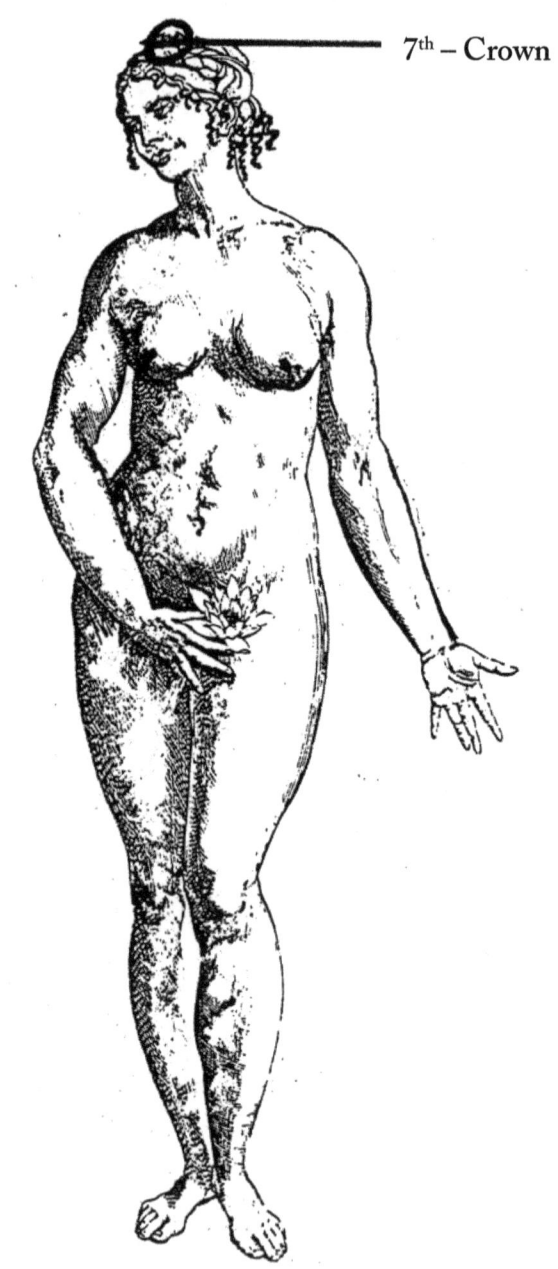

7th – Crown

7th ChakraAura: Crown – Spiritual Transformation

Chapter 20

INSPIRATION –
Spiritual Transformation

7th ChakraAura: Crown

ChakraSynergy: Inspiration

Shape: Polygon

Color: Violet

Stone: Amethyst

Number: Seven

Sound: eh

Goddess: Padma – Hindu Goddess
    of Spiritual Enlightenment

7th ChakraAura: Crown

Located at the top of the head, and encompassing the pituitary gland, the 7th ChakraAura is the Crown. It is perceived to be where we begin our evolvement towards spiritual enlightenment. Some cultures consider the soft spot (*fontanel*) on a baby's head when it is born, is where the Spirit of The Creator enters the physical body. The word fontanel is derived from the Latin word *font* means a receptacle for holy waters.

The longing for transcendence and union with Spirit rests at the 7th ChakraAura – Crown. This ChakraAura concerns itself with your higher purpose and your Soul's purpose. It is often referred to in Eastern cultures as the Thousand-Petalled Lotus. The Lotus flower is depicted in Eastern and Egyptian spiritual art as containing the wisdom of the Divine, and is believed to espouse the wisdom of the Creator. The more spiritual illumination you achieve, the more the Lotus unfolds, eventually guiding you to a final transcendence and union with the highest source of the Divine.

Some of the emotional indications that the 7th ChakraAura is out of balance are:

❖ apathy

❖ depression

❖ boredom

ChakraSynergy #7: Inspiration

The ChakraSynergy created for the Crown is named Inspiration, which helps to open and strengthen your spiritual energy. *This is your divine purpose on the Earth Mother.* At the same time, it is important to balance your spiritual energy with that of being human. In Buddhism, as the Thousand-Petalled Lotus rises from mud to glorify the dimensions above, we humans are here to integrate Spirit into the physical plane [here] on the Earth Mother. All of the essential oils in the synergy Inspiration support the 7th ChakraAura. The primary essential oils in Inspiration are:

- ❖ Cedarwood, Atlas (*Cedrus atlantica*)
- ❖ Chamomile, Roman (*Anthemis nobilis*)
- ❖ Frankincense, Somalia (*Boswellia carterii*)
- ❖ Ho Wood (*Cinnamomum camphora*)
- ❖ Jasmine Grandiflorum, CO_2 Extract (*Jasminum grandiflorum*)

7th ChakraAura Shape: Polygon

The Polygon is a symbol of infinity and is found in many cultures. It is a circle within a circle within circles. It is known in the East as a Mandala, to Native Americans as a Medicine Wheel, and to Native Hawaiians as a Menehune Ring. It symbolizes unity with individuation. In the search for our individual identity, we are reminded of our universal connection to he Divine that is our spiritual source.

7th ChakraAura Color: Violet

Violet is the color of broad-mindedness, inspiration, idealism, elegance, mystery, and royalty. It is the color representing meditation, telepathy, and spirit contact. Violet tunes into inner wisdom and the higher intelligences. It can energize your spiritual powers. Violet is said to be the color for the Aquarian Age. With the transformative energy of the planet Pluto becoming stronger, we will be fully immersed in the Age of Aquarius by 2024.

7th ChakraAura Stone: Amethyst

Amethyst is a crystal gemstone. The colors range from light purple to dark violet. It is a stone considered to be magical for thousands of years. Amethyst is the physical representation for *transformation*. It balances the energies of the physical, emotional, and intellectual bodies and has the ability to help you cut through illusion. Amethyst holds the energy of eternal peace. In Melody's book, *Love is in the Earth*, she says of amethyst that it is the "stone of spirituality and contentment." Amethyst is universally accepted as *the stone* for the Crown.

An additional stone that brings rationality to the intuitive and assists in exact communication of psychic information is Purple Fluorite. Additionally, it brings a methodical and conscious connection to both psychic and spiritual growth, further enhancing manifestation of dreams and vision into physical reality.

Other stones for the 7th ChakraAura are: Purple Fluorite, Iolite, Tanzanite, Alexandrite, Sugilite, Ametrine (Amethyst & Citrine), and Spodumene.

7th ChakraAura Number: SEVEN – Trust Inspiration

The fruit is beginning to appear in your garden; trust and faith is important. Know that the natural course of events produces the abundance. The number SEVEN is about things not normally seen. Don't force issues. Go inward for answers. This is primarily a time to meditate and to let the fruit ripen on its own now.

SEVEN is the balance of the masculine archetype (4, analytical) and the feminine archetype (3, intuitional). It is about finding the balance within your being on very deep, intuitional levels. The garden doesn't need a whole lot of focused attention right now. Be prepared for unexpected surprises.

SEVEN relates to the 7th ChakraAura – Crown. Inspiration comes from our Soul's openness to being guided and to opening to our spiritual nature. Have faith and trust.

7th ChakraAura Sound: *eh*

The sound for the 7th ChakraAura is *eh* – Tiwa for the head. (Refer to Chapter 9 *Sound* before you chant this word.)

7th ChakraAura Goddess:
Padma – Hindu Goddess of Spiritual Enlightenment

Padma (pronounced paad-maa) is the one who is everywhere – in jewels, coins, shells, rocks, trees, flowers, animals, and the unborn children. She is the embodiment of all the riches of the Earth Mother and of the Soul. Padma, in existence for all time, is the one who inspires everything in existence. Padma (also known as Lakshmi in India) is often seen resting on the top of a lotus flower, which represents spiritual enlightenment. She is the symbol of wealth on the Earth Mother and of the joy which spiritual prosperity brings to the Soul.

So we can learn life's lessons, Padma and her lotus flower are a symbol of the ever-unfolding openness of pure faith and of letting go of limiting beliefs. Faith is, simply stated, *complete trust*. Faith demands complete openness to the truth, whatever it might be. Faith in you is essential. Faith allows you to expand the scope of your world.

7th ChakraAura Goddess
Padma – Hindu Goddess of Spiritual Enlightenment
Artist Gail Marie

Meditation

To bring the energy of the Goddess Padma into your healing focus, use this meditation:

I embrace the eternal cycle of energy,
by opening my spiritual self to its Divine purpose.

Affirmations

I live in full expression of trust and INSPIRATION.

I have faith and trust in Divine Source and INSPIRATION.

I express unlimited INSPIRATION.

I INSPIRE others.

INSPIRATION is the creative force within me.

Your Affirmations for INSPIRATION—*Write your personal affirmations here:*

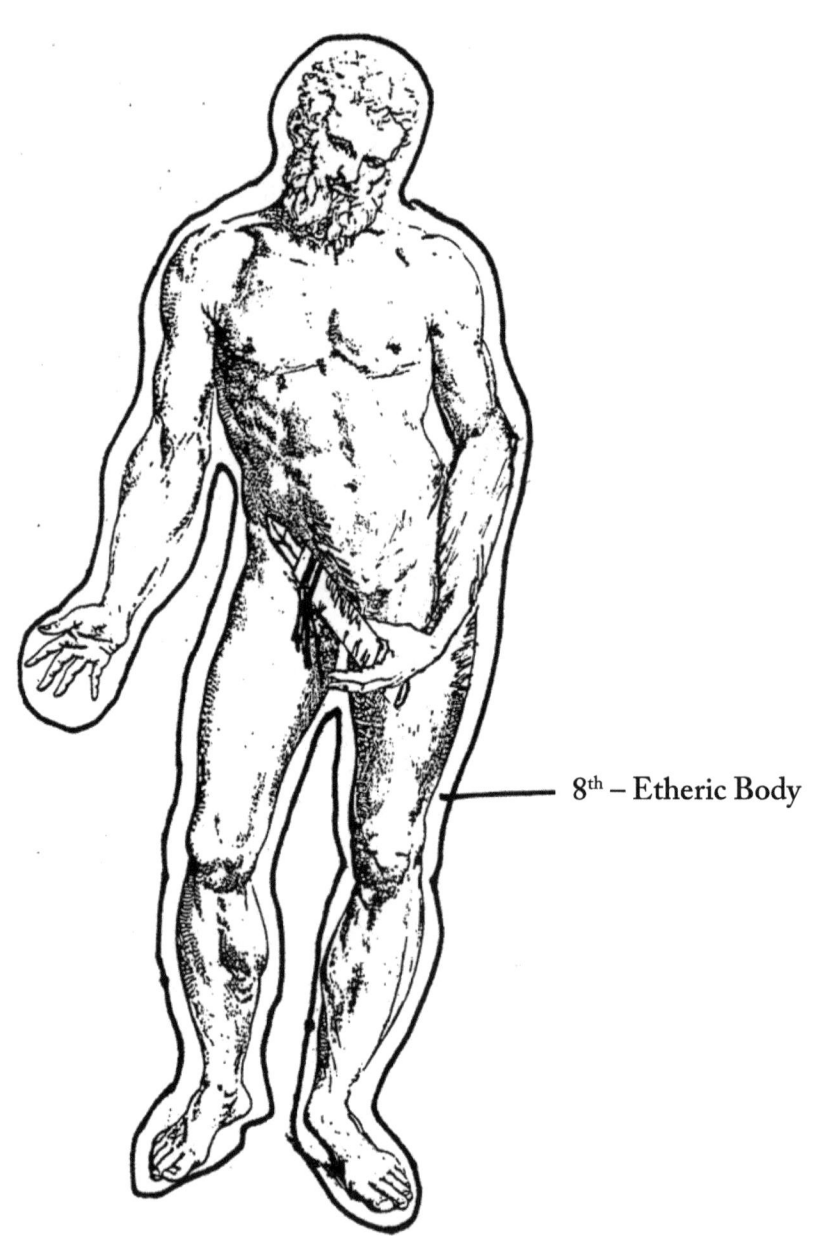

8th – Etheric Body

8th ChakraAura: Etheric Body –
Transforming Negativity & Blockages

Chapter 21

RELEASE –

Transforming Negativity and Blockages

8th ChakraAura: Etheric Body

ChakraSynergy: Release

Shape: Square

Color: Black

Stone: Onyx or Volcanic Lava

Number: Eight

Sound: eee oh eh

Goddess: Pasowee – Native American
Goddess of Endurance

8th ChakraAura: Etheric Body

The 8th ChakraAura is known as the Etheric Body. It is the first aura closest to the physical body. It relates to the sensations of the physical body, practicality, and our subconscious mind. The densest of all the auras, it helps to generate the electromagnetic energy and vitality for the physical body. The Greek word *thymos* refers to the Etheric Body.

The Etheric Body is like an ethereal twin to the physical body. It extends about one to two inches beyond the body; and it leaves the energy field of the physical body shortly after death. The Etheric Body assists with transformation by its possibility to filter out negativity or blockages before they reach the physical body.

Our physical body communicates through the Etheric Body by emanating an energy field that states its general wellness. Your body is the actual experience of your Spirit on the earth plane. "Pay Attention!" Use this attention along with your intentions to bring about transformation.

ChakraSynergy #8: Release

The ChakraSynergy for the 8th ChakraAura is named Release. The combination of these essential oils have the ability to disperse negativity and blockages in both the physical and energetic bodies. Release can be used to clear and balance the 8th ChakraAura. Release can also be used along with any of the other ChakraSynergies for clearing any blocked ChakrasAuras. When Release is used for another ChakraAura, it helps to remove blockages that are in the way of balancing that particular energy center. The primary essential oils in Release are:

❖ Cypress (*Cupressus sempervirens*)

❖ Ginger (*Zingiber officinale*)

❖ Grapefruit, Pink (*Citrus paradisi*)

- ❖ Mandarin, Red (*Citrus reticulata* Blanco)
- ❖ Pepper, Black (*Piper nigrum*)

8ᵗʰ ChakraAura Shape: Square

The Square symbolizes the four corners of the Earth Mother (north, south, east, west), the four seasons, the four solstices/equinoxes, and the four times of day (sunrise, midday, sunset, midnight). Each set of four is balanced within itself. The Square also represents down-to-earth truth and honesty. The Square has been perceived for thousands of years as a symbol of the masculine archetype and is associated with the number 4. Ancients greatly revered the number 7, because it is the unity of the numbers 4 (masculine/square) and 3 (feminine/triangle).

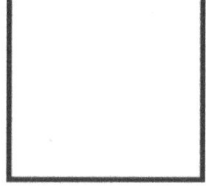

8ᵗʰ ChakraAura Color: Black

Black typifies the feminine archetype: the Divine Creative Essence. It represents the void and the darkness of the womb, where creativity and form begins. The female furnishes the womb and, in doing so, the substance for creation. As the renowned researcher Joseph Campbell so eloquently states, "By virtue of her obscuring power she occludes the Absolute Brahman (God), and by virtue of her projecting power she refracts the radiance of that Absolute in the forms of the world mirage, somewhat as a prism breaks the white light of the sun into the seven colors of the rainbow."

Black also represents protection and helps one to find the light within the dark. The opposite of Black is White. White represents the masculine archetype, the spark that manifests as Divine Life Essence. Divine Life Essence must have form through which to manifest in order to become visible on the physical plane. The perfect balance between the masculine and feminine archetypes is called polarity. Members of religious orders have worn Black because they ascertain that it *repels* negative energy that might be could be directed towards them.

8ᵗʰ ChakraAura Stone: Onyx or Volcanic Lava

Onyx is a mineral. It is predominately black. It helps to expel grief, motivate decision-making, and boost self-control. Volcanic Lava, formed from a volcanic eruption, offers great ability to instill a feeling of calm, followed by emotional tranquility and relaxation. Both stones help to remove and disperse negative energy, and to allow the recognition of any unnecessary energy that needs to be let go of. Removing negative energy allows you to reform your life's focus and begin anew.

Other black stones are: Black Coral, Jet, Obsidian, and Black Tourmaline.

8ᵗʰ ChakraAura Number: EIGHT – Achieve

The fruit is ripe and ready to eat. Success comes with patience, focus, and organization. Harvest your endeavors, your fruits! It takes planning and perseverance for the fruits to be ready for the marketplace. Self-confidence (particularly in the knowledge that your fruits are of the highest quality) pays off. Yet beware of greed. Know truly what you have and who you are. Don't blow it out of proportion and above all, don't be ruthless! There is enough abundance in the world for all to have what they *truly need*. If you don't keep these issues in mind, then your fruits could rot while you are planning the big score.

EIGHT is the energy of the first auric layer, the Etheric Body. It is about discernment and the aspect of removing hindrances wisely.

8th ChakraAura Sound: *eee oh eh*

The sound for the 8ᵗʰ ChakraAura is *eee oh eh* – Tiwa for the shoulders. (Refer to Chapter 9 *Sound* before you begin to chant this word.)

8ᵗʰ ChakraAura Goddess:
Pasowee – Native American Goddess of Endurance

Pasowee (pronounced pass-oh-wee) is the ability to see beyond appearances and cultural stereotypes. Pasowee is the Kiowa name for Buffalo Woman. The Native Americans hold that everything on the Earth Mother originating in Nature had its own essence and power – every person, twig, stone, animal and all plants.

Pasowee, stolen from her people, escaped her captors. On her way home, she found an old buffalo skin to keep her warm and to protect her from the cold, wind, and rain. Upon returning home, Pasowee taught her people how to honor the buffalo, to use all parts of an animal, and never to kill needlessly. She taught them how to survive and endure. She is endurance through adversity. Pasowee is both realistic and patient and, through her steadfastness, has the ability to disperse any interference in bringing her dreams and desires to reality.

Pasowee teaches that we are one in the web of life. Whatever we do to others, whether two-legged, four-legged, or winged, we do to ourselves.

8th ChakraAura Goddess
Pasowee – Native American Goddess of Endurance
Artist Gail Marie

Meditation

To bring the energy of the Goddess Pasowee into your healing focus, use this meditation:

I hold a clear vision of my deepest desires for change,
as I dispel any adversity on my path.

Affirmations

I RELEASE all fear and doubt.

I RELEASE what does not support my highest good.

I RELEASE it to the Divine.

I know my strengths when I RELEASE my fears.

I honor others and RELEASE control.

Your Affirmations for RELEASE—*Write your personal affirmations here:*

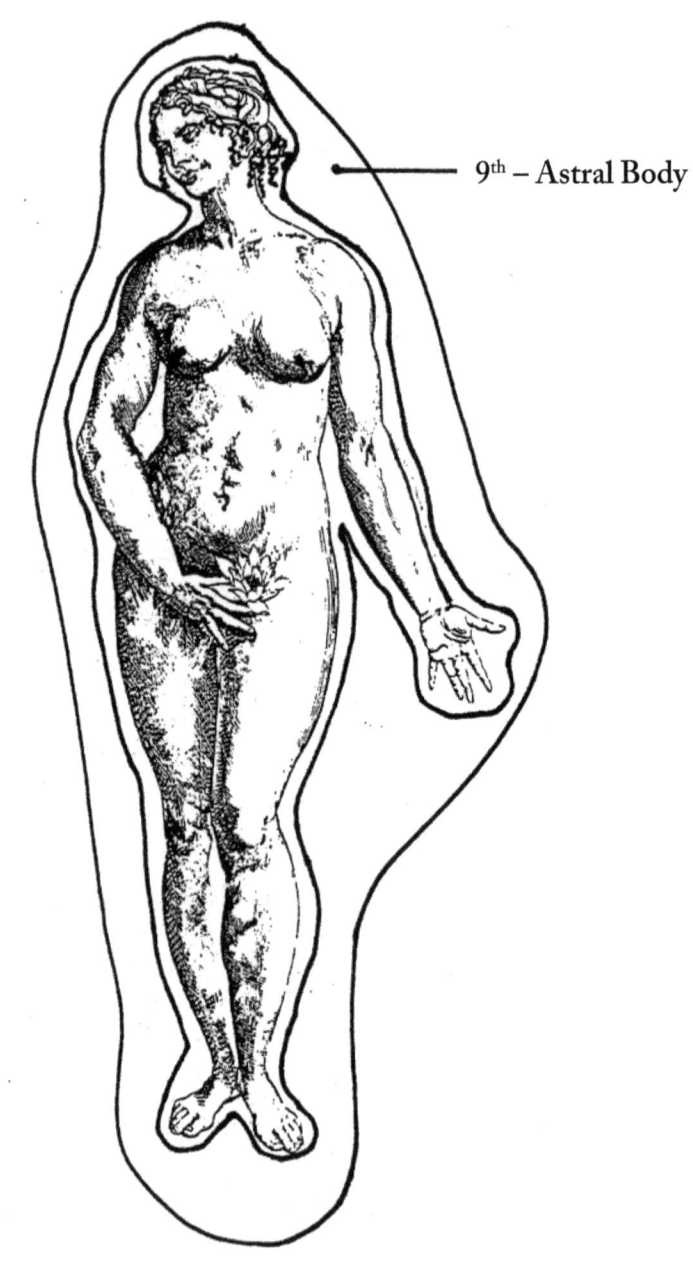

9th – **Astral Body**

9th ChakraAura: Astral Body – Transforming to Universal Love

Chapter 22

KNOWING –

Transformation to Universal Love

9th ChakraAura: Astral Body

ChakraSynergy: Knowing

Shape: Heart

Color: White

Stone: Moonstone

Number: Nine

Sound: aah eee

Goddess: Kuan Yin – Chinese Goddess
of Compassion

9th ChakraAura: Astral Body

The 9th ChakraAura is known as the Astral Body and is shaped more like an oval. It relates to our emotional body, aesthetics, and the subconscious. The Astral Body is home to our Soul. Our essence, the Soul (often called the psyche) gathers information lifetime after lifetime on the subconscious, conscious, and superconscious levels. The Soul is our guidance through Life and is the energy that carries on. The Soul is the vehicle for our Spirit and retains life experience and information.

In Kenneth Meadows book, *Where Eagles Fly*, he describes the Soul …. "Soul is to Spirit what bones are to the physical, the supportive structure at the spiritual level." He also describes the Soul Self as, "The intelligence or 'spirit' of the Soul – the most perfected aspect of a total being – whose knowledge and wisdom is a summation of experience gained through many lifetimes. Hawaiian shamans called it *Aumakua*."

Energetically, the Astral Body relates to Universal Love. Transforming to Universal Love means to move us out of the more carnal and erotic aspects of physical love (with its needs for personal gratification) and evolve into the higher aspects of spiritual and universal love. The Astral Body continues its existence after the death of the physical body. As the vehicle for the Soul and Soul Self, its energy is what carries on beyond each lifetime. It is the part of us that "goes to Heaven." It is the vehicle for the Light Body (our Spirit) to return to Source, to gather renewed life force, and, when the time is chosen to begin a new life, return again to physical form.

ChakraSynergy #9: Knowing

The ChakraSynergy for the 9th ChakraAura is named Knowing. It is particularly beneficial during any emotionally traumatic event in your life, such as a divorce, separation from a loved one, or a death. It aids in a peaceful, loving, and balanced transition. The Osha Root essential oil in Knowing offers the groundedness that acts as the balance and foundation for this synergy. Osha Root, also known as Bear Root, is wildcrafted in the Southwestern United States. Its energy enters strongly at the 1st ChakraAura – Base, and immediately shoots upwards to the 7th ChakraAura – Crown and into the auric layers.

It is important to embrace our humanness while reaching for spiritual unity. Knowing's purpose is to help bring acceptance and understanding of the Circle of Life creating a feeling of spiritual unity. All of the essential oils in this synergy support this purpose. The primary essential oils in Knowing are:

- ❖ Angelica Seed (*Angelica archangelica*)
- ❖ Melissa (*Melissa officinalis*)
- ❖ Neroli Bigarade (*Citrus aurantium*)
- ❖ Osha Root (*Ligusticum porteri*)
- ❖ Ylang Ylang (*Cananga odorata var. genuina*)

9th ChakraAura Shape: Heart

The Heart shape represents the heartbeat of the Absolute and the Infinite. Remember the sphere is symbolic of the Base of the Spine? This spherical shape also is a symbol for the unity of God, the Absolute, Divine Source. A Heart is a re-formed sphere shape. This sacred shape helps make the connection to the Divine who is both the spark within us and the Light Above us. Going beyond the earthly plane means expanding beyond the physical domain. By bringing into alignment our Will with Divine Will and by expanding our feelings beyond personal love, we can head towards Universal Love.

9th ChakraAura Color: White

White is the reflection of all colors. It is the reflection of Divine Light. White represents Divine Life Essence, purity, and knowing. There is a story from a treatise in 1542 that eloquently describes the essence of the color White and why it represents the 9th ChakraAura so perfectly.

The title of the story is *Solis Splendor,* which means Splendor of the Sun, or Light of the World. The treatise says, "The Spirit dissolves the body, and in the dissolution extracts the soul of the body, and changes this body into soul, and the soul is changed into Spirit, and the Spirit is again added to the body, for thus it has stability. Here then the body becomes spiritual by the strength of the Spirit."

9th ChakraAura Stone: Moonstone

Moonstone is a mineral. The color is various shades of white, cream, and ivory. It assists in sustaining and maintaining the understanding of your chosen destiny. It aids in further cleansing of negativity and enhances loving compassion. The energy of Moonstone relates to new beginnings. It is a stone for "feeling" and, like its namesake the Moon, reflects wondrous luminous light to the one in its presence. Moonstone enlivens spiritual nourishment throughout all the cycles of life. It can attune itself to all other gems and minerals. Moonstone carries all your dreams and visions and attunes them (for your highest good) to the purest of Divine Creation.

Other stones for the 9th ChakraAura are Diamond, Clear Quartz, Magnesite, Mother of Pearl, Snow Quartz, Danburite, Apophyllite and Selenite.

9th ChakraAura Number: NINE – Fulfillment

Your garden has completed its rightful purpose. Every number and aspect of life has its own distinct cycle. Yet your garden still continues to produce. Now is the time to finish cleaning out the dead weeds, to remove the dying branches and leaves, and to clean up so that new growth has the room it needs for future fulfillment.

This clean up is also a time to develop new concepts, new cycles, and new directions. They are now in the process and idea form. It is not the time to begin new projects or directions. It is the time to dream, to intuit, and to prepare for the new to come. Maybe there is something in your garden of which you have had enough … brussels sprouts, for example! So let your imagination go wild. What can you plant in its place next year? What will it take to grow a successful crop?

NINE is related to Universal Love, the Astral Body, and the 9ᵗʰ ChakraAura. It is about compassion, idealism, and humanitarianism. All of these aspects can be found within romance! In your wildest dreams, how do you want your garden to look? Dream now of what seeds you will plant for next year. Don't be impatient or temperamental; the time will soon come to plant new seeds.

9ᵗʰ ChakraAura Sound: *aah eee*

The sound for the 9ᵗʰ ChakraAura is *aah eee* – Tiwa for the eyes. I chose this because our energetic eyes or etheric eyes help us to see beyond the physical worlds into the Mystery of All Creation. (Refer to Chapter 9 *Sound* before you chant this word.)

9ᵗʰ ChakraAura Goddess:
Kuan Yin – Chinese Goddess of Compassion

Kuan Yin (pronounced kwan-yin) means *she who hears the weeping world*. Just as Catholic Christianity holds reverence for the Virgin Mary, Chinese and Japanese Buddhism has the feminine bodhisattva – Kuan Yin. A bodhisattva is one who is the essence of enlightenment and compassionately chooses to be in physical form to assist others. Herstory says that she was so concerned for humanity that, upon receiving enlightenment, she chose to retain human form rather than to transcend it as pure energy. Kuan Yin chose to be reborn again and again on the Earth Mother for the sake of humankind.

For the Chinese, the mere utterance of her name is supposed to protect you from physical and spiritual harm. Kuan Yin is the ultimate embodiment of compassion, peace, harmony, and generosity.

Kuan Yin has an affinity for nature and the Full Moon. She can often be seen in the forests when the moon is full, near water and willow trees. Kuan Yin helps us to find compassion. She assists our inner growth so that we can shine as full as the fullest moon. Sometimes seen with a sword in her hand, it depicts her ability to cut through illusion.

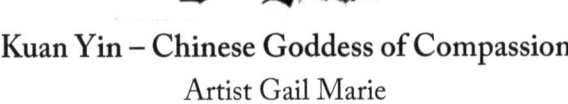

Kuan Yin – Chinese Goddess of Compassion
Artist Gail Marie

Meditation

To bring the dynamic of compassion into your life and the energy of the Goddess Kuan Yin into your healing focus, use this meditation:

I love and accept myself the way I am.
I choose growth as I shine my fullest brilliance.

Affirmations

I KNOW my connection to Divine Source.

I KNOW I have the ability to manifest my desires.

I am in full KNOWING of my Divine Self.

With KNOWING, I trust my choices.

I KNOW I can accomplish whatever I want to.

Your Affirmations for KNOWING—*Write your personal affirmations here:*

PART FIVE

Vibrational AromaTherapy

*In Vibrational AromaTherapy you find the myth, magic, and
mysticism of healing and transformation.*
– Ixchel Leigh

Meditation Using Vibrational Aroma Therapy
Artist Patricia Elder

Chapter 23

Ultimate Essence of Your Optimum Self

Hidden deep in the heart of things, Thou carest for growth and life:
the seed becomes shoot, the bud a blossom, the flower becomes fruit.
Tired I slept on my idle bed in the illusion that the work had an end.
In the morning I awoke to find that my garden was full of flowers.
– Rabindranath Tagore

Vibrational AromaTherapy by Ixchel™ is being used by individuals for their own transformational growth process, by doctors, hypnotherapists, and psychiatrists who use this modality with their patients, and by healing arts practitioners, such as: massage therapists, aromatherapists, acupuncturists, aestheticians, and somatic practitioners (Reiki, healing touch, polarity).

Vibrational Aroma Therapy has been created as a journey for self-discovery. It can be used for your personal meditations as a tool towards enlivening your Spirit. Healing begins with the self, YOU. Your day-to-day life concerns are based on desires and dreams of being all that you can be. You are here in this life for the experience and the learning it offers you.

Are you asking yourself, "Where do I begin?" Do you already have knowledge of some of the information in *Aromatic Alchemy*, yet still want to know how you can incorporate additional pieces into your life or work? *Aromatic Alchemy* introduces you to ways in which you can enliven your creativity, resourcefulness, imagination, and inspiration in order to reawaken your dreams and become all that you can be – the essence of your true self, your Essence Self.

You will find tools for self-responsibility towards your personal wellbeing. "Tools … self-responsibility! Yikes!" you may think. "I don't have time!" you might say. Don't fret! What is presented here is softer, a teeny bit sweeter, for people like you who live a hurried and full life. You will be given a guide to discovering the essence of who you really are and how you can express your Essence Self in the real world.

With assistance from Nature, the gifts and tools presented in this book can awaken your deepest inner dreams through your inner guidance – your intuition. Awakening your intuition on deeper levels enlivens your innate creative talents, which certainly brings more joy into your life.

HU-MANITY – HU is derived from a Sufi word meaning of Spirit. MANITY refers to mankind, one race – beings who inhabit the Earth Mother. Humanity therefore means: *the spiritual beings that inhabit the Earth Mother.* Since we began here on the Earth Mother, we *humans* have been evolving into our fullest and greatest possibility, that of being *humanbeings who are conscious of our spiritual selves.* We are evolving into beings that walk every step of our lives with the knowingness and the conscious awareness of our spiritual connection to Divine Source. We are integrating the spirit (hu) with the 'manity.' This is our potential, our possibility.

I love this quote by Soren Kierkegaard: "It is dangerous to go into eternity with possibilities which one has oneself prevented from becoming realities. A possibility is a hint from God."

Focused intent is very powerful and is the basis of alchemy. It has the ability to transform something ordinary into something extraordinary. Here is an everyday life example: If someone prepares a meal with the focused intent of nurturing and with great love, it tastes better than if it was prepared in haste and with little or no feeling behind it. Once you define and state your focused intent, bring your *attention* to your intention. Your intention needs to be supported by your attention …. Imagine a clear pathway leading to your intention, one free of hindrances. Better yet … *see your intention* as already a part of your life, rather than something that you are striving towards!

My focus and intention for this book is to assist you in rejuvenating your dreams … dreams of health, wellbeing, creativity, joy, success, happiness, abundance … the list can go on, for it is *your list*! My attention is activated in this book by giving you many choices, ideas, and suggestions for bringing your own attention to your intentions.

Socrates believed that if you have a problem, it is there to remind you that you also have the answer to the problem! How do you find the answer? You open your heart and your mind. Look deeply at who you are and what you want from life. Ask for assistance in your prayers or meditations. Take advantage of all the tools you have, your knowledge and the amazing gifts of Nature.

Individuation

What are your most intimate dreams? How do you see yourself in the world? First, find and define your personal identity, your particular gifts, qualities, and talents that make *you unique*. You are a unique individual, gifted from birth with special qualities that makes you unique. Once you define what your particular gifts and talents are, the next step is to integrate your personal identity (gifts and talents) into the world by discovering just where you fit in as the unique individual you are. This is *individuation* and it is a crucial aspect of your personal growth and transformation. The search for your individual identity and its worldly expression eventually leads to reminding you of your universal connection to a Divine spiritual source.

Re-membering

Have you denied or cut out a part of yourself in order to fit in? Have you shut off a portion of your feelings in order not to rock the boat? These dis-membered parts actually lie dormant, and can fester into dis-ease. Some of these parts are feelings or emotions that can be attached to some fairly painful memories ... ones which you would maybe prefer to forget. Some of these dis-membered parts could have crippled you emotionally or possibly made you physically ill. When you recognize that to feel whole within yourself you need to bring back those parts of yourself (which you previously denied, or dis-membered in order to suit someone else's agenda) then it is time to re-member!

When it is time to re-member, it does not necessarily mean that you need to relive painful memories! *Recognizing that you have lived too long denying a part of yourself*, this is your initial step. Have the courage to integrate the dis-membered part of yourself, to integrate it into your intrinsic nature. Re-member who you are! Re-membering leads towards your own personal and spiritual growth. Re-membering ultimately brings you back to remembering your deeper connection to a Divine Source, whatever your personal spiritual beliefs are. This connection reaffirms to your spirit that you are not alone, that you are loved, unconditionally, by the Supreme Creator, the Divine Source, God. *Feeling* this connection gives you the courage you need to be all that you can be and to be bold enough to live your dreams.

So Many Paths

There are numerous paths and tools for enlivening yourself towards personal growth and wellbeing. We live in an age when technology is expanding along with the methods for expanding and restoring health ... for open-minded seekers. The list of modalities is growing all the time and includes: homeopathic medicine, new research in allopathic medicine, osteopathy, naturopathy, traditional aromatherapy, *Vibrational AromaTherapy*, acupressure (Shiatsu), acupuncture, Chinese Medicine, reflexology, iridology, herbology, radionics, somatic therapies, Reiki, polarity therapy, kinesiology, sound therapy, color therapy, and more.

What feels right to you? What modality makes sense to you? Choose one modality or a combination that resonates with you and begin your personal growth on its deepest levels. *Aromatic Alchemy* comprises many new and ancient principles that can be used as tools for you to discover your individuation and to re-member who you are. In helping to restore balance and harmony to your spirit, soul, and psyche, you can bring wellness to your entire physical being.

Healing

Shelley von Strunckel, a long-time friend and noted author, astrologer and consultant, wrote an informative book way ahead of its time in 1990, titled *The No-Nonsense Guide to the Sixth Sense*. She says, "Healing means recovery. As the word is normally used, healing is regaining vitality, 'getting well.' When used in the metaphysical sense, 'the touch,' as healing is sometimes called, refers to the improvement of a condition, physical or otherwise, at a pace or in a manner beyond what is considered realistically possible … in the metaphysical realm, the unexpected can be an everyday event …. Healing occurs in the dimension beyond the physical. Though the effects we *see* are usually in the physical body, healing can equally result in a change of a condition to the mental or emotional nature."

You are responsible for your first steps to your healing, growth, and, ultimately, your transformation. Whether you seek healing from a common cold, a more serious disease, or a giant overall emotional or physical metamorphosis, you must decide for yourself what feels right to regain your vitality. The decision is yours. Even if full recovery of your vitality does not occur, what is important in the long term, are the steps you take towards your healing and growth.

Dr. Edward Bach, the English physician who was the first modern day physician to discover flower essences as a form of energetic medicine said: (printed in the book *Vibrational Medicine*, by Richard Gerber, M.D.):

"It cannot be too firmly realized that every Soul in incarnation is down here for the specific purpose of gaining experience and understanding, and of perfecting his personality towards those ideals laid down by the Soul. Let everyone remember that his Soul has laid down for him a particular work, and that unless he does this work, though perhaps not consciously, he will inevitably raise a conflict between his Soul and personality which of necessity reacts in the form of physical disorders …. From time immemorial it has been known that Providential Means have placed in nature the prevention and cure of disease, by means of divinely enriched herbs and plants and trees."

In the same book, Dr. Gerber references many studies by scientists of the effects of energy and its connection to healing. Dr. Gerber says that he has been "impressed by the commonality of loving intent amongst healers. They work primarily from a position of heart-centered, unconditional love when they work with another living being's energy field." Additionally, Dr. Gerber says, "The magnetic earthfield may thus provide a kind of added power to the innate energy-field projection of healers. Perhaps it is the increased magnetic or magnetoelectrical currents coming from the earthfield, and cascading down through the bodies of healers …. As the magnetoelectrical currents flow to patients, their energy fields undergo restructuring and repatterning that ultimately affect biochemical processes at the cellular level."

Honoring Life

I feel that as humans, we are placed on the Earth Mother to integrate all aspects of ourselves – our Body, Heart, Spirit, Mind, and Soul. If we don't use the precious resources gifted to us, we deny ourselves the experience of receiving their gifts. If we don't *honor* these natural resources as gifts from the Earth Mother, we deny the circle of healing which occurs from her to us. We must learn to use the Earth Mother's gifts, *Nature's Gifts*, wisely and consciously. Using her gifts wisely and consciously allows healing to occur, not solely for each human; yet additionally, the healing energy reverberates to all other beings, animals, and plants on the planet, *including* the Earth Mother herself.

Native Americans for generations have lived by a code of ethics called the *seventh generation principle* – no decision is made for the tribe (or community) without first taking into consideration how the effects of that decision will affect their children's children, for seven generations to come. This is honoring life in its greatest form.

Every cell in your body has a direct relationship with the Creative Life Force and each cell is independently responding. When you feel joy, all the curcuits are open, so the Life Force can be fully received. When you feel guilt, blame, fear or anger, the circuits are hindered and the Life Force cannot flow as effectively. Physical experience is about monitoring those circuits and keeping them as open as possible. Your cells know what to do; they are summoning the Energy.

– **Abraham Hicks**, *Ask and it is Given*

A Multi-Faceted Modality By Carol Corio

I was first introduced to *Vibrational AromaTherapy by Ixchel*™ in 1992 and use it in my personal journey of awareness and in my energetic healing practice. Since Ixchel Leigh introduced this work in this format at the first Live Seminar in Boston (November 1997), I have been drawn like a magnet to this incredible body of work and by my personal connection to Ixchel. She brings personal integrity, grace, intuition, passion, and divine energy to living her life's passion and she brings authenticity, strength, and humility to her work. Ixchel has been working with, receiving information about, and evolving the concepts of *Vibrational AromaTherapy* longer and in more depth than anyone I know of in the authentic aromatherapy industry. The vibrational and subtle qualities of the essential oils published in the 1st Edition were truly like a treasure chest of information never before available, In this edition, Ixchel has added 38 more essential oils (to the original 70); now we have a total of 108 available monographs to choose from.

Vibrational Aroma Therapy by Ixchel™ is a multi-faceted modality that is offered as a benefit for both individual transformation and healing bodywork practice integration. Even if you have never studied aromatherapy before, *Vibrational Aroma Therapy by Ixchel™* offers a simple, yet profound way to start incorporating essential oils into the energetic aspects of a personal meditation or professional bodywork practice. If you have studied aromatherapy with other teachers, it is a complement to those studies. In fact, it may ignite your passion about authentic and vibrationally-conscious essential oils and open you to continue the aromatic journey with additional studies.

My personal recommendation is to experience the ChakraSynergies. These ChakraSynergies have embraced the passage of time, almost twenty years, and your knowledge expands naturally with fluidity to include more of Nature's Gifts and Tools.

As a truly unique aspect, *Vibrational Aroma Therapy by Ixchel™* is offered as a standalone personal transformation approach to aromatherapy. If you know nothing about aromatherapy, you can read this book and practice the principles detailed within. If you prefer a more formal study option, find further information in "Resources" at the end of this book.

Chapter 24

Essential Oils – Spirit of the Plant

Aromatherapy belongs to the realm of natural therapeutics. As such it is based on certain principles … these principles … are based on man's interpretation of nature from his understanding of life.
– Robert Tisserand, *The Art of Aromatherapy*

Essential oils are often referred to as the life force of the plant. Their essence, or quintessence, is their scent, which is disemminated into the world where the plant is growing and living. It is this scent that attracts, repels, and acts also as protector for the plant. The scent of the plant carries with it the essence or spirit of the plant. Eliot Cowan in his book *Plant Spirit Medicine* says, "… plants have spirit, and that spirit is the strongest medicine. Spirit can heal the deepest reaches of the heart and soul."

Human beings can find alignment with the natural world and we can also affect it. In the 1960's, research was carried out in a university in the United States, which showed the effects that humans have on plants. One experiment involved people arguing vehemently in a room lined with plants. Later, electrodes were hooked-up to the plants, and when the same arguing people entered the room again, the plants were documented as registering levels of fear. This same alignment can work to our (and the plants) advantage.

True essential oils are extracted from botanicals (from Nature's laboratory) not created in human laboratories. These essential oils hold the energy and spirit of the plant and connect very synergistically to the spirit of each human. This is why any form of aromatherapy is so effective. The art and science of aromatherapy have developed many sub-fields of interests. You can find aromatherapy in hospitals, hospice care, healing centers, naturopathy, homeopathy, acupuncture, health services, and on and on.

Vibrational AromaTherapy Blending

True aromatherapy uses true essential oils – not synthetic aroma chemicals! Vibrationally-conscious essential oils are of great importance when focusing on vibrational healing and wellbeing. Using the highest quality, therapeutic-grade essential oils available will support all of your work with these delicious wonders.

Christine Malcolm of *Santa Fe Botanical Fragrances* explains, "There is a depth and dimension in essential oils that cannot be compared to aroma chemicals, no matter how similar the molecular structures. Essential oils themselves have long evolutionary and cultural histories that contribute to their multidimensionality."

Essential oils are extracted from various botanicals. During the day, the plant takes in, or breathes in, active solar energy. At night, the plant exhales passive lunar energy. As a result of this phenomenon, we can say that essential oils consist of *transformed solar energy*.

In traditional aromatherapy, the general percentage of essential oils in any given carrier oil or lotion (used for massage) is between 2% and 3% essential oil. The physical body is denser than our energetic body. Using these percentages for traditional aromatherapy will affect the physical body.

To reach the more subtle energy bodies, *use less*. As the ChakraAuras are energy centers, they are subtle and lighter than the mass weight of our physical body. When using essential oils for their energetic and vibrational effects, *less is more*.

Vibrational AromaTherapy Essential Oil Dosages

For Vibrational AromaTherapy, you will use 1% essential oil for any massage oil or lotion preparation. Glass bottles are preferred (save the planet). Fill the bottle one-half full with your preferred vegetable oil or lotion. Put in the required amount of pure essential oils (PEO) to equal 1%. Shake gently. Fill the remaining space in the bottle with the same vegetable oil or lotion. Shake again to use.

When you are blending for 1% essential oil in a massage oil preparation, use the "Vibrational AromaTherapy Dilutions" chart guide listed below. There is also a "Dilutions" chart to guide you for 2% dilutions.

Conversions

Below is a chart of sizes and how many liquid drops are in each size. This is approximate, as the size of the drop depends of what the viscosity of the liquid is:

- ❖ 1 ml (1/30th oz, 1/5 teaspoon) = 20 drops (liquid or PEO)
- ❖ 5 ml (1/6 oz, 1 teaspoon) = 100 drops
- ❖ 10 ml (1/3 oz, 1 ½ teaspoon) = 200 drops
- ❖ 15 ml (1/2 oz, 1 Tablespoon) = 300 drops
- ❖ 30 ml (1 oz, 2 Tablespoons) = 600 drops

Vibrational Dosages Formula

Generally you will be using 1% to 1 ½% PEO (pure essential oil/s) in your *Vibrational AromaTherapy* formulations.

For *Specific Use* (massage, shiatsu, acupressure, polarity, ritual) 1 %.
For Acute Use (acupuncture, energy work) 2 %.

This means that 1% to 1 ½% of your formula is PEO, the balance will be your chosen carrier oil or lotion. The following chart will tell you how many drops (or ml) of PEO you will need for each bottle size:

Bottle Quantity Size – Drops of PEO (pure essential oil)1% Dilutions

- ❖ 5 ml (1 tsp./teaspoon) = 1 drop of PEO
- ❖ 10 ml (2 tsp) = 2 drops PEO
- ❖ 15 ml (1/2 oz) = 3 drops PEO
- ❖ 30 ml (1 oz) = 6 drops PEO
- ❖ 60 ml (2 oz) = 12 drops PEO
- ❖ 120 ml (4 oz) = 24 drops (1 ml + 4 drops) PEO
- ❖ 240 ml (8 oz) = 48 drops (2 ml + 8 drops) PEO)
- ❖ 480 ml (16 oz) = 96 drops (4 ml + 16 drops) PEO
- ❖ 2 % Dilutions
- ❖ 5 ml (1 tsp./teaspoon) = 2 drops of PEO
- ❖ 10 ml (2 tsp) = 4 drops PEO
- ❖ 15 ml (1/2 oz) = 6 drops PEO
- ❖ 30 ml (1 oz) = 12 drops PEO
- ❖ 60 ml (2 oz) = 24 drops (1 ml + 4 drops) PEO
- ❖ 120 ml (4 oz) = 48 drops (2 ml + 8 drops) PEO
- ❖ 240 ml (8 oz) = 96 drops (4 ml + 16 drops) PEO
- ❖ 480 ml (16 oz) = 192 drops (9 ml + 16 drops) PEO

Very Important!!!

Use only the highest quality pure and true, therapeutic-grade essential oils for Vibrational Aroma Therapy. You are affecting the subtle energy system. You want to use only those essential oils that have the highest vibrational and energetic properties ("vibrationally-conscious"), and essential oils without other chemical (human-made) interferences.

Vibrational AromaTherapy Formulations

Vibrational AromaTherapy Bath:

Run the water first, whether you want cool, tepid, or very warm (hot). When you are ready to soak, add the essential oils and swirl them around with your hand to blend in water. Use 2 to 4 drops PEO in a full tub. Alternately, you can add the pure essential oils to castile soap or fractionated coconut oil for easier dispersal in water.

VibrationalSynergy (for Healing Anoint or Massage):

Glass bottle. Add 12 drops essential oil in 2 ounce bottle. Fill bottle with your chosen carrier (oil or lotion). Gently shake and use.

VibrationalMist:

In 2 ounce glass bottle, add 1ml of fractionated coconut oil. This is coconut oil that has been processed (fractioned) to create shelf-stable oil and will allow the essential oils to easily disperse into water. Add 12 drops of essential oil to the coconut oil. Fill up bottle with spring water, distilled water, or the hydrol you choose (to assist overall wellness, as guided by your chosen essential oils and focused intention of your completed formula). Shake before each use.

ChakraSpritz:

This is a term created for using with *Vibrational AromaTherapy*. A ChakraSpritz is a vibrationally effective aromatherapy mist purposefully created for use with the modality of *Vibrational AromaTherapy by Ixchel™*. In a 2-ounce glass bottle, add 12 drops of fractionated coconut oil. This is coconut oil that has been processed (fractioned) to create shelf-stable oil and will allow the essential oils to easily disperse into water. Add 10 drops of ChakraSynergy (or essential oils) to the coconut oil. Fill up bottle with spring water or distilled water. Shake before each use.

Creative ways to use the Vibrational AromaTherapy ChakraSpritz:

- ❖ Spray healing room before and after a session, clears space
- ❖ Spritz face of person receiving treatment, allows luxuriating in scent
- ❖ Spray mist on face and body, supports each ChakraAura's healing

Specific Use (massage, shiatsu, acupressure, ritual):

- ❖ 1% PEO dispersed in lotion or carrier oil

Acute Use (acupuncture and energy work):

- ❖ 2 % PEO, or
- ❖ Acupuncture – 2 drops PEO in 1teaspoon sweet almond oil
- ❖ Energy Work – (Not touching the body, inhalation only) 1 drop PEO in the palm of your hand

Formulating for Traditional Aromatherapy versus *Vibrational AromaTherapy*

Above, I have given you the percentages for using PEO when creating a *Vibrational AromaTherapy* formula (or the alchemical and esoteric use of pure essential oils for transmutation and transformation).

Listed below, you will find a chart of the normally accepted percentages when creating formulations for specific uses in Traditional Aromatherapy (for comparison with above information):

- ❖ 4 drops PEO in 1/3 ounce (10 ml) carrier lotion or oil
- ❖ 13 drops PEO in 1 ounce (30 ml) carrier lotion or oil
- ❖ 25 drops PEO in 2 ounces (60 ml) carrier lotion or oil
- ❖ 50 drops PEO in 4 ounces (120 ml) carrier lotion or carrier

Chapter 25

Hydrosols – Liquescent Treasures

*Hydrosols represent the highest benefits of the combination
of herbal-therapy and aromatherapy.
The elixir of life infused with the spirit of a plant.*
– Jeanne Rose

Hydrosols (aka. Hydrolates) are waters, pure distillates that carry the properties of plant. A true hydrosol is a by-product of the steam distillation process used when distilling essential oils from botanicals. They are this ONLY! A floral water is NOT a hydrosol. Floral water can be *any* water that has scent added to it (the scent may or may not be essential oils). When using a hydrosol for energy work, make sure that it is a true hydrosol (NOT floral water). Always use organic hydrosols when available.

The word hydrosol means a water (hydro) solution (sol). Hydrosols contain micro-molecules of essential oils, as well as minute particles of the botanical from which they are distilled. To prevent them from turning or going off, keep them in cool, dark places. If the hydrosol has turned, it smells rather sour or mildewy. The hydrosol is relatively inexpensive compared to its essential oil counterpart; so if it "goes off," or smells sour, use it to water a plant, rather than yourself!

Suzanne Catty, an aromatherapist in Canada, specializes in hydrosols. She says of hydrosols, "Gentle and safe in their pure state, highly effective in extremely low dilutions, and with few contraindications or safety precautions, here is the subtle, constitutional form of aromatherapy." Ms Catty says, "new medical research indicates that weak or compromised immune systems can sometimes respond negatively or shut down in response to powerful treatments. Hydrosols may offer safer, less stimulating health support in these cases and many trials are exploring this possibility."

(from a paper by Ms. Catty, delivered at the Pacific Institute of Aromatherapy sponsored Conference on Aromatherapy in October 1998 in San Francisco)

Using Hydrosols for Energetic Work

Hydrosols are perfect when used for energy work. Hydrosols may appear as merely water, or presented as a mist; yet they have power! Extremely effective in a subtle way, hydrosols are easy and safe to use. They are particularly effective and easy for babies, the aged, or invalids. They are also great to use for animals and pets such as cats, birds, and dogs.

In a paper written by Jeanne Rose called *Two Products of Distillation*, and published in *The World of Aromatherapy Book*, Ms. Rose quotes Christoph Streicher, "During the distillation process, the ascending steam dissolves the essential oil contained in the plant, temporarily associating with it in a highly aromatic ethereal oneness of opposite values: water and oil, which normally do not associate ... in recent times it has become more and more evident that the hydrosols are also exceptional carriers of intelligent vibrational impulses of plant life."

You can use hydrosols before a meditation. Mist a hydrosol directly on your (or your client's) face, or you can mist the area of the ChakraAuras. Misting a hydrosol is done for many purposes. Sometimes, it can be cleansing or purifying; other times, it can assist the individual's wellness in an emotional or physical manner. All depends on your choice of hydrosol and its particular healing properties.

I encourage you to discover further the tremendous benefits and uses of true hydrosols. You will find books for further investigation in "Resources." Choose the hydrosol you use based on your intentions. As a hydrosol is a by-product of the steam distillation process for essential oils, it derives its properties from the essential oil used. A hydrosol has the same vibrational qualities and healing properties as the essential oil of the same botanical name.

Chapter 26

Vibrational & Energetic
Monographs for Essential Oils

The individual is not the sum of his common impressions but of his unusual ones. Thus familiar mysteries are created in us which are expressed in rare symbols. It is near water and its flowers that I have best understood that reverie is an ever-emanating universe, a fragrant breath that issues from things through the dreamer.
– Gaston Bachelard, Water and Dreams

It is *extremely* important to respect essential oils, especially when using with a particular focus for healing or for their vibrational and energetic uses. Essential oils are one of the most potent of Nature's Vibrational Medicines. Important to consider:

❖ Listed first is the common name for the essential oil.

❖ The *italicized* word (immediately to the right of the common name for the essential oil) is that oil's Latin binomial, or botanical name.

❖ The number(s) are the ChakraAura(s) that the particular essential oil relates to with the strongest vibrations.

❖ Please invest in pure, therapeutic-grade essential oils. Organic, wild-crafted and biodynamic, when available, are also preferred. These carry the highest quality vibrational signature possible. Most of these PEO's are steam distilled, cold pressed, or CO_2 extracts (suitable for aromatherapy). Healing is worth it!

❖ This list includes the essential oils listed as ingredients in all of the ChakraSynergy formulations for *Vibrational AromaTherapy*, and additional essential oils. In *Vibrational*

AromaTherapy I do not recommend the use of any essence that is not suitable for therapeutic-grade (medical-type) healing.

❖ The description for each essential oil is its Vibrational Monograph: A specialist body of writing created by Ixchel Leigh, over decades of work, through research and as received through meditations, while sitting in contemplation with the specific botanical essence.

❖ "Note" is the fragrance classification for each essential oil: Head Note (Top Note), Heart Note (Middle Note), Soul Note (Base Note), or Fixative.

(Special Note: Please use essential oils with respect and caution. If you are unsure of the use of any essential oil, please seek further advice from a professional who has credible experience and credentials. The author and publisher are not responsible for any individual's careless misuse or overuse of essential oils. The following information is for educational purposes only. It has not been evaluated by the U.S. Food and Drug Administration.)

108 Essential Oils or CO₂ Extracts
With Their Vibrational Monograph

Absinthe *(Artemesia absinthium)* **4**

From the flowering tops. (Recommended purveyor: Vetiver Aromatics.) Scent: very lusciously verdant, vanilla-like, warm, smooth. Remember the dreams you had for your life? It's never too late! It is always the Now today, so begin the process towards your freedom and joy.

Note: Heart

Agarwood *(Aquilaria crassna)* **1, 7, 9**

From wood, steam distilled. Scent: deep, rich, ancient, smoky, sweet tobacco, opulent, otherworldly. Used for both aromatherapy and parfumerie, highly revered since antiquity, known as Oud. Life is full of difficulties and challenges, but at the same time it's very sacred. You are here to meet the challenges (they are gifts to help you grow). Remember the sacredness of Life.

Note: Soul, Fixative

Ambrette *(Abelmoschus moschatus)* **2, 7, 9**

From seeds, CO_2 extract. Scent: fertile, musky, floral, animalic, sensual, and leathery. Mimics a musk scent that people love, from a botanical! Carries an angelic signature that eases stress and tension, and offers balance to all of the senses: smell, taste, touch, sight, and hearing.

Note: Soul, Fixative

Amyris *(Amyris balsamifera)* **3, 5**

From wood. Scent: soft, woody, balsamic sweetness, dash of peppery ginger and wisps of vanilla. Calming and soothing, helps light your path for expanded personal explorations. Opens you to renewal and regeneration. Eases stress, anxiety, and promotes sleep (insomnia).

Note: Soul, Fixative

Angelica *(Angelica archangelica)* 1(Angelica root), 9 (Angelica seed)

From either the root or the seed. Scent: herbaceous, spicy, woody, pungent, very little goes a long way! Highly grounding, while at the same time, allows you to see things in a new way. Stirs things up energetically. Cleanses and purifies the blood. Restores and revitalizes while alleviating feelings of hopelessness. Helps to ground your spirituality into the physical world for those who do a lot of meditation or separate their spiritual life from their physical life.

Note: Heart

Aniseed *(Pimpinella anisum)* 2, 3

From the seed. Scent: sweet anis-like, warm like soft sunshine. Helps to dispel criticism and judgment of self or of others, particularly when there is resulting guilt felt on either side. Also helps to stimulate the sexual glands while allowing you to go beyond the mere physical world to that of spirit.

Note: Head

Basil *(Ocimum basilicum)* 3

From an herb. Scent: surprising green penetrates with first whiff, herbaceous, slight anise sweetness. Reduces mental fatigue. Stimulates the conscious mind and sends creative energy to the conscious mind. Enhances creative awareness. Helps to repel the "evil eye," or when you sense that someone is jealous of you.

Note: Head, Heart

Basil, Holy *(Ocimum sanctum)* 7

From the herb. Scent: green, very herby, spicy, balsamic, deeply sweet. Offers to protect you in your home or while travelling, mentally, psychically, and physically. Considered extremely sacred for the Hindu religion.

Note: Head

Bay Leaf *(Pimenta racemosa)* **3**

From the leaves of the allspice tree. Scent: reminiscent of pumpkin pie, green with hints of clove. Bay Leaf promotes positive change. Bay Leaf is used when there is a need for protecting an individual's physical or energetic space. It is associated with the energy of Fire. Consequently, it helps to "light the fire" or stimulate personal growth. This is a different species from Bay Laurel, which associates itself with the 6th ChakraAura – Third Eye.

Note: Heart

Bay Laurel *(Laurus nobilis)* **6**

From the dried leaves and branches. Scent: slightly spicy, herbaceous, earthy and peppery. Bay Laurel offers protection of psychic space, thus giving you a feeling of strength and acceptance of your own creative essence, intuition, and psychic abilities. It can also enhance prophetic ability. Bay Laurel helps to stimulate a renewed interest in life. Assists with the assimilation of new ideas. Helps to calm feelings of hysteria.

Note: Heart

Bergamot *(Citrus aurantium, ssp bergamia)* **4**

Zest from the peel. Cold-pressed from the skin (rind). Scent: freshly soft citrus that is crisp, with floraly green delight. The color of Bergamot is green and is associated greatly with the 4th ChakraAura – Heart. Aids grief and is uplifting. Helps to instill feelings of joy and calm. Bergamot ushers in the space for the individual to be open to receiving love and to be open to their highest potential.

Note: Head

Buddha Wood *(Eremophila mitchelli)* **7, 9**

From the heartwood. (Recommended purveyor: White Lotus Aromatics.) Scent: creamy smooth, slightly mossy and of old worldy leather. With wisdom, you follow your guidance, every step of your journey – you are rewarded. Offers the tenacity when needed, to go beyond your physical concerns; to see beyond the physical body, that you are a spiritual being. Enhances meditation.

Note: Soul, Fixative

Cannabis (Hemp) *(Cannabis sativa)* **1, 2, 3**

From the leaves and tops. The scent initially is slightly woody, fruity yet pungent, then becomes extremely herby, lasting a very long time and this continues into the drydown. Use sparingly as it can be overpowering. Eases anxiety, tensions, pain (physical and emotional) and anxiousness. Can calm migraines and soothe over-worked muscles. Helps you to feel grounded and connected to the Earth. Mood-altering, offers an outlook of positivity, uplifting, and gives a lightness to your being (unrestraint).

The cannabis I use comes from Eden Botanicals. Their "in-house GC/MS analysis found no THC or CBD present." CBD (cannabidiol- not psychoactive) and THC (delta-9 tetrahydrocannabinol) are considered non-volatiles and **do not** appear in the essential oil. ("Mediaville, Vito and Simon Steinemann. 'Essential oil of *Cannabis sativa L. strains*,'J International Hemp Association, 1997, 4(2):80-82.")

Note: Heart, Soul

Cananga *(Cananga odorata or Canangium odoratum)* **5**

From the flowers. Scent: sweet, spicy and hay-like. Helps to stimulate the adrenals, the thymus gland, and the immune system. Helps emotional expression so that the thymus and the adrenals aren't "stuck." Uplifting and enhances a youthful feeling.

Note: Soul, Heart

Caraway *(Carum carvi)* **2, 8**

From the seed. Scent: like freshly crushed seeds, woody, spicy, and warm. Caraway helps you to renew your interest in life. It refreshes the conscious mind and enhances alertness. It assists in removing negativity, strengthens memory, and encourages fidelity.

Note: Heart

Cardamom *(Elettarria cardamomum)* **2**

From the seed (fruit). Scent: mouth-watering, distinctively sweet spiciness, warm, rich, and long lasting (where's the cup of chai?). Cardamom is the second most expensive spice (the first being saffron). Stirs the creative energies, as well as helping the individual to overcome blockages that could be preventing the opening of creative or sexual expression. Cardamom is good during visualizations for drawing love or intimate relationships closer to you.

Note: Heart

Carrot Seed *(Daucus carota)* **6**

From the dried seeds. Scent: rooty, wet earth, woody, slight spice. Helps to dispel anger, fear, or denial. Carrot Seed assists in renewing a youthful vigor and lustful feeling about life. Assists in opening your inner vision, or intuition, allowing for the highest truth to be ascertained, even in the midst of confusion. Helps to remove blockages that can prevent the free flow of energy, especially between the 3rd ChakraAuras – Solar Plexus and 4th ChakraAura – Heart.

Note: Heart

Cassia *(Cinnamomum cassia)* **2, 3**

From the leaves, stems, and twigs of the evergreen (indigenous to southern China). Scent: cinnamon, warm, penetrating spiciness. Helps to balance the pancreas and to stabilize the Solar Plexus. Aids in controlling emotions when obsessive feelings become overwhelming. Also stimulates sweetness related to feelings of love in life. Cassia instills the feeling of control or stimulation, depending upon what the individual needs.

Note: Heart

Cedarwood, Atlas *(Cedrus atlantica)* **1, 7**

From the wood, also known as Atlas Cedarwood. Be mindful of your supplier. Look for sustainability of endangered biological species. Scent: deeply sensuous, woody, resinous balsamic, comforting. Enhances spirituality and strengthens an individual's feelings of connection to the Divine. Helps you to maintain a sense of balance and control in life. Great for cutting through any mental catarrh (unwanted stuff!) that may clog the mind. Cedarwood helps to purify a room, home, office, healing or meditation space. When you feel that your personal space (the energetic space around you) feels unclean, Cedarwood helps to clear it.

Note: Soul, Fixative

Cedarwood, Himalayan *(Cedrus deodorata)* **7, 9**

From tree wood, wild growing. Scent: slightly camphoraceous, before becoming sweet, woody, and warm. This tree's life is an example for humanity …. Thrive - don't just survive. It takes a very different mindset to get off a treadmill of living from one disaster to another. Being flexible, shake off what binds you, and raise your head high.

Note: Soul, Fixative

Celery Seed *(Apium graveolens)* **2, 6**

From the seed. Scent: warm and powerful with some spicy freshness. Celery seed exhibits properties with completely opposite qualities: it can assist with insomnia and also aids concentration. In order to assist concentration, it helps the analytical left-brain to achieve what it focuses on. Celery Seed uplifts the spirit, enhances psychic abilities, and initiates lustful qualities.

Note: Heart

Chamomile, German *(Matricaria chamomilla)* **5**

From the flowers of the herb, aka Blue Chamomile. Scent: sweet, warm, herby and somewhat tobacco-like in dry-down, feels like a deep blue mountain lake. Helps you to communicate without anger, harmful ego, or animosity. German Chamomile assists in lessening emotional tension, and related physical tensions such as a nervous stomach, headache, and insomnia.

Note: Heart

Chamomile, Roman (*Anthemis nobilis*) **7**

From the flowers of the herb, aka English Chamomile. Scent: herby and fruity, deep, rich, very green, and tenacious. One of the original sacred herbs to the Saxons, which they called *maythen*. This chamomile has similar vibrational properties as its relative German Chamomile, yet it takes these same properties to a higher octave. English or Roman Chamomile aids healing on the highest of spiritual levels. It is effective for very deep meditation, insomnia, and deep soothing from emotional pain. It assists in seeking higher spiritual truths and assists channeling information into your awareness.

Note: Heart

Champa, White Flower (*Michelia alba*) **9**

From the flowers. Scent: beautiful, gracious, sensuous, sweet floral, tropical, herby, wisp of fruitiness. Imbues a sense of elegance and otherworldly charm. Helps you keep cool, calm, and collected; no unruffling of your feathers, you remain ethereal.

Note: Heart, Soul

Cinnamon Bark (*Cinnamomum zeylanicum*) **1**

From the dried bark. Scent: sweet and spicy, very warm, with lasting memories of celebrations. Invites prosperity into your life. It lifts your physical energy and the energy of your spirit. It lights the flame to renewed interest in life, with a desire to create new foundations upon which to grow.

Note: Heart

Cistus *(Cistus ladaniferus)* **3, 6**

Extracted from the leaves and twigs. (For Labdanum, see Parfumerie Essences.) Scent: penetrating sweet warmth, sweetly balsamic. In Dr. Edward Bach's remedies (Bach Flower Remedies) the same plant is known as Rock Rose. It helps to quiet the nerves, especially when you feel that are totally ineffective in life due to a nervous state of mind. Cistus elevates the emotions, is good for insomnia, and has positive uplifting effects on the pineal gland.

Note: Soul, Fixative

Clary Sage *(Salvia sclarea)* **2, 6**

From the leaves and the flowers. Scent: slightly bitter, raw herby, slender sweetness. Known as a "feminine balancer" because of its affinity to assist women's health. For overly emotional or fluctuating emotions and hyper-sensitivity; when women's hormones are out of balance. Clary Sage is also good for men who are in an extremely emotionally sensitive state. Esoterically its properties aid balancing of emotional energy and helps to recall dreams, to allow you to see (things, truths) more clearly.

Note: Heart, Fixative

Clementine (*Citrus reticulata Blanco var. Clementine***) 4**

From the peel. Soft, fresh, mouthwatering, citrusy, sweet with a hint of floral. Offers you the sweetest expression of joy. The truth of innocence in its highest spiritual form of expression.

Note: Head

Clove Bud *(Syzygium aromaticum)* **3**

From the buds. Scent: strong and tenacious, bitter, intense, yet sweet. Clove helps to eliminate negative feelings or pessimism. It gives a sense of protection and the courage to take the steps required at the moment. Clove aids comfort and healing from bereavement. It can purify physical space.

Note: Heart

Coriander Seed *(Coriandrum sativum)* **6**

From the seeds. Warming, spicy, light sweetness, balsamic-woody, slightly peppery, with a similar to Rosewood odour. Speeds up the healing processes, which is enhanced when accompanied with visualization. Helps you to apply focus to your intentions.

Notes: Heart, Head; Fixative

Cypress, Blue *(Callitris columellaris)* **6**

From the wood and bark. In 1990 it was identified that the color can vary from blue to dark green when both the wood and bark are steam distilled together. From Australia, this wonderfully intoxicating and obsessive essential oil gives feelings of wanting to experience more of life! It helps you to deeply plant your roots on the Earth, allowing you to embrace the totality of who you are in all of its magnificence. "Have the strength to find your heart's desires."

Notes: Heart, Head; Fixative

Cypress *(Cupressus sempervirens)* **4, 8**

From the needles and twigs. Scent: green, resinous, smoky, fresh, and woody. Cypress purifies physical and energetic space; this can apply to the actual body or an area. Perfect for times of transition. This ever-living tree vibrationally gives comfort and strength to an individual who has experienced the loss of someone close.

Note: Heart

Davana *(Artemesia pallens)* **4, 8**

From the leaves and tops of the herb. Scent: earthy-balsamic, woody, slight camphor-like, powerful, tenacious. If you feel strangled by life, Davana helps you to purge what is eating at you, allowing you to open a pathway for renewal and freedom.

Note: Heart

Dill *(Anthum graveolens) 2, 8*

From the seed (fruit) and the herb itself. Scent: fresh, warm, green spiciness. Dill is another protection essential oil. Helps to protect your energetic space from the envy of others. It stimulates lust and desire, both sexually and in attracting wealth.

Note: Heart

Elemi *(Canarium luzonicum) 1, 7*

From the resin/gum of the tree. Scent: spicy, peppery, woody, green-balsamic. Elemi in ancient civilizations, carried the nickname "as above, so below." It is grounding and helps you feel grounded, secure, and connected to all life. It also assists in connecting the physical to the spiritual, helps bring to fruition dreams and desires, and helps you bring form and foundation to your dreams and desires. Elemi enhances an individual's ability to feel a part of the whole.

Note: Heart, Head, Fixative

Eucalyptus Blue Gum *(Eucalyptus globulus) 1, 3, 8*

From the leaves and twigs. Scent: camphor-like (medicinal-cineolic), penetrating, and green; you want to inhale into your lungs. Fortifying, cleanses and purifies the air you breathe and energetically. Helps speed recovery after arguments, conflicts, and verbal battles or fights. Clears negativity.

Note: Head

Fennel, Sweet *(Foeniculum vulgare) 3*

From the seeds. Scent: licorice-like, earthy, peppery, sweet. Offers protection when there are feelings of being attacked psychically (evil eye). It helps to give strength and courage when needed. Sweet Fennel encourages longevity in any situation when desired. Use also for feelings of over sensitivity.

Note: Heart, Head

Fir, Douglas *(Pseudotsuga menziesii)* **3, 8**

From the needles. Scent: beautiful light fir, soft, fresh. Offers protection of your physical and psychic space. Hardiness. Longevity. Clears your mind of too many thoughts and endless obsessing.

Note: Head

Fir, Siberian *(Abies sibirica)* **3, 6**

From the needles and twigs of the wild tree. Scent: evergreen, pine-like, relaxing balsamic sweetness. Acts as a gentle sedative to allow your conscious mind to take a vacation. This allows for fresh, insightful guidance to come to you with a renewed conscious awareness.

Note: Head, Heart

Fragonia TM* *(Argonis fragrans)* **1, 4, 7, 8**

From the white flowers of the tree. The scent is pine-like, sweet and fruity, almost makes your head spin and your mouth water. Greatly balancing for emotional stress, as it can calm, while allowing you to feel like inhaling deeply, affirming the physicalness of life, and at the same time it invites you to connect with your spiritual self (Essence Self). Truly *AlcheMystical*, the essential oil, can balance, yet goes beyond its individual chemical components … it becomes alchemical taking you to the spiritual gold. Helps you to Let Go! Assists to release old and tenacious emotions (or ideas) that interfere in your life and have been preventing you from feeling carefree.

*A relative newcomer in essential oil repertoires, it is the only one to carry the trademark symbol (2001). It is said to "strengthen the immune system when the oil is applied to the skin over the lymphatic nodes in the side of the neck" (oilsofnature.com.au). Dr. Penoel, leading essential oil medical doctor and researcher, offers that it improves the immune system, calms emotions and adds, "I was amazed to find out that the sacred number known as the golden proportion was expressed almost perfectly through the chemistry of this essential oil."

Notes: Head, Heart

Frankincense, Somalia *(Boswellia carterii)* **7, 9**

From the resin. Scent: ancient, sacred, smooth, woody, balsamy resinous. Aids deeper meditations and prayers. Enhances spiritual aspirations. Assists one in connecting to the divinity inside them and to connect to the greater divinity of the Divine. Opens a personal space to experience the eternal energy available in the universe.

Note: Soul, Fixitive

Galbanum *(Ferula galbanifera)* **4, 6**

From the oleoresin/gum. Scent: deep green, richly earthy, woody, This is a CO_2 extract usually, but suitable for aromatherapy. Galbanum is harmonizing and balancing for the psyche and spirit. It helps to open the 6th ChakraAura – Third-Eye (the pineal gland) and assists intuitive capabilities. Galbanum is warming and soothing to the 4th ChakraAura – Heart energy.

Note: Head, Fixative

Geranium, Rose *(Pelargonium rosium asperum)* **4**

From the leaves, stalks, and flowers. Scent: delicate herbaceous, minty, very fesh, rosy. Also known as Rose Geranium, it assists in giving you courage, strength, and protection. Geranium helps to imbue a sense of grace, beauty, and balance. It is perfect for transitions of any sort. Geranium brings in a quality of the softer side of love into your heart.

Note: Heart

Geranium, Bourbon *(Pelargonium graveolens)* **4, 5**

From the leaves, stalks, and flowers. Scent: sweet rosiness, herbaceous, delicious fruitiness, overlaying fresh green. This is deeply rich and offers its smooth advice just before being pushy, for Geranium Bourbon is always graceful in any situation.

Note: Heart

Ginger *(Zingiber officinale)* **2, 8**

From the root. Scent: pungent, warm, fresh spicyness. Ginger is sometimes nicknamed "I Create" and carries very magical energy. A firey spice, it stimulates the physical body to be open to intimacy. It helps the physical and energetic bodies to maintain energy in general. Ginger assists you in attracting abundance.

Note: Heart

Grapefruit, Pink *(Citrus paradisi)* **3, 8**

From the fruit (peel). Scent: very fresh, citrusy (mouthwatering), but softer and sweeter than other grapefruit essential oils. Are you overly critical (or those around you are)? Is your Ego getting too much in your way (very stubborn and it's interfering in your life)? Grapefruit! It assists in the digestion of new concepts or ideas. Used for cleansing, clarity, and helps to remove negativity. All three Grapefruits hold the same vibrational properties, but Pink Grapefruit acts more like a feather in delivering the message; White Grapefruit is more direct, and Red Grapefruit even *more intensely clear* in its message!

Note: Head

Helichrysum *(Helichrysum italicum)* **6**

From the flowers (commonly called straw flowers), aka Immortelle or Everlasting. Scent: extremely earthy, tea-like, herby, rich, pungent. Helichrysum is true to its name and also vibrationally everlasting. It promotes longevity in any situation. Helps an individual "to remember" past parts of themselves that have been lost (feelings, un-requited dreams, etc.) and are needed to be reunited to your Essence Self for wholeness. Helichrysum activates the right brain and enhances intuition and creativity. Valuable for meditation, it also aids visualizations. Enhances feelings of compassion, personal growth, healing, and enhances feelings of your personal connection to the creative arts.

Note: Heart, Head

Hinoki *(Chamaecyparis obtusa)* 4

From the heartwood. Scent: very green, deeply resinous, precious. Encourages you to take a deep, healing breath. Offers support to minimize anxiety, repel what is ailing you (emotionally, psychically), and brings softness (less rigid ideas) to your heart.

Note: Soul, Fixative

Ho Wood *(Cinnamomum camphora)* 6, 7

Sustainable sourced from the wood, aka Shiu Oil. Scent: warm, slightly woody, floral, fresh scent, delicately sacred; allows me to feel it's "A Walking Prayer". Its properties vibrationally and energetically take you to a much deeper and also a much higher sense of self and place. Ho Wood opens and balances 6th ChakraAura – Third-Eye (pineal gland) and the 7th ChakraAura – Crown (pituitary gland). It helps to call forth an individual's highest spiritual aspects, aiding one to "walk your talk." Helps to ease fears. Opens to clear, open, unrigid (removing any Ego attachment) intentions. Ho Wood assists in the highest of aspirations for healing, personally and for the planet.

Note: Heart

Hyssop, Decumbens *(Hyssopus officinalis)* 4, 8

From the flowering tops and leaves. Scent: powerful, sharp, spicy, yet warming. Since ancient times, Hyssop has been used to purify sacred places. It can purge negativity. It can help you, figuratively, to take a deeper breath of life, renewing your commitment to your life. When you feel beaten by life, try Hyssop.

Note: Heart

Jasmine Grandiflorum, CO$_2$ Extract *(Jasminium grandiflorum)* 2, 7

From the flowers. My *most favorite Jasmine*! Scent: earthy sweetness, green depth, sensuous richness, like planting my face in the fresh flowers. Stands for the unity of opposites – yin/yang, feminine/masculine archetypes (principles). It can help to create polarity (balance). This exotic flower is a creamy white color, very delicate (symbolizing feminine energy) yet it is also a very hardy, sturdy plant (exuding masculine energy) that yields a dark brown colored essence. Jasmine Grandiflorum enhances spiritual development and assists uplifting yin and yang towards Universal Love. This particular Jasmine is considered the only one suitable for aromatherapeutic purposes, because it is a CO$_2$ extract, using benign solvents. It is highly revered also for quality parfumerie.

Note: Heart, Soul

Juniper Berry *(Juniperus communis)* **6, 8**

From the berries and the twigs. Scent: woody, green, pine-like, slightly fresh. Juniper cleanses, detoxifies, and helps to clear negative energy. One aspect of this essential oil is its affinity to help clear feelings of uncleanliness (in particular from rape) due to past actions, whether done to the individual or by the individual. Juniper gives strength to the body, mind, and spirit. It assists clairvoyance, particularly when used for unselfish purposes.

Note: Head, Heart

Lavender, Alpine (High Altitude) *(Lavendula augustifolia)* **4**

From the flowers of the herb. Scent: sweet and lush, soft green depth (not at all penetrating). The most highly recommended type of lavender for vibrational work is the High Altitude or Alpine Lavender. This essential oil is calming, cleansing, and balancing. Assists in bringing the lower and higher chakras into harmony. Use Lavender to deepen your meditations, for deeper trance channeling work, and for integration of spirituality into daily life. Lavender sings the harmonious song of the heart.

Note: Heart

Lavendin Grosso *(Lavandula x intermedia)* **2**

From the flowers. Scent: very sharp scent that almost feels like burning to the nose, with hints of familiar lavender, yet not. Unfortunately, many irreputable companies sell this hybrid and mark the bottle: Lavender. Watch out, Lavendin is a hybrid created by crossing two plants – true lavender and spike lavender. It is primarily an energetic purifier and an energy boost for sluggish individuals. Surprisingly however, it also helps to put your sexual desires into an appropriate perspective for your life.

Note: Head

Lemon *(Citrus limon)* **1, 8**

From the fruit's peel/rind. Scent: intensely fresh, citrus-lemony, tangy. Lemon is for overall health, healing, and physical energy. When the etheric energy system or the actual physical system is low, use Lemon. It dispels sluggishness. It helps to clear negative blockages and revitalize the energy. It opens you to renewal.

Note: Head

Lemongrass *(Cymbopogon citratus)* **5, 6, 8**

From a grassy herb. Scent: lemony citrusness, soft grassy green. Clears pathways for psychic awareness and increases sensitivity to your intuition. Encourages balance for thyroid. Cleansing, sedative, and overall balancing of wellbeing.

Note: Head

Lime *(Citrus aurantifolia)* **8**

From rind/peel. Scent: freshly tart, zesty limey sweetness, feels like a tropical vacation. Lights the fire energy needed for healing, protection, and love. Dissolves negativity, ill feelings, and blockages, while protecting against an evil eye (jealously with resentment focused at you from someone).

Note: Head

Lovage *(Levisticum officinale)* 2

From the roots, leaves and stalks. Scent: green, fresh, earthy warmth. Lovage instills a robust energy rooted in the 2nd ChakraAura – Sacral and related to your creative fire. Does your creative flame need rekindling? Lovage. It also attracts love to you with a fervor as if having been awakened from a deep hibernation and says … let's eat!

Note: Heart

Mandarin, Red *(Citrus reticulata Blanco)* 4, 8

From the fruit (peel). Scent: smooth, sweetly floral, orange-citrus tartness, smells like summer. Red Mandarin is a softer scent than other Mandarins (Green: very tart; Yellow: less sweet). However, all of them speak to your child within. It helps you get in touch with your playful, non-critical inner self and its ability to see the world as a child does, with more innocence and less criticism. It assists individuals in clearing out clogged ideas. It helps you to reach the highest of the spiritual child (also known as the christ-child consciousness). This is a child-like innocence that sees only the most positive life has to offer.

Note: Head

Manuka *(Leptospermum scoparium)* 1, 8

From the leaves and twigs. Scent: fresh, herby, tangy, penetrating, with a green softness. It originates in New Zealand, and Manuka Honey is derived from these plants. Offers you protection from all the varied forces inside and outside of you that can knock you off track (shake up your day!). Whether they are viruses, radiation, microbes, or people acting out. It assists you and your ChakraAuras to build up immunities (energetically or literally).

Note: Head, Heart

Marjoram, Sweet *(Origanium marjorana)* **2**

From the flowers. Scent: pungent, herby, fresh, and lightly medicinal. This essential oil offers protection on a vibrational level from grief, anxiety, and irritability. It will not eliminate these things, yet it softens the angst. Sweet Marjoram enhances the probabilities for attracting love, happiness, health, and wealth. What a wide range! Use with caution. Prolonged use over an extended time can deaden the emotions! Sweet Marjoram is also beneficial for those going into a period of celibacy, as it modifies an over-active sex drive.

Note: Heart, Head

May Chang, *(Litsea cubeba)* **3, 8**

From the small ripe fruits. A fresh, intensely lemony and peppery scent with a hint of floral woodiness. Opens a clear, clean path and sparks the ability to get things accomplished.

Note: Head

Melissa *(Melissa officinalis)* **4, 9**

From the leaves. Scent: rich, fresh, honey-like, green, wisp of lemon. Melissa is most comforting for individuals who have experienced the death of a close loved one. It helps to dispel fear and regret and bring acceptance and understanding in any situation. Melissa helps you to remember past lives. It brings in a spiritual unity into your awareness. Melissa, which means "heart's joy" in Swedish, is truly that – it instills a joy of heart.

Note: Heart, Head

Mugwort *(Artemesia vulgaris)* **5, 6**

From the flowers of the plant. Scent: subtly sweet, powerful herby, a dream weed that encourages visions. Used for smudging and known as POTENT! Use with care and attentiveness. Has been used extensively in many Native American cultures to encourage dreams and visions. Deepens the dream state, can call in guides, and awakens your deeper unconsciousness. Scott Cunningham, in his book *Encyclopedia of Magical Herbs*, suggests that Mugwort has the ability to facilitate astral projection as it encourages separation of the consciousness from the body, allowing it to travel at will. I have experienced much of the magic of this herb and essential oil when used in particular to enhance and recall my dreams.

Note: Heart

Myrrh, Somalia *(Commiphora myrrha)* 1, 5, 7

From the resin/gum. Scent: very earthy, sweet, slight spicy scent, feels deeply hallowed. One of the sacred herbs of the Bible, Myrrh enhances and strengthens spirituality. It assists healing when used before a healing session. It fortifies the 1ˢᵗ ChakraAura – Base, helps to clear stuck emotions, and gives you the courage to speak when you have been feeling fear or a lack of confidence. It does the same for the spirit, allowing you to clear out the old and fly ahead with a new sense of your own essence and purpose.

Note: Soul, Fixative

Myrtle *(Myrtus communis)* 2, 3

From the leaves. Scent: fresh, camphoraceous, herbal sweetness. Myrtle is an essential oil full of opposites. It has the ability to enhance gentility and strength and it allows you to hold your space through any adversity, keeping the Ego and Will in a healthy, balanced state. It vitalizes both the body and spirit. Myrtle permits you to go with the flow. It aids in increasing fertility, attracting love, helping to keep love alive and strong, and attracting money and abundance.

Note: Head, Heart

Nagarmotha, Cypriol *(Cyperus scariosus)* **5, 9**

From the roots. Scent: dirty, smoky, mossy, woody, rich earth, hints of cinnamon. What's my wisdom? I will gently share it. Speaks to your Soul, your Essence Self, and allows you to vulnerably share from the depths of your being. It aids in seeking the mysteries of life; observing that times are changing; and feeling connected to your emotions.

Note: Soul

Neroli *(Citrus aurantium)* **2, 7, 9**

From the flowers, aka Orange Blossom. Scent: barely bitter green quickly launches into a powerful, rich sweetness. Living in a valley plentiful with orange trees, my favorite time of year is spring when the trees are bursting with blossoms. Just before dawn, and after sunset, I ritually stand outside and inhale deeply, 'til my nostrils can't absorb more, before I exhale the sweet, green, fresh, powerful scent. Neroli stands for the purity of the highest aspect of yourself. It enhances deeply the creative energies of the 2nd ChakraAura – Sacral and helps you to spiritualize your sexual relations. Music, painting, and writing are creative energies that Neroli has an affinity for and, in fact, helps facilitate all creative activities when they are inspired by spiritual aspirations. Consequently, Neroli assists in bringing both the spiritual aspirations of the individual and their more expanded self into unlimitedness.

Note: Head

Nutmeg *(Myristica fragrans)* **2, 7**

From the seed. Scent: spicy sweetness, warming, slightly woody, mouthwatering. To be respected (research safety data). Nutmeg allows the fervency and exhilaration of the passion for life to be expressed with wild abandon, yet at the same time, it is deepened by vision, insight, and wisdom typical of a lifetime of experience.

This can be experienced, however, by an individual of young years, for this kind of depth is brought in by the Soul. Nutmeg ignites the remembrance of the wisdom, with a renewed sense of freedom from old thought patterns.

Note: Head, Heart

Orange, Sweet *(Citrus sinensis)* 3

From the peel/rind. Scent: smells like fresh, tangy, gloriously happy oranges. Sweet Orange helps to instill generosity, joy, and happiness. It confirms the blessedness of being you and your gifts. It allows you to expel any sour feeling in your Heart or Soul. Sweet Orange attracts good fortune and luck.

Note: Head

Orange, Blood *(Citrus sinensis)* 1, 4

From the rind/peel. Scent: richer sweetness than Sweet Orange, deep zesty and piquant. When these are in season in Ojai, California (late spring to early summer) I can't get enough of them. I slice them in half, then plunge my mouth in and devour. Great with quality artisan tequila! Blood Orange takes you to the depths of generosity, joy, and happiness, experienced through feelings that you are connected to the pulse of life. Allows you to feel intensely connected to the experiences of this physical world.

Note: Head

Oregano *(Origanum vulgare)* 5, 8

From flowering tops of the herb. Scent: spicy, warm, deeply pungent with a fresh green, herby and woody scent., deeply earthy, smells of healing. (In the same family Labiatae, as rosemary, lavender, and thyme.) When something is eating at you, annoyingly clinging on, and you need to expel it. Purging. When something is holding you hostage or nagging at you (like a parasite hanging on), and you want/need to speak out. Helps rid of these feelings. (**Precaution:**

consult safety data before use in aromatherapy.) Use sparingly (1-2 drops) in perfumery.

Note: Heart, Head

Osha Root *(Ligusticum porteri)* **9**

From the root. Scent: woody, very earthy like wet dirt, slight hint of celery. Other names are Bear Root (Native American) and Porter's Lovage, not to be confused with Lovage *(Levisticum officinalis)*. Osha Root is about catharses. This rare essential oil first comes in energetically at your foundation, your root and your 1st ChakraAura – Base, where it immediately shoots upwards with a vibrational force that demands expansion. When this essential oil is intentionally used in transformational work with the focused intention of an artist, it can promote intense spiritual renewal. Even a healer is an artist of sorts; a physician at one time was called an artist!

Note: Heart

Owyhee *(Artemesia ludoviciana)* **9**

From the leaves and blossoms. Scent: subtly spicy, strongly fruity, somewhat herby sweet. A rare and exotic oil that grows indigenously in the Western United States (its name derives from the ancient name for Hawaii). Owyhee's message: I lift you up out of despair. I am light hearted. I dance in the sun, sip the rain, and celebrate life in every moment. I will ease your tensions and allow you to flow with the winds of change.

Note: Heart

Palmarosa *(Cymbopogon martinii)* **6**

From the herb (a grass). Scent: light rosy, citrusy, green, smooth, fresh. With focused intent and visualization, Palmarosa speeds up healing. It helps to assist the individual begin her/his healing path towards approval of the self. Palmarosa holds the promise for someone to stop self-hatred and to begin a new transmutational path.

Note: Head, Heart

Palo Santo *(Bursera graveolens)* 1, 7

From aged, dead hardwood. Scent: penetrating aroma, fruity sweet, woody, slight citrus, spicy, minty, with a tendril of frankincense scent. You are (or want) to feel rooted and connected to the Earth Mother, yet open and inquisitive to the cosmos. You are in the midst of change and transformation on all levels (Body, Mind, Spirit). Encourages deep contemplation, meditation, and prayer.

Note: Heart

Patchouli *(Pogostemum cablin)* 1, 2

From the leaves. Scent: intense, rich, pungent, sweet, and earthy. (You either love it or hate it!) Patchouli essential oil is found in a Dark (deep brown color and stronger) or as a Light (golden amber color and less intense). Associating it with the Earth Mother, it is very grounding to an individual, especially those who tend to float somewhere in the ethers. It helps to root you or to help you maintain your connection with the physical body. As we are both physical and spiritual beings, we need to find our balance. Patchouli helps with individuation, which is defined as finding that special part of you which is an individual, discovering and knowing how you relate to others, and what is special about your expression of self in the world.

Note: Soul, Fixative

Pepper, Black *(Piper nigrum)* 3, 8

From the dried fruits. Scent: sharp, spicy, and warming. With its firey energy, Black Pepper is for alertness. Enhances the desire to get going on a new project or with a new direction in your life. Helps to bring daydreams into reality. Helps to prevent falling asleep during meditation. Assists in removing blockages in the energy fields. Helps in freeing the Mind from envious thoughts.

Note: Heart, Head

Pepper, Pink *(Schinus molle)* **7, 8**

From the dried fruits. The Peruvian Pepper. Scent: sharp, spicy, sweet, slightly floral, smoky, and warming. Lights the fires within you and your desire for renewal. Grace, flexibility, sturdiness, allowing you to – flow with the go – of life.

Note: Heart, Head

Peppermint *(Mentha piperita)* **3**

From the herb. Scent: strong, penetrating, minty fresh. A type of peppermint was found in tombs in Egypt, dating back to 1000 B.C. Possibly, the ancient Egyptians thought that this herb would help expedite the deceased into the next world. Peppermint helps to dispel the Ego. Peppermint also assists in overcoming feelings of inferiority. It is cleansing and helps those who want to live an ethical life and hold true to their convictions.

Note: Head

Petitgrain *(Citrus aurantium var. amara)* **3**

From the leaves and twigs of the bitter orange tree. Scent: Fresh green, slightly floral, barely bitter, leafy green. Petitgrain assists with mental clarity. It helps to ready the conscious mind for change, while clearing out any mental cobwebs. Helps you feel the passion of life. It imbues a sense of overall wellbeing.

Note: Head

Ravensara *(Ravensara aromatica)* **8**

From the leaves. Scent: pungent, hay-like, green-fruity, and camphoraceous. Ravensara helps to eliminate negativity and blockages energetically, just as it rids the physical body of toxins in traditional aromatherapy. It also instills feelings of strength. These toxins or negativity can hinder the fulfillment of joy in your life.

Note: Head

Rhododendron *(Rhododendron adamsii)* **3, 4**

From the leaves and flowers. The scent is fruity, very fresh, and green, with slightly wine-like and woody drydown. It's message: "Life has challenges, I'm here to help you find the balance between your heart and these challenges."

Note: Heart, Head

Rosa Alba, White Rose *(Rosa alba)* **1, 4**

From the white rose flowers. Scent is a slightly green and honeyed Rose, with a peppery zing. This special White Rose declares: "I AM!" It announces you are here, affirming life and your existence in it. It is unreserved and celebratory. It supports your heart's ease through any transitions.

Notes: Heart, Head

Rose Otto *(Rosa x damascena)* **2, 4, 9**

From the flowers. Scent: yes rosy, but deeply sensuous, warm, rich, like real rose. (unlike synthetic rose). Rose Otto is truly of the Goddesses, such as Aphrodite and Venus. Yet no matter whose name is associated with the rose, it is truly and undeniably a sacred oil. Rose has the capacity to heal. It calls forth both Divine and earthly love. Grief, sorrow, and despair are assuaged with Rose. It aids conception – of children and ideas. Enhances connection to all creativity, the arts, and beauty. (See PART SIX – AlcheMystical Aromatics, for other rose profiles.)

Note: Heart

Rosemary ct Cineole *(Rosmarinus officinalis)* **6**

From the leaves. Scent: penetrating, intense, clean, fresh, and pungent. Used in ancient Greece and during the Middle Ages for fumigation, to ward off evil spirits, and for protection against the plague. Rosemary is a psychic protector and a protector of spaces. It helps to promote clear thought, clear sight or vision, and to develop clairvoyance.

Note: Heart

Rosemary ct Verbenone *(Rosmarinus officinalis)* **6, 7**

From the leaves. Scent: balsamic, penetrating, intense, pungent. This Rosemary (ct Verbenone) helps you to hear "the truth." It helps to dispel anger. If you feel someone is jealous of you and they covet something you have, it can act as an evil eye (symbol to repel someone's jealousy). It revitalizes and regenerates body, mind, psyche, and spirit.

Note: Heart, Soul

Rosewood Leaf *(Aniba rosaeodora)* **1,4**

From the leaves and twigs. Scent: bitter woody-green, slightly rosy, fresh - a scent that mellows in dry-down. Rosewood is now available in this version essential oil as a superior alternative to the previous version (PEO distilled from the wood, causing the tree to now be on the endangered list). It helps to balance your Heart and Soul's desires with your physical needs and desires. Rosewood has a calming and soothing effect and brings forth a light-heartedness of being.

Note: Heart, Head

Sage *(Salvia officinalis)* **1, 8**

From the leaves. Scent: extremely strong, camphoraceous, herby, and green. This Sage is grounding (scattered no more), helps relieve anxiety, and stress. Assists clearing away (with focused intention) negative energies and obsessive mental pictures.

Note: Heart, Head

Sage, White *(Salvia apiana)* **8, 9**

From the leaves. Scent: fresh, penetrating, camphoraceous, deeply green, hardy earthy. The favored Sage for smudging. Grows wild in

California. Helps clear pathways from clinging, nagging feelings, and old habits. This clearing makes way for new openness to see things differently. It dissolves blockages, and re-enlivens positive energy fields. Its message: Live life fully.

Note: Heart, Head

Sandalwood Mysore *(Santalum album)* **1, 2, 7**

From the roots and wood. *This tree is endangered and extremely valuable due to over-harvesting. See alternative sustainably sourced Sandalwoods below.* Every drop is more sacred than ever. Scent: extremely rich, warm, slightly sweet, erotic sensuousness, great tenacity. It has been used for more than 4,000 years. Ancient and precious, it stimulates the imagination and quiets mental chatter (the kind that drives you absolutely batty)! It prepares you for healing. It softens feelings of emotional, sexual, and mental dysfunction. Sandalwood helps you to focus during meditation. It works with the 1st ChakraAura – Base and the 7th ChakraAura – Crown by encouraging you to remember your spiritual connection to the Divine.

Note: Soul, Fixative

Sandalwood, Royal Hawaiian *(Santalum paniculatum)* **1, 4, 7**

From the heartwood of the tree/shrub, sustainably grown. Scent: rich, woody, full-bodied, sensuously sweet. A wonderful alternative to Mysore! Prepares you for healing to take place by quieting mental chatter. It allows your heart to feel less rigid so you are open to making the needed changes.

Note: Soul, Fixative

Sandalwood, New Caledonia Extra *(Santalum austrocaledonicum)* **2, 7**

From the heartwood. Scent: lovingly warm, woody, smooth, softy sweet. This Sandalwood gets to influence your creative energies. Carries similar vibrational properties (as other Sandalwoods), quieting down the excess chatter in the mind. This allows for your creative gifts and talents to show their face to you so you can access them and dance your joy!

Note: Soul, Fixative

Spearmint *(Mentha spicata)* I, 5

From the leaves. Scent: powerful, penetrating, sweetly minty (softer than peppermint). Offers psychic protection while sleeping. Opens communication channels of energy. Strengthens the foundational 1st ChakraAura – Base.

Note: Head

Spikenard *(Nardostachys grandiflora)* 4, 9

From the roots, aka Nard or Jatamansi. Scent: extremely rooty and earthy, animalic, woody, brings you to your knees. Spikenard is strengthening and comforting to the Heart and Soul. It helps to calm feelings of being overwhelmed by life and gives strength for the tasks that lie ahead. Spikenard can also deepen your feeling of the Soul's need for more meaning to life and your connection to a divine purpose. Spikenard was used by Mary Magdalene to anoint Jesus' feet before the crucifixion.

Note: Soul, Fixative

Spruce, Black *(Picea mariana)* I, 4

From the needles. Scent: sweet and mild evergreen, deep, with a hint of smokiness. From the depths of the sacred northern forests, inhale life. Breathe deeply, letting your lungs fill completely. Balances adrenals, relieves anxiety and stress, and offers life-affirming nuances.

Note: Soul, Fixative

Tagetes *(Tagetes minuta)* I

From the flowers. Scent: very, very pungent, strong, green, lightly fruity. It is a marigold, contrary to its sometimes mistaken identity as a calendula. It is hardy and offers this quality vibrationally. Tagetes

exudes the attribute of longevity amidst adversity.
Note: Head, Heart

Tanacetum, Tansy *(Tanacetum annuum)* **5**

From the leaves and tops. Scent: intense blue aromatic, herby, green, penetrating, camphoreous, mildly warming. Tanacetum relates to purging and cleansing. It helps you clear any stuck emotions, which may feel like they are attached to you, or clogged within your energy fields. With focused intention, Tanacetum can be very powerful when used in conjunction with meditation. It allows you to let go for the moment and release concerns of your day-to-day life allowing your meditations to be grander.
Note: Head, Heart

Thyme ct Linalool *(Thymus vulgaris)* **1, 5**

From the flowering herb. Scent: peppery, green, slightly sharp, sweet, herby, soft woodiness. Thyme helps individuals who have separated from the world (especially in an extended retreat) to re-enter and return. Helps you to eliminate old habit patterns, stubbornly still clinging on. It is strengthening and energizing.
Note: Heart, Head

Tumeric *(Curcuma longa)* **3**

From the rhizomes, a continuously growing underground root. Scent: pungent, identifiable with Indian food, slightly gingery, spicy, warming, and woody. Tumeric asks you, "Who are you in the world?" It stimulates your ability to hold your footing in a very stable and strong manner. You can become rooted when you need to be, even when adversity is directed toward you.
Notes: Heart, Head

Vanilla CO_2 *(Vanilla planifolia)* **2**

From the bean pods. Scent: very rich, warm, sweet, smooth,

intoxicating. Produces a magical, strong vibrational electricity emitted by the one who uses/wears it. Instills feelings of sensuous loving with effortless emotion. Revitalizes. Arouses loving sexuality.

Note; Soul, Fixative

Verbena *(Lippia citriodora)* 3

From the leaves. Scent: crisp, lemony, slightly fruity, herbeacous, appealing soft floral. Reminds you that life is to be treasured with gratitude. Picks up your spirit, instilling freshness of mind and attitudes.

Note: Head

Vetiver *(Vetiveria zizanoides)* 1, 3

From the root. Scent: intense, deeply earthy, pungent, smoky, lasting. Vetiver balances the entire ChakraAura system by grounding the 1st ChakraAura – Base and protecting the 3rd ChakraAura – Solar Plexus from over sensitivity. It aids those who feel like a psychic sponge or those who feel too sensitive to outside forces.

Note: Soul, Fixative

Wintergreen *(Gaultheria fragrantissima)* 8

From the leaves and twigs. Scent: penetratingly intense, soft mintyness, sweet, creamy, cooling. When something is repeatedly irritating, Wintergreen helps you to let go and to trigger the dissolution of it. Helps to break something holding you back from where you want to go. Offers protection and positive energy towards your healing.

Note: Heart

Yarrow, Blue *(Achillea millefolium)* **5, 8**

From the leaves and tops. Scent: green herbaceousness, sweet, deep, fresh, woody. Yarrow helps to heal emotional wounds that have been resistant to healing. As it heals these wounds, it allows for a new courage and awareness of love of self. It also opens you to your intuitive or psychic abilities and the ability to express them.

Note: Head, Heart

Ylang Ylang *(Cananga odorata var. genuina)* **2, 9**

From the flowers. Scent: intensely sweet, extremely floral, bright, fruity, hint of spice, feels like dancing. There are many types of Ylang Ylang on the market today (Ylang Ylang Extra, Complete, I, II, III, & Fine). An exotic flower with an equally exotic pronunciation: *e-long, e-long*. They all hold the same vibrational and alchemical signature. Ylang Ylang can help to dispel anger and negative emotional states. It assists you to overcome sexual dysfunction or concerns. It helps to alleviate over excited emotions or feelings that are contradictory to your wellbeing, and allows you to soar with your Soul.

Note: Head, Heart, Fixative

Yuzu *(Citrus Juno)* **2, 7**

From the citrus peel. Scent: citrus with a wisp of sweet, fresh flowers and tangy, mild grapefruit at opening; surprising drydown mildly balsamic! Grows wild in Tibet and Central China; cultivated in Japan and Korea. Instills fresh ideas and thoughts into your present thinking. Gives you a boost and feelings of a fresh new start to your current life's path. "I'm here for you," says Yuzu. "Let me offer you a new way."

Note: Head

Essential Oils in the ChakraSynergies

Here is a list of the forty-five essential oils that are used to create the ChakraSynergies, designed specifically for Vibrational AromaTherapy.

ChakraSynergy #1 – Courage

Elemi (*Canarium luzonicum*)
Lemon (*Citrus limon*)
Patchouli (*Pogostemum cablin*)
Tagetes (*Tagetes minuta*)
Vetiver (*Vetiveria zizanoides*)

ChakraSynergy #2 – Create

Cardamom (*Elettarria cardamomum*)
Dill (*Anthum graveolens*)
Lavendin Grosso (*Lavandula x intermedia*)
Marjoram, Sweet (*Origanium marjorana*)
Sandalwood Mysore (*Santalum album*)

ChakraSynergy #3 – Manifest

Basil (*Ocimum basilicum*)
Bay Leaf (*Pimenta racemosa*)
Cassia (*Cinnamomum cassia*)
Cistus (*Cistus ladaniferus*)
Myrtle (*Myrtus communis*)

ChakraSynergy #4 – Joy

Bergamot (*Citrus aurantium, ssp bergamia*)
Galbanum (*Ferula galbanifera*)
Lavender, Alpine (High Altitude) (*Lavendula augustafolia*)
Rose Otto (*Rosa x damascena*)
Spikenard (*Nardostachys granduflorum*)

ChakraSynergy #5 – Truth

Cananga (*Cananga odorata*)
Chamomile, German (*Matricaria chamomilla*)
Mugwort (*Artemesia vulgaris*)
Tanacetum, Tansy (*Tanacetum annuum*)
Thyme ct Linalool (*Thymus vulgaris*)

ChakraSynergy #6 – Vision

Carrot Seed (*Daucus carota*)
Clary Sage (*Salvia sclarea*)
Helichrysum (*Helichrysum italicum*)
Juniper Berry (*Juniperus communis*)
Palmarosa (*Cymbopogon martinii*)

ChakraSynergy #7 – Inspiration

Cedarwood (*Cedrus atlantica*)
Roman Chamomile (*Anthemis nobilis*)
Frankincense (*Boswellia carterii*)
Ho Wood (*Cinnamomum camphora*)
Jasmine Grandiflorum, CO_2 Extract (*Jasmine grandiflorum*)

ChakraSynergy #8 – Release

Grapefruit, Pink (*Citrus paradisi*)
Cypress (*Cupressus sempervirens*)
Ginger (*Zingiber officinale*)
Mandarin, Red (*Citrus reticulata* Blanco)
Pepper, Black (*Piper nigrum*)

ChakraSynergy #9 – Knowing

Angelica Seed (*Angelica archangelica*)
Melissa (*Melissa officinalis*)
Osha Root (*Ligusticum porteri*)
Neroli (*Citrus aurantium*)
Ylang Ylang (*Cananga odorata var. genuina*)

108 Essential Oils Organized by ChakraAura

All of the essential oils, organized by the ChakraAura they associate with.

1st ChakraAura – Base of Spine – Courage

Agarwood, Angelica root, Cannabis (Hemp), Cedarwood Atlas, Cinnamon Bark, Elemi, Eucalyptus Blue Gum, Fragonia™, Lemon, Manuka, Muhuhu, Myrrh Somalia, Orange Blood, Palo Santo, Patchouli, Rose Alba (White Rose), Rosewood Leaf, Sage, Sandalwood Mysore, Sandalwood Royal Hawaiian, Spearmint, Spruce Black, Tagetes, Thyme ct. Linolool, Vetiver.

2nd ChakraAura – Sacral – Create

Ambrette, Aniseed, Cannabis (Hemp), Caraway, Cardamom, Cassia, Celery Seed, Clary Sage, Dill, Ginger, Jasmine Grandiflora CO_2 Extract, Lavandin Grosso, Lovage, Marjoram-Sweet, Myrtle, Neroli, Nutmeg, Patchouli, Rose Otto, Sandalwood Mysore, Sandalwood New Caledonia Extract, Vanilla CO_2, Ylang Ylang, Yuzu.

3rd ChakraAura – Solar Plexus – Manifest

Amyris, Aniseed, Basil, Bay Leaf, Cannabis (Hemp), Cassia, Cistus, Clove Bud, Eucalyptus Blue Gum, Fennel Sweet, Fir Douglas, Fir Siberian, Grapefruit Pink, May Chang, Muhuhu, Myrtle, Orange-Sweet, Pepper Black, Peppermint, Petitgrain, Rhododendron, Tumeric, Verbena, Vetiver.

4th ChakraAura – Heart – Joy

Absinthe, Bergamot, Clementine, Cypress, Davana, Fragonia™, Galbanum, Geranium Rose, Geranium Bourbon, Hinoki, Hyssop Decumbens, Lavender Alpine (High Altitude), Mandarin Red, Melissa, Orange Blood, Rhododendron, Rose Alba (White Rose), Rose Otto, Rosewood Leaf, Sandalwood Royal Hawaiian, Spikenard, Spruce Black.

5th ChakraAura – Throat – Truth

Amyris, Cananga, Chamomile German, Geranium Bourbon, Lemongrass, Mugwort, Myrrh Somalia, Nagarmotha Cypriol, Oregano, Spearmint, Tanacetum Tansy, Thyme ct Linolool, Yarrow Blue.

6th ChakraAura – Third Eye – Vision

Bay Laurel, Carrot Seed, Celery Seed, Cistus, Clary Sage, Coriander Seed, Cypress Blue, Fir Siberian, Galbanum, Helichrysum, Ho Wood, Juniper Berry, Lemongrass, Mugwort, Palmarosa, Rosemary ct Cineole, Rosemary ct Verbenone.

7th ChakraAura – Crown – Inspiration

Agarwood, Ambrette, Basil Holy, Buddha Wood, Cedarwood Atlas, Cedarwood Himalayan, Chamomile Roman, Elemi, Fragonia™, Frankincense Somalia, Ho Wood, Jasmine Grandiflorum CO_2 Extract, Myrrh Somalia, Neroli, Nutmeg, Palo Santo, Pepper Pink, Rosemary ct Verbenone, Sandalwood Mysore, Sandalwood Royal Hawaiian, Sandalwood New Caledonia Extra, Yuzu.

8th ChakraAura – Etheric Body – Release

Caraway, Cypress, Davana, Dill, Eucalyptus Blue Gum, Fir Douglas, Fragonia™, Ginger, Grapefruit Pink, Hyssop Decumbens, Juniper Berry, Lemon, Lemongrass, Lime, Mandarin Red, Manuka, May Chang, Oregano, Pepper Black, Pepper Pink, Ravensara, Sage, Sage White, Wintergreen, Yarrow Blue.

9th ChakraAura – Astral Body – Knowing

Agarwood, Ambrette, Angelica Seed, Budda Wood, Cedarwood Himalayan, Champa White Flower, Frankincense Somalia, Melissa, Nagarmotha Cypriol, Neroli, Osha Root, Owyhee, Rose Otto, Sage White, Spikenard, Ylang Ylang.

Chapter 27

Rejuvenation – Supportive Recipes

At the heart of each of us, whatever our imperfections,
there exists a silent pulse of perfect rhythm, a complex of wave forms
and resonances, which is absolutely individual and unique,
and yet which connects us to everything in the universe.
The act of getting in touch with the pulse can transform our personal
experience and in some way alter the world around us.
– George Leonard

Rejuvenation can be as easy as a hot bath after a long hard day, or come from a week in an exclusive resort. Yet true rejuvenation comes from deep within us – out of the depths of our Soul and is a daily experience. We experience rejuvenation when we feel joy in our heart. When we approve of ourselves. When we feel what I can only describe as "my Spirit and Soul in harmony with my physical body."

I remember feeling this … I felt happy within myself; I was doing what I loved to do; I was receiving acknowledgement from my peers for what I was doing. I felt the joy of life. For the first time in my life, I felt *totally* connected – Body, Heart, Spirit, Mind, and Soul. For the first time in my life, I felt complete harmony within myself – I was not fighting myself in any way! Physical body weight that I had put on over ten years literally fell away! Stress had added the weight … joy subtracted it! I wouldn't say I had lost the weight … because when you lose something you usually want to find it again. I certainly did not want to *find that forty pounds!* But somewhere along the line, fear and doubt returned and with it some of the weight. A wise being once said to me, "Fear and doubt knock it out!"

Rejuvenation. What rejuvenates you? Trust and faith in yourself and your life does. Trust and faith that by honoring who you are, and what you came into this life to do, you will be supported in all ways by Infinite Source.

I now phrase and think of things differently. Remember what I said two paragraphs ago … "I *felt* happy within myself; I *was* doing what I loved to do; I *was* receiving acknowledgement from my peers for what I *was* doing. I *felt* the joy of life" … Today I phrase things differently, even goals or desires for my future. In my prayers and meditations I say them as though they are part of my *present everyday life*. So, I say:

"I *feel* happy within myself; I *am* doing what I love to do; I *am* receiving acknowledgement from my peers for what I *am* doing. I *feel* the joy of life." Say it with feeling. Get all of your senses involved:

❖ What does it feel like?

❖ How does it taste?

❖ How does it smell?

❖ Is there a song?

❖ What colors does it emit?

Sometimes you have to pretend that something is real, until it actually is. You have to go into the "pretend" and feel it with all of your senses. Eventually, your body, thoughts, or your life will catch up!

*   *   *

In this section of the book are some suggestions for healing sessions as treatments, using the concepts presented in *Aromatic Alchemy*, and utilizing the modality of *Vibrational AromaTherapy by Ixchel*™. Design what works for you personally. You can self-study, do these at home alone. Or you might gather a few friends together, and share with each other. If you are a healing arts practitioner and you want to incorporate the information into your client's sessions, you can design what works best.

Vibrational AromaTherapy Sessions

Vibrational AromaTherapy uses many different components (essential oils, color, gemstones, etc.). I recommend that you begin using the blessed essential oils, as these are probably what drew you to this material.

Feel The Essential Oils

Set the intention for the focus of your (healing) session. Meditate on it. Meditation is a passive act. The purpose of meditation is to calm your Mind of chatter. Take three deep breaths:

Breathe …

- ❖ IN and OUT … Release your thoughts.
- ❖ IN and OUT … Let go of today's events.
- ❖ IN and OUT … Release again, clear your mind of it's chatter.

When your Mind is calm, focus your attention on the individual essential oil (or a ChakraSynergy that associates with the chakra or aura you are focusing on).

After a while, you move into prayer. Prayer is an active act. In prayer, you ask for answers or guidance to your questions. Ask this about the oils:

- ❖ What do I *feel* when I smell this essential oil or ChakraSynergy?
- ❖ Do any pictures or images come to me?
- ❖ How does this benefit or balance me?

PAY ATTENTION! It is not easy to do this when you are just beginning. It takes patience and focus. *Focus* can be described as a state of being that allows clear perception. In the early stages of focusing, meditation, and prayer, we hear some not so helpful messages like … "I have to get toothpaste at the health food store." Or "Why is that dog barking?" Or "I forgot to pick up the dry cleaning." This *is life*. Part of being human is just as much the mundane as the arcane. FOCUS! PRACTICE PATIENCE!

Powerful Essential Oils

Many people ask about the influence of the essential oils during a *Vibrational Aroma Therapy* Session. Essential oils act as a catalyst for healing. They offer balance and open the *space* for your energetic system to shift to wellness and healing. When your energy system is open, your physical body can move into healing mode.

Science has researched and proven that aromas influence our emotions. Essential oils can affect the wellbeing of your physical body. When essential oils subtly affect your state of wellness, your intentions set off a chain reaction for you to begin to make real physical, emotional, and mental changes.

Outside Influences

People who share their gifts (work) in fields that support others' wellbeing (doctors, health practitioners, nurses, etc.) must also pay attention to their own health. If you have travelled on a plane, they tell you to "Put the oxygen mask on yourself FIRST!" If you have concerns such as, taking on the energies, issues, or sicknesses of the individuals you work with, here are some suggestions:

❖ You can visualize white light, the pure energy from the Divine, and surround yourself before you begin a session. Give gratitude and release it when you finish the healing session.

❖ When you complete a healing session, shake your hands three times quick and hard; it is almost like the snap of the wrist with a limp hand. This stops the flow of energy and "shakes off" the giving and receiving of energy. Rinse your hands in cold water. Water is a cleansing agent, and it purifies.

Your Imagination as a Guide

Continuing with the session, after you have used your ChakraSynergy (self-created synergy, or single note PEO) you can add more Vibrational Tools such as:

❖ Shapes

❖ Gems and minerals

❖ Bring in color with chakra colored cloth or silk scarves

❖ Add sounds in the form of special music or the Tiwa Sounds

❖ Invoke the Goddess Meditation for the ChakraAura as a focus.

❖ Make your own ChakraSpritz or use a true hydrosol to mist and cleanse the room, refresh your face (or your client's face) to clear the ChakraAuras.

Use your imagination and your intuition will guide you through each *Vibrational AromaTherapy* Session. Each client brings her or his unique energy, beliefs, and issues to each session; therefore, each *Vibrational Aroma Therapy* Session is unique, uses different (yet always appropriate) ChakraSynergies, and offers creativity to use any or all of the Vibrational Tools for Transformation. There is no limitation to the combinations of tools and vibrational medicines that are available to use in a session. You can use as many different tools for your personal healing (or to help facilitate and guide others). If you are a healing arts practitioner, you can incorporate any of these tools and combine them with whichever healing modality is your specialty. Healing has many paths.

RejuveTreat – A Rejuvenation Treatment

Want to bring that long needed *spa vacation* to you? With the RejuveTreat Treatment, it's possible. All you need is soft music and candles to set the mood, and vibrationally-conscious essential oils (or a ChakraSynergy). RejuveTreat is an experience that enhances personal transformational work. RejuveTreat becomes a gift you give yourself, or someone you would like to pamper.

If you are a healing arts practitioner, RejuveTreat can be added easily to your healing sessions, no matter what modality you prefer.

RejuveTreat is a combination of foot reflexology, energy balancing, and facial shiatsu. RejuveTreat is rejuvenating to your body and acts like *a natural face-lift* for whoever receives it!

- ❖ **Steps 1-5,** the reflexology, is for balancing the body.
- ❖ **Steps 6-10** are energy balancing techniques (similar to polarity, Healing Touch, or Reiki).
- ❖ **Steps 11-14** are classical oriental facial shiatsu or acupressure for rejuvenating the facial tissues, resulting in a natural face-lift!

Although this kind of pampering feels better when given to you by someone else ... you *can* administer most of this treatment to yourself. Try it! Both the foot reflexology points and the facial acupressure points are the same as when giving the treatment to another person, you just have to approach them a bit differently if self-acupressure is applied.

For self-pampering, giving yourself a RejuveTreat session: sit in a chair, or comfortably on the floor, or sofa (back supported). You may have to adjust your hands for the facial shiatsu. You will feel it as you go along.

Getting Ready

Create a sacred space for your healing session, one that feels comfortable and nurturing. To cleanse the energy in the room:

❖ Smudge the room very lightly with a sage bundle. A sage bundle is formed of the dried herb bound together with a fine string. You can find sage bundles in many health food stores or herb shops.

❖ Light a candle.

❖ Another way to clear the energy for your healing space is to use an essential oil diffuser. There are many styles available in health food stores, herb shops, or online. Choose an essential oil with relaxing properties (such as lavender) and place some of the pure essential oil in the diffuser.

❖ Play soft music and lower the lights.

❖ Place a lavender eye pillow over the eyes.

❖ Prepare a glass of spring water to drink when finished.

How to Proceed

If you are giving this treatment to a loved one (or if that loved one is yourself) read all of the steps and adjust them to suit *you*. Set your healing space as a true healing sanctuary, a place where you feel relaxed, cared for, and nurtured. If you are administering the RejuveTreat treatment to yourself (or special friend or loved one), determine your focus and intention.

What do I mean? I often set aside an evening just to pamper myself. Many times my focus is to rejuvenate my creative juices, which relates to my 2nd ChakraAura – Sacral. If this is my focus, I use the ChakraSynergy #2 – Create. Or, if I don't have this with me, I may pick one of the essential oils that relates to the 2nd ChakraAura. Choose the synergy or a single essential oil that you like and that relates to the number of the ChakraAura that you have chosen as your focus for your treatment. (If you are a healing arts practitioner, help your client to choose which ChakraAura to focus on for their treatment. Although many ways to do this have already been discussed in previous chapters, here are additional suggestions:

❖ Use a divination method to choose randomly which ChakraAura you will focus on.

❖ Talk to your client and determine which ChakraAura to balance.

❖ Use your pendulum, intuition, applied kinesiology, muscle testing, or any other method you feel comfortable with to determine which ChakraAura you will make your focus.

Once you have determined which ChakraAura to focus on during the RejuveTreat, next choose the appropriate ChakraSynergy (or essential oil).

Foot Reflexology - Steps 1-4

Note: If you are administering this Foot Reflexology to yourself, sit on the floor, in a comfortable chair, or on a sofa where you can easily reach your feet.

Step 1. Energetically set the tone and ambience. Mist the body with a true hydrosol or a vibrationally appropriate ChakraSpritz. The gentle mist cleanses the aura in an aromatic and relaxing way.

Step 2. Begin with the feet. The feet are crucial to your balance. You use your feet to stand on the Earth Mother. Although this is an obvious fact, the simplicity of it is quite profound. Your feet support and balance your physical body and symbolically are the foundation for your inner balance. Foot reflexology is based on this principle. Lie on your back (face up on the massage table) or sit in a chair or on the floor.

Put one drop of the chosen ChakraSynergy (or essential oil) in the palm of your hand. Mix it with a few drops of unscented massage oil/lotion. Ask your client to take a total of five (5) slow, deep, cleansing breaths – in through the nose and out through the mouth. As she or he does this, gently rub the blend onto the bottom of each foot, one foot at a time.

Next, hold the bottom of each foot with full hand contact (your RIGHT hand on bottom of their LEFT foot and your LEFT hand on bottom of their RIGHT foot) as the cleansing breaths are completed. Continue holding for about two and-a-half (2 ½) minutes on each foot. Step 2 takes approximately five (5) minutes to complete both feet.

Step 3. Reflexology for the Right Foot. Place one drop of the ChakraSynergy (or essential oil) on the finger administering the reflexology (shiatsu). Begin to apply firm (not hard or painful) pressure on each of the points in the diagram for the RIGHT foot. There are a total of five (5) points on the RIGHT foot. Hold each one for about thirty (30) seconds. Step 3 takes approximately two and-a-half (2 ½) minutes to complete.

Step 4. Reflexology for the Left Foot. Add another drop of ChakraSynergy (or essential oil) to your finger administering treatment. Begin applying firm (not hard or painful) pressure on each of the points in the diagram for the LEFT foot. There are a total of six (6) points on the LEFT foot. Hold each one for about thirty (30) seconds. Step 4 takes approximately three (3) minutes to complete.

See **Foot Reflexology Diagram** *with points on the next page.*

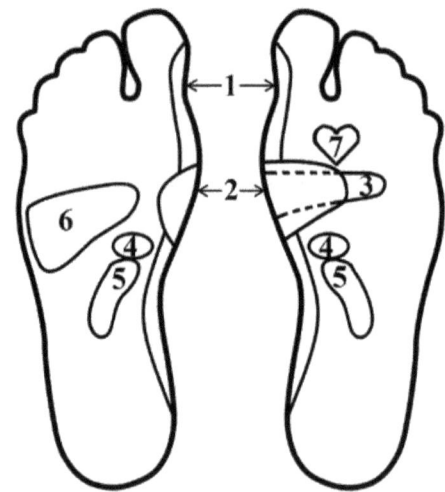

Right   Left
Foot Reflexology View of Bottom of Feet

Description of the foot reflexology points:

❖ *Point 1.* Spine (the back bone of your being-right &
left foot)

❖ *Point 2.* Stomach (helps assimilate ideas and life-right
& left foot)

❖ *Point 3.* Pancreas (helps process ideas and life-left foot)

❖ *Point 4.* Adrenals (balances nervous system-right &
left foot, on top of Kidneys)

❖ *Point 5.* Kidneys (helps ease frustration, fear and
anxiety-right & left foot)

❖ *Point 6.* Liver (helps balance anger and depression-
right foot)

❖ *Point 7.* Heart (for eliminating grief and lack of joy-
left foot)

Energy Balancing and Healing – Steps 5-10

Step 5. Abdomen Massage. Using the chosen ChakraSynergy (or essential oil), place one drop in the palm of your hand, add a little massage oil or lotion. Gently massage the abdomen CLOCKWISE for one (1) minute with your RIGHT hand. Your intention as you massage is to help stimulate the colon, which can help to eliminate fatty deposits. This step can also help to clear overall energy in the body. If your client is clothed, do this same motion of clockwise circles, above the area of the abdomen, but outside the sheet/blanket.

Step 6. Clean your hands. Before proceeding with Step 7.

Step 7. ChakraSynergy for treatment. Place two drops of your client's chosen ChakraSynergy (or essential oil) in your hand and gently mix it with the massage oil or lotion.

Step 8. On top of the 3rd ChakraAura – Solar Plexus. Just in the hollow of the ribcage, gently massage: COUNTER-CLOCKWISE for one (1) minute with your RIGHT hand. Your intention, as you massage, is to help to stimulate the main nervous system, making the rest of the treatment even more effective. As before, if your client is clothed or with a sheet/blanket over this area, do the same movements above the coverings.

Step 9. On the back of the 3rd ChakraAura – Solar Plexus. Adding one drop of ChakraSynergy (or essential oil) to massage oil/lotion, dispers it to both hands. Slide your RIGHT hand underneath your client (either touching the body directly or by slipping it between the sheet and the table). Position your RIGHT hand on the back directly underneath the area of the 3rd ChakraAura – Solar Plexus. Your intention, as you hold this position, is to balance the 3rd ChakraAura, to encourage wellness, and to stimulate the main nervous system. Hold your LEFT hand on or slightly above the Solar Plexus on the front of your client's body. Hold this position for about three (3) minutes.

Step 10. Gently place BOTH hands on or slightly above the 4th ChakraAura – Heart. Your intention, as you hold this position, is to balance and assist your client's equilibrium by allowing her or him to feel your full loving intention with this treatment. Hold for one (1) minute.

Note: If you are giving this treatment to yourself, do the best you can to reach each Step, or adjust it to suit you, or eliminate it altogether.

Facial Shiatsu Face-Lift – Steps 11-15

This treatment acts as a natural facelift for all of the muscles in the face. You can see differences within a few sessions. The word shiatsu is derived from the word *shiatsuryoho* and refers to a type of massage treatment using the thumbs, fingers, and palms of the hand. *Shi* means finger and *atsu* means pressure. You can apply this treatment to your own face, or you can apply the mild pressure to another's face for the treatment. Shiatsu is also known as acupressure. It is generally mild pressure administered with the fingertips. (Foot reflexology is a similar technique of acupressure, using pressure applied by the hands and fingers and administered to the feet.)

Note: If you are giving this facial shiatsu to yourself, sit in a comfortable chair, with your back supported, and adjust each step to suit you.

Step 11. Prepare for the face-lift treatment. Sit comfortably on a stool or chair near your client's head. Put two drops of a light face cream or lotion on the palm of your hand. Add one drop of one of the following essential oils: Rose, Chamomile, Roman, or Neroli (your choice).

Step 12. Place BOTH hands lightly on the face, with the nose untouched. Sitting behind your client (if self, adjust), place the palm of your hands on the cheeks, and around the jaw with your fingertips resting on the chin. Have the nose to breathe in the aroma freely. Hold for about 45 seconds.

Step 13. Begin the actual facial shiatsu pressure points. Described below as Points 1-5 (see the Facial Shiatsu Points Diagram). Each point should be lightly, gently massaged and held for one (1) minute each (count slowly to 60 to give you the exact timing).

See **Diagram and Description of Facial Shiatsu Points** *on next page.*

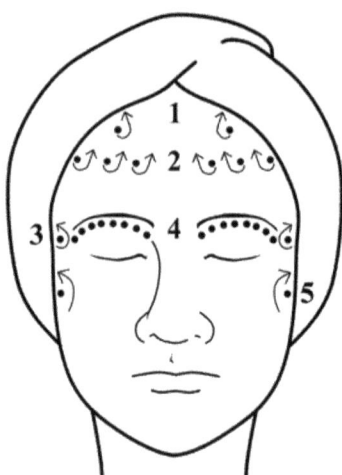

Diagram of Facial Shiatsu Points

Description of Facial Shiatsu Points

- ❖ *Point 1.* Directly above the eyes, at the hairline: Use steady pressure and make small inward circles. Known as *Mei Jung,* this point opens up the energy into the face and classically is used to treat headaches.

- ❖ *Point 2.* Just below, between the hairline and the eyebrow: Massage with small inward circles. This point helps prevent wrinkles by stimulating the muscles here to support the skin. The oriental name is *Yang Bai* and is traditionally used for treating migraines and insomnia.

- ❖ *Point 3.* Located at the outside corner of the eye, in the hollow: Massage with small outward circles. This point helps to tone, energize, and invigorate the small muscles around the eyes and enhances circulation. The skin becomes soft and supple, which helps to eliminate "crow's feet." This point is called *Wai Ming* and has also been found helpful in treating dry or irritated eyes.

❖ *Point 4.* The inside of the eye sockets, near the nose: Using the thumbs, press lightly, yet firmly, making small inward circles and continue along the inside of the brow bone to the outside of the eye socket. This point activates the flow of energy around the eyes, nose, and the center of the face. Known as *Zan Zhu*, it has traditionally been used for headache, eyestrain, and sinuses.

❖ *Point 5.* At the hinge of the jaw (near the ear) find the depression on the side of the cheek: This point is tender for those who experience TMJ (Temporomandibular Joint) sensitivity. Ask your client to let her or his mouth open slightly. Using your index fingers on both hands (or the first two fingers on both hands), massage in small circles toward the back of the head. This point helps relieve any tension in the jaw and is called *Cheng Jiang*.

Finishing the Treatment

Step 14. End the mini Facial Shiatsu Massage. Put one drop of ChakraSynergy (or essential oil) in your palms, rubbing gently together to disperse. Place BOTH hands lightly on the face (as in Step 12, leaving the nose exposed) and hold for one (1) minute. Your intention, as you hold this position, is connecting with the client to signal the near completion of the session.

Step 15. Suggest that your client take a few deep breaths, inhaling through the nose (allowing the belly to rise) and exhaling through the nose (allowing the belly to sink in). This particular breath is excellent to help move lymphatic fluid (see more below). Finish by drinking a glass of water. Meditate or contemplate (or journal) on your experience.

The Importance of the Lymphatic System

Recent studies by Stanford University show that 80% of women over 40 have sludgy lymph systems! Dr Bruno Chikly, M.D., D.O., director of the Lymph Drainage Therapy & Brain Therapy Programs in Scottsdale, Arizona (USA) says, "When lymph flow is slow and congested, it leads to an accumulation of body fat .... A slow lymphatic system can no longer properly transport fat where it needs to go ... Greater lymph flow may reduce your risk of plaque buildup in arteries, high cholesterol, and inflammatory bowel disease."

"Your breath acts as one of the largest pumps in the body, pulling lymph fluid from the lower parts upward and supporting healthy lymphatic flow .... Carrying around these extra pounds triggers inflammation – a problem for both your immune system *and* your waistline .... As part of its role as a superhighway, the lymphatic system carries immune cells through your body to infection-fighting lymph nodes. But inflammation thwarts this process by reducing lymph flow," says Jenna Macciochi Ph.D., who is a lymph expert.

Scientists at the University of California Los Angeles (UCLA) have reported that taking calming, deep breaths several times throughout a day helps torch 27% more fat, particularly for women.

Five Tibetan Rites for Life – ChakraAura Balancing

The *Five Tibetan Rites for Life*, are a series of five exercises (asanas in yogic terminology) for overall rejuvenation, for balancing the energy centers, and for energizing, strengthening, and adding flexibility to your physical body. These exercises are highly recommended for personal wellbeing. If you make the time to do them daily (takes 10-20 minutes), you will be impressed with how you look and feel!

The *Five Tibetan Rites* are both physically and spiritually enhancing. Doing all Five Rites helps to balance the ChakraAuras, helping you have vibrant, radiant health. They can enhance every aspect of your life. Enjoy their benefits and when you see the results, share them with others!

When you begin practicing the *Five Tibetan Rites*:

- ❖ Begin with three repetitions of each Rite per day for the first week.

- ❖ Every week, increase the number of repetitions by two. So, beginning at 3 repetitions a week, the next week you will do: 5; then 7; 9; 11, and so forth, up to 21.

- ❖ When you are doing 21 of each of the *Rites* – HOLD it at that for your practice. *Doing more than twenty-one is NOT recommended.* It will take ten weeks to increase your repetitions from 3 to 21 per Rite.

- ❖ It is recommended to do the Rites daily.

- ❖ First Week: 3 each
- ❖ Second Week: 5 each
- ❖ Third Week: 7 each
- ❖ Fourth Week: 9 each
- ❖ Fifth Week: 11 each

Sixth Week: 3 each
Seventh Week: 15 each
Eighth Week: 17 each
Ninth Week: 19 each
Tenth Week: 21 each

Tibetan Rite for Life # 1

Standing straight put both arms out shoulder height.

❖ Hold your LEFT hand with the palm UP with fingertips pointing towards the Sky. Hold your RIGHT hand with palm DOWN and fingertips pointing towards the Earth Mother.

❖ Watch the palm of your LEFT hand, slowly twirl your entire body (*not* too fast in the beginning) around in a COUNTER CLOCKWISE direction (to your left) for 3 full revolutions.

❖ Keeping arms outstretched, reverse your hand positions. Hold your RIGHT hand with palm UP, fingertips pointing towards the Sky. Hold your LEFT hand with palm DOWN, and fingertips pointing towards the Earth Mother.

❖ Watch the palm of your RIGHT hand, slowly twirl your entire body around in a CLOCKWISE direction (to your right) for 3 full revolutions.

❖ Now STOP. Place your hands in a prayer position over the heart area of your chest and stand still until you stop feeling dizzy. Bring your breath to a normal breathing pattern. Repeat 3 times.

This exercise strengthens the vestibular system (the balancing mechanism in the inner ear). It connects to your sense of balance and spatial orientation and helps with your overall balance. With regular practice, any dizziness stops. After awhile your spin becomes easy, smooth, and fluid, even if you get up to a moderately fast spin. This is the same motion as practiced by Islamic Dervishes or Sufi Mystics.

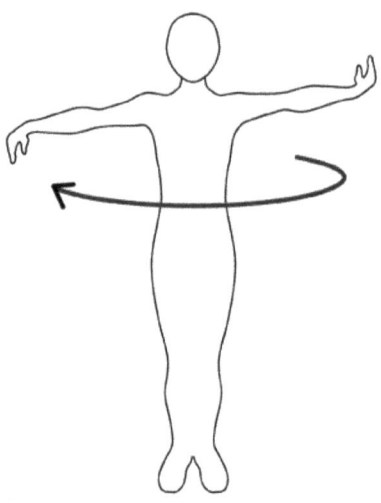

Diagram of Tibetan Rite #1

Tibetan Rite for Life #2

Lie flat on the floor with your legs extended, feet flexed, and ankles touching.

❖ Place your hands under your hips with palms down.

❖ Lift your head and legs *at the same time.*

❖ INHALE through your nose, lift your head up, and your chin in toward your chest. Keeping your lower back FLAT on the ground, lift your legs up to a little past 90-degrees above your torso and point your toes to the sky. This motion is done at the same time in one smooth motion.

❖ EXHALE through your nose (or mouth) as you bring your legs back to the flat and extended starting position.

❖ Repeat 3 times, INHALING as you bring your head and legs up and EXHALING as you bring them back down again.

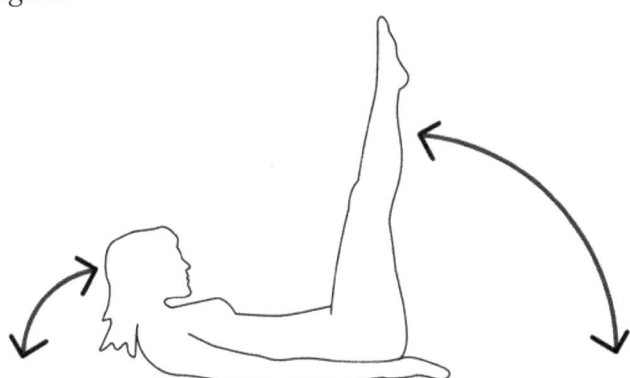

Diagram of Tibetan Rite #2

Tibetan Rite for Life #3

Kneel with your torso perpendicular to the ground, the balls of your feet resting on the ground, and your knees about shoulder width apart.

- ❖ Look at your knees (they should be about 4-6 inches apart).
- ❖ Place your palms on the backs of your thighs (just below the buttocks). Your spine should be erect.
- ❖ INHALE through your nose, lift your head up and drop it back as far as you comfortably can, trying to look up at the sky.
- ❖ EXHALE through your nose (or your mouth) and bring your chin down to your chest.
- ❖ Repeat 3 times.

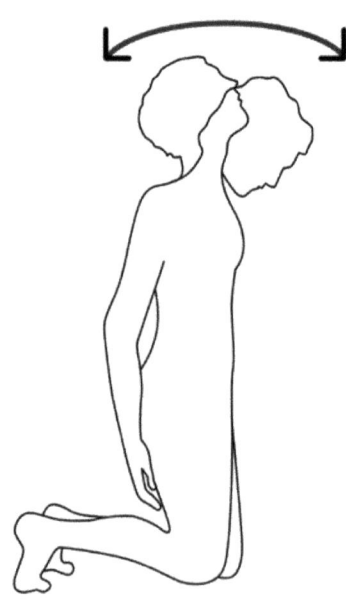

Diagram of Tibetan Rite #3

Tibetan Rite for Life #4

Sit up straight with your legs outstretched in front of you and shoulder width apart.

- ❖ Place your hands on the floor BESIDE your hips, fingers facing forward.
- ❖ EXHALE through your nose (or mouth) and allow your chin to drop to your chest.
- ❖ INHALE through your nose, lift your head up and drop it back so it makes a straight neck with your spine.
- ❖ LIFT YOUR HIPS and body up. Your feet will be shoulder width apart and flat on the ground. You are now balanced on your hands and feet with your body in the air facing the sky. Your arms should be straight. Your body should eventually look like a TABLE.
- ❖ EXHALE through your nose (or mouth) and lower yourself down to your starting position.
- ❖ Repeat this Rite 3 times.

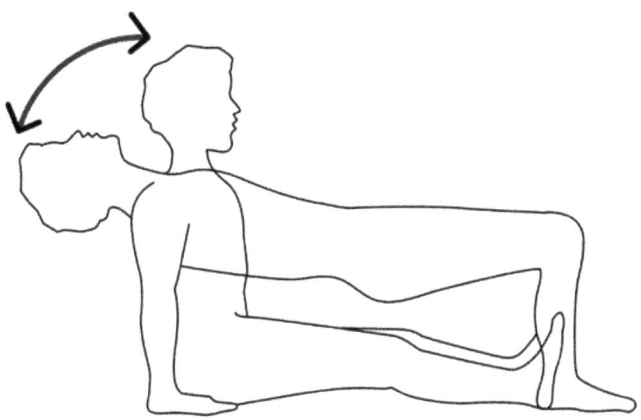

Diagram of Tibetan Rite #4

Tibetan Rite for Life #5

Support your body on the palms of your hands and the balls of your feet. Both of your arms and legs are about two feet (24 inches) apart and are straight.

- ❖ Your body is in an upside-down "V" (see diagram below).
- ❖ INHALE through your nose and push your body down so you are parallel to the ground.
- ❖ EXHALE through either your nose (or mouth) and return to the starting upside-down "V" position.
- ❖ Repeat this Rite 3 times.

Diagram of Tibetan Rite #5

PART SIX

AlcheMystical Aromatics

Look in the perfumes of flowers and nature
for peace of mind and joy of Life. .
– Wang Wei, 8th century

Chapter 28

AlcheMystical Parfumerie

Mysteries and secrets, the soul of perfume.
– Serge Lutens, Fragrance Industry Conference in Grasse, France 1995

AlcheMystical Awakening

As humans, we are experiencing a new era of *alchemystical awakening.* Many of you are feeling a desire or need to live a life that acknowledges your physical body and blends it with your spiritual self. If this sounds like something you have been feeling or thinking about … this is *AlcheMystical.*

The ultimate goal of formulating scents in *AlcheMystical Parfumerie* is to compose fragrances that are focused on raising overall vibrations. The perfumes offer support and encourage communication with your soul. Aspirations that may have lain dormant (maybe for eons) are possibly aching to be realized. Humans globally are craving to see changes in the world and this begins with each one of us in our – Body, Heart, Spirit, Mind, and Soul.

When I prepare an *AlcheMystical Parfum*, a *SoulParfum*, I am truly creating one that has *AlcheMystical* properties. I compose a fragrance with conscious intent or focus to create a formula that has enhanced positive, therapeutic, and wellness qualities for the purpose of transformation. The whole, or end result, is a product greater than its individual parts, which can trigger a path for change for those who wear it and potentially those who smell it.

In 1960, Frater Albertus, a German alchemist, published a book titled *The Alchemist's Handbook: Manual for Practical Laboratory Alchemy*. He summarized his book with the "Alchemical Manifesto." I offer a portion of this summary here for your contemplation:

"Since no Alchemist covets praise or glory, it should not be hard to understand that there is no need for personal acknowledgement … the work itself is the important thing, never personalities.

Not everything that greets our senses is met with full understanding on first contact. Psychologists have likened our conscious mind to that visible portion of an iceberg that represents only a fraction of its actual dimensions …. Meditation will open up what has been, and for some still is, concealed from our understanding. This is the key that will open the portal to the new world of the Alchemists, a world that you are already aware of and acquainted with, through karma, through previous incarnations, or whatever terms may be applied.

May the Cosmic Light guide and direct you in your sincere endeavors, and may you be one of those to glorify the works of the Divine by becoming an administrator of the heavenly bounties among mankind.

Surely it is better to be one of those actively engaged in the Hermetic work, leaving for posterity a record of accomplishment, than to remain an outsider who only *reads* about others and what they have been able to perform.

May a deep and abiding PEACE permeate your whole being, and may you be engulfed in the radiations from the endless Love of the God of your Heart."

AlcheMystical Soul Parfums

As with many paths I embark on in my life, composing a *Soul Parfum* was birthed from my own cravings. In the early 1980's, I was using aromatherapy to help both me, and my toddler son. I created blends for simple issues like calming (him) or boosting energy (me). I have always been a seeker. Even in my teens, I searched for spiritual meaning to my life. One day I looked at my three-dozen or so essential oils and felt an intense pull to create a concoction for myself that might support my spiritual yearnings.

I sat down in a room far away from my thirty-six essential oils. I went into a meditation, taking a few breaths in, and suddenly I smelled essential oils. *But they are not near me? How is this possible?* The aromas continued. Able to identify the odors, I wrote each one down. I was given information about each of the essences (as an inner knowing). It was as if each essential oil had been invited to the party and they were telling me why they were there! They also told me how each of them offered their personalized assistance as part of the whole composition of the fragrance.

I wrote down everything. I let my intuition also guide me for how many drops of each were going into the beautiful Egyptian perfume bottle that I had saved for something special. The "something special" was me ... I was special enough (this was initially hard to accept) to create this intoxicating fragrance. It would guide my path as a friend. After this experience, I have a ritual each year of creating a new fragrance for myself on the solstices and equinoxes.

Eventually, I shared what I was doing with a friend, who then asked me to make one for her. I felt shy. It was one thing to do this for me. An entirely different thing to admit what I was doing to a friend. And yet another thing to make her one! But I gathered my courage and composed her a scent: "This is special for this moment-in-time." I shared more with her of her personalized information supporting the essences in her perfume. And, "It will accompany you for 3-4 months, assisting you with the goals and dreams you told me about. After that, things will have changed in some way in your life, and you will feel ready (or you will feel the need) for a new scent." One friend, led to another friend, and eventually others have come to me, and the *SoulParfums* have travelled the world.

My repertoire of essential oils keeps growing. Today I have hundreds in my apothecary at my personal *atelier* (studio). Every time I receive a new one, I sit in meditation with the essence and ask what is its purpose. I still have my original yellow legal pad with notes for each essence. Finally, with writing this new second edition of *Aromatic Alchemy – Recipes for Transformation*, I am turning the faded, frayed limp pages into a digital list on my computer.

Over the years, as I keep morphing, so too have the names for these bespoke (custom) fragrances: "Fragrance for a Moment-in-time, Alchemical Parfum, AlkemicalFragrance, Parfum Alkemie …." Now, in this book for the first time, I'm sharing with you my secrets for composing a *Soul Parfum*. Yes, the name morphed again. It even has a .com: SoulParfum.com. The fragrances I personally compose for someone, I call: *SoulParfums*.

I've seen over the years some magical and mystical things happen for people who have invited these parfums into their lives. (You can read some of the testimonials in the "Addendum" at the end of this book.) In actuality, I guess everything I've ever created with essential oils, from my first company (Essence AromaTherapy) with its "Crystal CandleEssence" to my current company (Artisan Parfums) and the collection of nine ChakraSynergies (*Vibrational AromaTherapy by Ixchel™*) and nine *Parfums with Purpose*, have all incorporated the concepts of creating fragrances to inspire transformation.

Modern Perfumery

Modern perfumery actually began in the mid to late 1800's. Up until this time, all fragrances were composed of raw materials from Nature (from plants and animals). Chemists in 1855 created the first synthetic molecules: Benzyl acetate. By the late 1800's these synthesized chemicals became the foundation of today's perfumes.

Early in the 1920's, Gabrielle "Coco" Chanel, already a well-known fashion designer, approached a perfume supplier and asked for a fragrance she could offer to her customers. She said, "If I were a perfumer, I would put everything into the perfume, and nothing into the presentation … and to make it inimitable [incapable of being imitated], I would want it to be extremely expensive." In 1921, she presented to the world: *Chanel No 5*.

Most of today's perfumes are composed based on notes: top notes, middle notes, base notes, and fixatives (for endurance of the scent) and on scent families (florals, citruses, herbs, resins, woods, etc.). Usually a perfumer will begin with the base notes, working their way up to the top notes. In *AlcheMystical Parfumerie*, I prefer: *Head Notes* – Top Notes, *Heart Notes* – Middle Notes, and *Soul Notes* – Base Notes.

❖ Top Notes/*Head Notes*: 30 % of the formula. The lightest of the essences used, these open up the perfume at first whiff, but they also disappear the quickest. They are the most volatile. Examples: bergamot, coriander, lavender, rosemary, lemon, and other citruses.

❖ Middle Notes/*Heart Notes*: 50 % of the formula. These essences are also referred to as the heart of the perfume and they can last for a few hours. They become apparent after the top notes have faded and are the core of the perfume. Examples: geranium, rose, juniper, ylang ylang, and jasmine.

❖ Base Notes/*Soul Notes*: 20 % of the formula. When the perfume begins to settle, after you have put it on your skin or blotter paper, this it what will remain after the previous notes disappear. Usually resins and woods, examples: frankincense, myrrh, cedarwood, and sandalwood.

❖ Fixatives: Percentages generally included in the 20% for Base Notes. These are used to help hold the perfume together and to create a scent with endurance so it stays around longer.

Perfumes of today use mostly synthetic materials, with few natural essential oils. Many times, if the perfume says there is Lavender, the fragrance contains synthetic chemicals chosen to represent "Lavender." This is because synthetics are more cost effective and are consistent in their chemical constituents, thus more reliable to use year after year. Botanical ingredients from Nature can be fickle. The naturals from Mother Nature (not human laboratory created nature-identicals) will change each season due to growing conditions: droughts, heavy rains, less or more sun, grown in lowlands or altitudes. All alter somewhat year-to-year the chemotype of the essential oil. Chemotypes are plants from the same species and genus – they look alike, however the chemical constituents of the essential oil change due to fluctuating growing conditions.

Accords in Perfumery

An "Accord" in perfumery composition is two or more scented ingredients, expertly blended together so that the composition of the two (or more) smells, is different than each individual scent. I am a self-taught *parfumeur* (perfumer). Early in my aromatherapy explorations, I created my first parfum for me. In 1989, I composed a perfume from all white flowers, purely from essential oils, in a jojoba carrier. I named it: Sonata. It became part of my offerings with my company at the time, Essence AromaTherapy.

In 2018, I reformulated all nine of my parfums for *Artisan Parfums.* I revamped *Sonata,* and in it is a Floral Accord: Magnolia, Champaca, Champa, Tuberose, Angelica, Osmanthus, and White Rose.

Yet this blend didn't explain what was in my mind and what my nose was conceiving. Researching modern perfumery didn't divulge what I was looking for either. I wanted to make a specialized perfume concentrate that was a mélange of one botanical – different types of that botanical. Say a mélange of different: Roses, Jasmines, Lotuses, Myrrhs, and Frankincenses. I have chosen to call these mélanges: a Melody = a scented expressive quality of one essence, i.e. Rose.

I have three "Melody" creations in my parfum collections for *Artisan Parfums:*

- ❖ *Illume Parfum* has a Frankincense Melody
- ❖ *Passion Parfum* has a Lotus Melody
- ❖ *Harmonie Parfum* has a Jasmine Melody

In all of these parfums, the Melody is just one part of the whole composition. There are many other essences that make up the perfume concentrate, which are blended with the carriers, to be bottled for the wearable parfum.

Here is an example of a Frankincense Melody:

- ❖ Frankincenses old and rare … collected over time
- ❖ Frankincense Somalia, *Boswellia carteri* - Hydrodistilled
- ❖ Frankincense Somalia, *Boswellia carteri* - CO_2 Extract
- ❖ Frankincense Somalia, *Boswellia carteri* – Organic/ Hydrodistilled
- ❖ Frankincense Oman, *Boswellia sacra* - Hydrodistilled
- ❖ Frankincense India, *Boswellia serrata* - CO_2Extract
- ❖ Frankincense Frereana Somalia, *Boswellia frereana* – Hydrodistilled

What Goes with Which?

Learning what scents blend harmoniously with which other scents takes a long time and a great deal of experience. If you have some aromatherapy experience, you have a head start. I can really encourage you to start experimenting. Here is a suggestion: Take three bottles of three different essences. Remove the caps. Hold all three in your two hands and pass them quickly under your nose … what does it smell like? Appealing? Annoying?

When beginning to formulate aromatherapy blends or perfumes, use sparingly the strongest essences (roots, woods, resins), medium scented (florals and some herbs) used in moderation, and the citruses (or citrusy scents like lemongrass) can be used according to how prominent you want the concentrated blend of essences, but they are also head notes and will disappear fastest. Don't be shy, keep playing and experimenting.

There are books on perfume blending (see: Suggested Reading). There are also several websites who sell essential oils and essences, and they have information on what blends with which other essences. Some I recommend: EdenBotanicals.com and WhiteLotusAromatics.com.

AlcheMystical Parfumerie

Modern methods of composing perfumes are very different than how you approach *AlcheMystical Parfumerie*. I am going to focus from here onwards, on sharing with you how you can create a *Soul Parfum*, based on how I compose my *SoulParfums*. In a sense, you will need to throw out some of what you may know of modern perfumery blending (to get into your intuitive and creative left-brain). However, you may be more comfortable using your analytical right-brain.

I have listed different ideas below for formulating your *Soul Parfum* fragrances if your right-brain wants them! As always, there are several paths to one end. The Dalai Lama says, "People take different roads seeking fulfillment and happiness. Just because they're not on your road doesn't mean they've gotten lost."

Composing Parfums

Some different approaches to composing *AlcheMystical* scents might be:

❖ Choosing the raw materials by building percentages based on Notes: 20% *Soul Notes* & Fixatives, 50% *Heart Notes*, 30 % *Head Notes*.

❖ Building your *Soul Parfum* fragrance based on the esoteric properties of the raw materials, listed in the vibrational and energetic monographs sections of this book.

❖ Choosing what type of a scent you want by category (aka classification): oriental, floral, citrus, woody, spices, fruits, etc.

❖ Find your starting point from inspirations experienced through your senses: color (a tropical bird for example), sight (sunset from a mountain top), taste (oranges dipped in chocolate), or sound (your favorite dance tune or inspirational music).

❖ Choose which ChakraAura you want to influence, and then from the essential oils listed in Chapter 26 for each of the ChakraSynergies, compose a *Soul Parfum*.

❖ Follow other modern perfumery approaches to composing, and include using your intuition when you feel comfortable.

Jean-Claude Ellena, in his book *Perfume-The Alchemy of Scent* says: "The aim of perfumery, as of all the arts, is to create products that arouse sensual pleasure. As a man and as a composer of perfumes, I must feel pleasure in order to give it. The pleasure of surprising, of evoking, of suggesting, of hinting. Perfume is a story in odours, sometimes a poetry of memory."

I compose my *SoulParfums* **totally** from my psychic and intuitive abilities. I trust them now after using them regularly and deeply for over fifty years in many areas of my life and creative work. However, you may create your own *Soul Parfums* using whatever approach you feel comfortable with.

Another difference between my compositions and modern perfumes, even some "natural perfumes" are:

❖ I use ONLY raw materials from Nature, or from natural sources.

❖ I do not blend my parfums in alcohol, but prefer vegetable oils and waxes, like the ancient Egyptians used.

❖ I set my intentions, then I create *SoulParfums* and *Parfums with Purpose.*

In my approach to composing parfums I have two distinct differences in the types of ingredients that are used:

❖ *SoulParfums*, specifically composed for an individual, couple, or specific group, usually are composed from 100% therapeutic-grade essential oils (suitable for medical aromatherapy) and CO_2 extracts.

❖ *Parfums with Purpose (Artisan Parfums Collections)* use the same therapeutic-grade essential oils (suitable for medical aromatherapy) but also include some rare and unusual absolutes, dry-distillations, ruhs, attars, and mélanges (natural blends).

All Composers of Perfumes

So what are we doing when we compose a perfume? We are expressing our passions, our senses, and our desires into a physical form – through scent. We want to inspire others to feel connected to this grand experience we call Life. As a perfumer, we hope that our creations will stand out as different and that the components of the scent make a difference to the individual who chooses to wear the fragrance.

Composers of *AlcheMystical Parfums*

The added dimension, differentiating *AlcheMystical Parfums* from other perfumes, is to design a scent that at least triggers transmutation and, at its ultimate best, is transformational. Ancient alchemy's promise is that the fragrance has the potential to open doors and open possibilities for an individual to become the gold, the ultimate essence of their Essence Self.

What is this "Essence Self?" It's a term used to describe the individual who has gained wisdom from their experiences in life.

They never stop consciously morphing and growing, they feel balance within themselves; they have balanced (married) the feminine and masculine archetypes in their psyche, and they have created a new expression of themselves – their optimum self, the perfected form of themselves … they have **become** the gold.

A Formula to Enthuse You – Inspired by Ancient Egypt

Ancient Egypt initially used scented oils for ritually anointing statues of their deities, as a greeting to the goddesses and gods each day. Mummification was carried out to preserve the body of the dead, along with their inner organs, helping them on their journey into the afterlife. Eventually, these scented oils were made into cones of wax, placed on their heads, as they would sit in the hot sun and let the wax melt and drip down the head and body – scenting the body with precious oils. Cleopatra enticed Mark Anthony with carpets possibly two-feet thick of rose petals, sails on her watercraft imbued with oil, bathing in milk and roses, and intoxicating body oils to seduce.

In 2015 at the *Tell Timai* excavation site, near the ancient Egyptian city of *Thmuis* (founded in 4,500 B.C.), they uncovered original amphora with residuals of its ingredients. What a magnificent discovery! Through chemical analysis scientists were able to identify the ingredients (that had long lost their scent). This was the first time in over 2,000 years that these bottles of antiquity had been uncovered.

What was detected in the amphora? Myrrh, cardamom, cinnamon, and olive oil, which would have been used as an anoint in the form of a heavy resinous oil.

I have been inspired to create a *SoulParfum* honoring the Temple of Isis on the island of Philae, on Lake Nasser in Egypt. During ancient times, Philae was the center for the worship of Isis. In February 2010, my mother and I visited Egypt. This trip was on her "bucket list" of places she longed to visit. I too desired for decades to visit these ancient lands. Egypt was exceptionally memorable and unforgettable, deeply moving my soul and heart.

Inspirations for a Soul Parfum

My inspirations – the smells of time immemorial: musty, fresh, hot, cold stone, and bright sunlight. Ancient temples, pyramids, and structures reach up to mid heaven, it almost hurts your neck to keep your head up and looking so high. Vivid colors of cottons and silks: purple, yellow, green, orange, blue, and red. Jewelry designed intricately with 22-carat gold or silver. The green Nile, freshly filled with rain, its waters lapping at the sandy banks. Attars in the souks: Rose, Jasmine, Amber, Lotus, and Myrrh.

What's in my *Philae Revisited* formula? I wanted to create something that used ingredients easily available for you, and that are listed in this book with their vibrational monographs. Here is the formula:

Philae Revisited

The parfum opens exhibiting fresh, green notes and pine-like undertones. Its heart is spicy and warm, with an intoxicating richness of citrus, floral, and a voluptuous fresh rose sweetness. The Soul of the parfum deepens and enfolds with sacred essences from ancient worlds.

Soul Notes & Fixatives: 20%
3 drops Frankincense *Boswellia sacra*
5 drops Myrrh *Commiphora myrrha*
2 drops Spikenard *Nardostachys jatamansi*
Heart Notes: 50%
3 drops Cardamom *Elettaria cardamomum*
3 drops Carnation Absolute *Dianthus caryophyllus*
2 drops Cinnamon *Cinnamomum verum*

4 drops Lotus Absolute *Nelumbo nucifera*

7 drops Orange Blossom Absolute *Citrus aurantium*

6 drops Rose de Mai Absolute *Rosa x centifolia*

Head Notes: 30%

5 drops Galbanum *Ferula galbaniflua*

8 drops Geranium, Rose *Pelargoneum graveolens*

2 drops Juniper *Juniperus communis*

This composition totals 50 drops. A 15 ml bottle will take a total of 30 drops of perfume concentrate (combined essences) for a 10% dilution.

Philae Revisited is a "Parfum with Purpose" and as a *Soul Parfum* it has its own distinguishing characteristics. Would you like to remember something from your past or maybe even a past life? Would you like to feel supported with one of your current dreams or goals? *Philae Revisited* is a fragrance composed for renewal and to spark remembering. Combined with your focused intentions, it can help you reveal some of your own secrets! One or two drops under your nose before bed or during meditation or prayer. On your wrist during the day, the parfum will help you keep your focus.

Composing Soul Parfums

What you'll need:

- ❖ Choice of Essential Oils/Raw Materials.
- ❖ Organic carriers such as: Jojoba (liquid wax), almond oil, grapeseed oil, or sunflower oil.
- ❖ Glass beakers (or bottle) for blending into.
- ❖ Glass bottles chosen for finalized *Soul Parfum.*
- ❖ Notebook to track your formula.

I recommend using a 10% dilution of essential oils/raw materials blended into your chosen carrier(s). This gives you a fragrance stronger than the dilutions for *Vibrational AromaTherapy* (1%-2%). The ideal perfumes are smelled on you only when someone gets close to you. It is really invasive when someone's perfume trails after them leaving a heavy track of scent that permeates the entire room, and your clothes if you hug them! Especially true for some of the synthetic fragrances in modern perfumery that are intentionally created to stick around for days.

Essential oils are powerful and you probably won't need a stronger dilution of essential oils/raw materials than 10%. This is 1 drop of scented essence and 9 drops of carrier; or 1 part scented material and 9 parts carrier. If you prefer your fragrance stronger (or lighter) you can adjust the chart below for a 5% or 15% dilution, respectively.

Dilutions Chart for Soul Parfums for 10% Fragrance

Bottle Size - Pure Essential Oil (PEO)
- ❖ 5 ml (1 tsp./teaspoon) – 10 drops (½ ml) of PEO
- ❖ 10 ml (2 tsp) – 20 drops (1 ml) PEO
- ❖ 15 ml (1/2 oz) – 30 drops (1 ½ ml) PEO
- ❖ 30 ml (1 oz) – 60 drops (3 ml) PEO
- ❖ 60 ml (2 oz) – 120 drops (6 ml) PEO
- ❖ 120 ml (4 oz) – 240 drops (12 ml)) PEO

Compose Your Raw Materials for Your Perfume

Track what you do in the notebook. Put your beaker (or glass bottle) on your work table. Note **every drop** of each individual essence you use. You will adjust and build your composition. Start with only 1 or 2 drops of each. Sniff and inhale after adding each essence. Adjust … a drop of this, 2 drops of that ….

When you have finalized the perfected scent to suit your nose, record this on its own page of the notebook. Sometimes you may have to label (for history) and set aside a composition that just doesn't come together the way you want. (Or throw it away! I dig a small hole in my backyard for discarded oils, which aren't many.) Keep all the notes of what it took to get to the accepted scent. This is your historical log in case you need to refer back at a later time. Give your composition a name.

This combination of ONLY essential oils/raw materials is called a perfume concentrate. From the perfume concentrate, you can fill any size bottle for the final bottled *Soul Parfum*. Your perfume concentrate will mature over time. It will mellow, allowing each individual ingredient to create a harmonizing perfume.

In a glass perfume bottle (using the above chart) for a 5 ml size you will drop into the bottle 10 drops (or ½ ml) essential oil/raw material of perfume concentrate. Fill the remainder of the space in the bottle with your chosen carrier and put the lid on. Shake very gently, almost rolling the bottle in your hands.

Bottle Size Conversion Chart

❖ 1 ml (1/30ᵗʰ oz, 1/5 teaspoon) = 20 drops (liquid or PEO)

❖ 5 ml (1/6 oz, 1 teaspoon) = 100 drops

❖ 10 ml (1/3 oz, 1 ½ teaspoon) = 200 drops

❖ 15 ml (½ oz, 1 Tablespoon) = 300 drops

❖ 30 ml (1 oz, 2 Tablespoons) = 600 drops

Chapter 29

Vibrational & Energetic Monographs for Parfumerie Essences

Rose can be used to bring our consciousness closer to our angels, and to the angelic self that dwells within us. To inhale rose is to inhale the love and kisses of angels.
– Valerie Ann Worwood, *Aromatherapy for the Soul*

Choosing Raw Materials for Composing *Soul Parfums*

In *AlcheMystical Parfumerie,* you can choose from any of the essential oils and CO_2 extracts in Chapter 26 (for *Vibrational AromaTherapy*). For aromatherapy, where physical health is the primary concern, you may choose to be on the safe side and not use perfume oils or absolutes, especially if there are any serious health concerns for the individual(s) wearing the parfums. Essential oils are collected through steam distillation, or by hydro-distillation or cohobation. Citrus oils are collected by cold-pressed extraction. CO_2 Extracts are extracted using carbon gas under pressure (no petrochemicals used).

The raw materials world is yours when you create from naturals for perfumes. Absolutes, Attars, Concretes, Ruhs, and Dry-distillations, all are used for perfumery (but **not aromatherapy)**. *Important Note:* Some materials have residues of petrochemical solvent vapors from their solvent extraction. Others will have waxes and residues in them from the different methods used to collect the scented essence. If pregnant, breastfeeding, or with serious health concerns, please research safety data before use.

(Additional Note: If you want more in-depth information on the extraction methods for essential oils and perfume oils, I suggest further research and recommend *EdenBotanicals.com* and *WhiteLotusAromatics.com* websites, as educational sources.)

I have chosen to incorporate both essential oils and natural perfume materials in my collections for *Artisan Parfums*. However, for my bespoke *SoulParfums*, I use primarily essential oils, yet occasionally my intuition (or direct knowledge) will guide me to use natural perfume materials too.

For any *Soul Parfums* you choose to compose, you make the decision as to which materials to use, taking into consideration everything you know about how the parfums will be used and by whom.

27 Natural Parfumerie Essences With
Their Vibrational Monograph

Almond, Bitter (*Prunus armeniaca*)

From the nut. Rich scent of marzipan (almond), nutty and sweet, with cherry overtones. Something exciting and new is on its way into your life; or this plants the seed for you to open up your mind for something new to come into your life.

Note: Head, Heart

Amber, Fossilized (*Oleum succini*)

Dry Distillation from 35 million year old Himalayan fossilized tree resin. Scent: smoky, resinous, tar-like, woody, leathery, with slight pine and balsamic notes. Connects you deeply to your life on the Earth Mother. Increases the fertility of your creative expressions and brings in an abundance of light into your being.

Note: Soul, Fixative

Beeswax Absolute (*Cera alba*)

From bee's honeycomb. Scent: very warm, almost resinous, with notes of honey, pollen, and a sweetness with a hint of outdoors, hay-like. Message: Bee-lieve in yourself! Live your dreams. Also carries the vibration and energy of our magnificent bees (who work so diligently to pollinate). Bees are the true original alchemists and are imperative to the survival of humanity.

Note: Heart, Soul, Fixative.

Black Currant Bud Absolute (*Ribes nigrum*)

From the flowers buds. Scent: tangy, green, slight fruity, warm like wine, rich earth, with an animalic or phereomone surprise. This type of scent creates an aphrodisiac and erotic effect, often unconsciously. Message: "Let your hair down, kick up your heels, run naked through the forest … abandon your inhibitions and whatever is holding you back from your dreams."

Note: Heart, Base

Cassie Absolute (*Acacia farnesiana***)**

From the yellow blossoms. Scent: sweet, warm, green and fresh, with touches of violet and balsam. Message: "Don't let day to day life overwhelm you. You are fragile, strong, and vital. Seek your assets, known as your innate gifts and talents, and find your unique expression in the world. I can soften feelings that may overwhelm you."

Note: Heart, Soul

Carnation Absolute (*Dianthus caryophyllus***)**

From the flowers. Scent: almost spicy like clove, honey-sweet, herby and very tenacious. It is warming to floral notes. Carnation instills feelings of comfort, celebratory joy, and carefree freedom. It's an expression of love.

Note: Heart

Champaca (aka Champa) Red, White (*Michelia champaca***)**

From the magnolia flowers. Scent: a sultry and rich panoply of scents, like everyone came to the party: earthy green tea, berries, apricots, sweet floral, minty, herby, tobacoo. Just very erotic and yummy! Boosts your courage. Helps to eliminate old forms of protection that you have continued out of habit, but they are outdated and no longer needed. Instills feelings of peace. Balancing to all systems and energy centers. Being rooted to the Earth Mother, yet open to the cosmos. The White Champaca is slightly sweeter than the Red Champaca.

Note: Heart

Choya Loban (*Boswelia serrata***)**

From the resin, a dry distillation of Frankincense. Scent: slightly smoky, sweet resinous, with balsamic woodiness. Renews your faith in yourself. Message: "Through the smoke from cleansing fires, you emerge to embolden and reaffirm your sacredness."

Note: Soul

Choya Nakh (Seashells)

From the dry distillation of dry roasted seashells. Message: "Through the waters and the seas, you are cleansed and purified. Breathe in new life."

Note: Soul

Cacao Absolute (*Theobroma cacao*)

From the cocoa seeds. Yes chocolate! Scent: rich, warm, slightly spicy, decadent, enticing and hard to resist. Comforts your mind and gives you feelings of elation and overall wellbeing. Lets you know that you can do anything you set your heart and mind on.

Note: Heart, Soul

Coffee Bean CO₂ Extract (*Coffea Arabica*)

From the roasted beans. Scent: smells like freshly roasted rich coffee, smoky and strong. Helps you to open your eyes to see what is Truth before you, possibly something you couldn't see before. It also helps you to light your inner fire to get going on a project or deeply held desire.

Note: Heart, Soul

Crysanthemum Absolute (*Chrysanthemum x morifolium*)

From the flowers. Scent: fresh, slightly camphorous, floral, soft, smooth, with a hint of fruity sweetness. Message: "With eternal longevity and wellbeing, you see the Truth of what Life is. Your mood is elevated, lightened, and euphoric. You understand that every moment is here for your benefit, to raise your energetic vibration to feel one with Infinite Source."

Note: Soul

Fir, Balsam Absolute (*Abies balsamea*)

From the needles. Scent: warm, balsamic, fresh, green, fruity and rich. Oh so mouthwatering, like fresh conifer trees! A gentle sedative allows your mind to take a vacation. Gives you guidance and opens you to a fresh, clear, and insightful perspective on things.
    Note: Heart, Soul, Fixative

Jasmine Sambac Absolute (*Jasminium sambac*)

From the flowers. Scent: hints of sweet green, floral, honey and tea, almost a little smoky. A very rich scented jasmine. The power to transform physical love from an earthly grounded expression into its highest form of spiritual energy. The spiritualization of sexuality.
    Note: Heart

Labdanum Absolute (*Cistus ladaniferus*)

From the oleoresin, the sticky resin that is found on the entire plant. (Long ago, the resin was collected by wearing leather pants, rubbing against the plant so the resin would attach itself to the leather, and then scraping the resin off of the leather. Scent: deeply resinous, sweet, slightly marine-like, animalic and richly balsamic. Stimulates higher consciousness. Encourages you to see beyond what seems real. Deeply sedating. (Also called Rock Rose, the resin comes from the same genus as the essential oil of Cistus that comes from the tops of leaves.)
    Note: Fixative, Soul

Lotus, Pink & White Absolute (*Nelumbo nucifera*)

From the flowers. Pink Lotus: Scent:very soft, creamy sweet, deeply floral, and earthy. Enhances love to strengthen relationships and spiritual communication, connection within relationship. White Lotus: Scent: very similar, but bolder, greener, and not as sweet as the Pink. Enhances spiritual connections with Divine Source and allows you to feel the purity of this connection.
    Note: Heart

Orange Blossom Absolute (*Citrus aurantium var. amara*)

From the flowers. Scent: a sharp green, citrusy floral, deeply sensuous and rich, yet not cloying, very warming. Enriches life's pleasures and joys, deepens connections to others and to daily experiencing of life.

Note: Heart, Fixative

Osmanthus Absolute (*Osmanthus fragrans*)

From the flowers. Scent: very long lasting scent, fruity, green, floral, honey-apricot, with wisps of rich dried deeply colored fruits, and a hint of leather. An alchemical essence that focuses on transformation: spiritual essence into the embodiment of the human experience, transmuting matter (physical form). "The Sweet Nectar of Life" equals Love.

Note: Heart, Soul

Pear, Organic Extract (*Pyrus communis*)

From the fruit, aka Williams Pear, Bartlett Pear, European Pear. Scent: sweet, like ripe, fresh picked pears, slightly green, light, and bright. The one I use I bought in Paris at *Aroma Zone*, whose main offices are in Avignon, Provence, France. It's message: "Life is sweet and innocent, enjoy its moments."

Note: Head

Rose de Mai Absolute (*Rosa x centifolia*)

From the flower petals, from an antique rose, the cabbage rose. Scent: voluptuous and sweet with deeply delicate sweetness, not cloying, and hints of honey and green freshness. Helps you to see the larger picture of any situation. Directly speaks to your heart, so you can discern this message from that of your mind.

Note: Heart

Seaweed Absolute (*Fucus vesiculosus*)

From the whole plant. Scent: pungent, green, earthy, salty, slightly woody and leathery, smells like being at the seaside. Message: "Through the magnificent seas of the Earth Mother, the great trees of the oceans offer you cleansing from what is old, obsolete, and of no service to you, purifying your body, mind, psyche, spirit and soul."

Note: Heart, Soul, Fixative

Tobacco Absolute (*Nicotiana tabacum*)

From the leaves. Scent: tenacious and deeply scented of pipe tobacco, rich, warm, smoky. Helps you to connect with the deeper aspects of yourself, to see clearly who you are. Takes you to profounder spiritual levels to support your dreams and desires.

Note: Soul

Tonka Bean Absolute (*Dipteryx odorata*)

From the dried beans (seeds). Scent: caramel sweetness, rich, slightly powdery, warm with a hint of tobacco. If you think you aren't worthy of the pleasures and joys of life – this introduces you to them without being overly sentimental. For those who are *very proud* of their accomplishments (both of mind and material things) it offers balance.

Note: Soul, Heart, Fixative

Tuberose Absolute (*Polianthes tuberosa*)

From the flowers. Scent: extensively rich sweet floral, which hangs around for a long time! In India, known as *Rat-ki-rani* "Mistress of the Night." Calms and soothes the emotions, stills raging passions, invites love, expands existing love … love of self, a beloved, or others. Very expansive and opening.

Note: Heart, Soul

Vanilla Absolute (*Vanilla planifolia*)

From the bean pods. Scent: deep, sweet, warm, and very rich. Love energy with very fluid and watery emotions. The magic of sexual arousal, loving sexual energy, and revitalization of a relationship. Produces increased bio-electrical energy.

Note: Soul, Fixative

Violet Leaf Absolute (*Viola odorata*)

From the leaves. Scent: unlike the sweet powdery perfumes or candies, offers crushed wet green leaves, a hushed woody-earthiness with a grassy depth. Helps dispel doubt and shrinking from your magnificence. Renewal with tenacity. The ability to hold the essence of who you are, and offer it to others as a gift. The simplest of pleasures offer a key to enjoyment of life.

Note: Heart Soul

Water Lily, Blue Absolute (*Nymphaea caerulea*)

From the flower. Often called a Lotus, actually a Lily, an incredible blue/purple with golden center. Scent: spicy undertones beneath a delicate soft watery floral, with a hint of powder. Message: About celestial connections. We all can feel this from time-to-time, some stronger than others. This oil is about rejuvenation, clairvoyance, healing, and balance, and deepening your meditations to light the spark of these connections.

Note: Heart

Resources

When you recover or discover something that nourishes your soul and brings joy, care enough about yourself to make room for it in your life.
– Jean Shinoda Bolen

Aromatherapy Today Magazine

PO Box 477
Elanora, Queensland 4221
Australia
Phone:+61 7 5534 5434
Fax:+61 7 5534 5434
Website: aromatherapytoday.com
Email: admin@aromatherapytoday.com
Letters to editor email: deby@aromatherapytoday.com
    International aromatherapy journal, lecture tours, and
    aromatherapy book publishers.

Aromatic Plant Project (APP)

219 Carl St.
San Francisco, CA 94117 USA
Phone: 415.564.6337
Website: JeanneRose.net
Website: Jeanne-blog.com
Website: aromaticplantproject.com
Email: info@JeanneRose.net
    Jeanne Rose is a well-known international authority on the
    therapeutic uses of herbs, essential oils, and hydrosols; author
    of 25 books; Instructor and Aromatherapy teacher. Ms. Rose
    publishes a monthly blog about essential oils (www.jeanne-
    blog.com); offers classes and perfumery workshops. The APP
    supports local and organic production of aromatic plants and
    provides resources for growers and distillers, to ensure high-
    quality aromatherapy products and to educate consumers as to
    the appropriate and beneficial uses of these aromatic products.

Artisan Parfums

226 West Ojai Ave. 101-420 (post/mail only)
Ojai, CA 93023 USA
Websites: ArtisanParfums.com & IxchelLeigh.com
Email: fragrancealkemist@gmail.com
Instagram: @IxchelLeigh

Ixchel Leigh is the founder of Artisan Parfums and Creator-Founder of *Vibrational Aroma Therapy by Ixchel™*. She is a purveyor of "ChakraSynergies," "ChakraSynergy Elixirs" and "Parfums with Purpose," available at select stores and on the above website.

For further information on educational possibilities for *Vibrational Aroma Therapy* or *AlcheMystical Parfumerie*, please go to ArtisanParfums.com, click on: "Academie" listed on the very bottom of the pages (in small print). Carol Corio is Education Director for *Vibrational Aroma Therapy by Ixchel™*. For inquiries to experience a bespoke *SoulParfum* by Ixchel, please contact Ixchel through the website. Find the heading "CustomScents" at the top of the page under the website name (ArtisanParfums).

Ixchel is available for guest speaking engagements, and educational inquiries. You can connect with her through website: ArtisanParfums.com.

Press Kit download available on IxchelLeigh.com.

Atlantic Institute of Aromatherapy

1618 Saddlestring Drive
Tampa, FL 33618 USA
Phone: 813.265.2222
Website: atlanticinstitute.com
Email: info@atlanticinstitute.com

Founded by Sylla Hanger in 1989, Nyssa Hanger has come on board to continue her Mission: Further education standards for all aspects of aromatherapy by providing a comprehensive resource for the professional or lay person interested in holistic aromatherapy.

College of Botanical Healing Arts, The

4170 Gross Road Ext Suite 5
Capitola, CA 95010
Phone: 831.462.1807; Fax: 831.462.9307
Website: cobha.org
Email: cobhasantacruz@gmail.com

> Founded by Elizabeth Jones (aka Elizabeth Van Buren), who is also the Director. The college is the first aromatherapy college in California to receive state approval and offers the first nationally approved 300-hour program in aromatherapy.

Eden Botanicals

3820 Cypress Drive #12
Petaluma, California 94954 USA
Phone: 1.707.509.0041; Toll free: 855.333.6645
Fax: 1.707.949.2526
Website: edenbotanicals.com

> Supplying premium quality essential oils, absolutes, CO_2 extracts, organic extracts, rare and precious. Retail and Professional prices. (See Orris Perfumery "Resource" listing for more information about the exclusive showroom and retail store in Los Angeles, showcasing Eden Botanicals products.)

Elizabeth Van Buren Aromatherapy

Phone: 1.800.710.7759; 831.425.8218
Website: ElizabethVanBuren.com
Email: sales@evb-aromatherapy.com

> Therapeutic-grade essential oils, blends, hydrosols, massage, carrier oils, lotions, skincare, and more. Every batch GC/MS analyzed on-site!

Fragrant Earth

5a The High Street
Glastonbury
Somerset, UK BA6 9DP
Head Office:
Unit 21 The Beckery
Glastonbury
Somerset, UK BA6 9NX
Phone: +44(0)1458 831216
Website: fragrantearth.com
Email: sales@fragrantearthint.com
> Founded by Jan Kusmirek. Offers professional aromatherapy, skin care, and life-style products. Includes pure essential oils, herbal oils, hydrolats, synergies, vegetable oils, bases. Jan Kusmirek is also available as a Consultant.

Peter Holmes LAc, MH

Snow Lotus Aromatherapy, Inc.

Snow Lotus Inc.
47 Foley St.
Santa Rosa, CA 95403 USA
Phone: 800.682.8827 or 707.546.3706 - Fax: 707.546.3851
Email: info@snowlotus.org
Website: snowlotus.org
> Founded by Peter Holmes Lac, MH. Aromatherapy, Education, Inspiration.Snow Lotus Aromatherapy specializes in sourcing genuine essential oils from organically grown or ethically wild-crafted plants from producers worldwide.

International Journal of Professional Holistic Aromatherapy, The (IJPHA)

528 Folklore Avenue
Longmont, CO 80504 USA
Website: ijpha.com
Email: editor@ijpha.com

Ixchel Leigh

226 West Ojai Ave. 101-420 (post/mail only)
Ojai, CA 93023 USA
Websites: ArtisanParfums.com & IxchelLeigh.com
Email: fragrancealkemist@gmail.com
> Instagram: @IxchelLeigh
> Ixchel Leigh is the founder of Artisan Parfums and Creator-Founder of *Vibrational Aroma Therapy by Ixchel*™. She is a purveyor of "ChakraSynergies," "ChakraSynergy Elixirs" and "Parfums with Purpose," available at select stores and on the above website.
>
> For further information on educational possibilities for *Vibrational Aroma Therapy* or *AlcheMystical Parfumerie*, please go to ArtisanParfums.com, click on: "Academie" listed on the very bottom of he pages (in small print). Carol Corio is Education Director for *Vibrational Aroma Therapy by Ixchel*™. For inquiries to experience a bespoke *SoulParfum* by Ixchel, please contact Ixchel through the website, or find the heading "CustomScents" at the top of the page under the website name (ArtisanParfums).
>
> Ixchel is available for guest speaking engagements, and educational inquiries. You can connect with her through the website: ArtisanParfums.com.
> Press Kit download available on IxchelLeigh.com.

Lotus Light Enterprises

P O Box 1008,
1212 Pryor Street,
Silver Lake, WI 53170 USA
Phone: 800 548 3824 (toll free order line),
Phone: 262 889 8501 (office phone)
Email:oshadhi@lotuspress.com
> Oshadhi products are imported in North America by Lotus Light Enterprises, Inc., a majority woman-owned, family business since 1981.

Krishna Madappa

7106 NDCBU
Taos, NM 87571 USA
Website: KrishnaMadappa.com
Email: essence@taosnet.com
> Krishna Maddappa is a shaman, Ayurvedic specialist, educator, essential oil clinician, researcher, and storyteller. Based in Taos, New Mexico, USA.

Christine Malcolm
Santa Fe Fragrances LLC
Ascent Aromatics

1874 Candela Street
Sante Fe, NM 87505 USA
Phone: 505-231-6713
Website: santafebotanicalfragrances.com
Email: info@santafefragrance.com
Store: www.etsy.com/shop/ScentualJourney
> Botanical fragrance development; Wholesale bulk manufacturing; Retail and wholesale: Essential Oils, TherArome bath & diffusor, essential oil blends, Perfumes, and Colognes.

Miron Glass (aka Violet Glass) USA

US Offices: 1248 N. Mariposa ave.
Los Angeles, CA 90029 USA
Phone: 323.467.0558
Website: miron-glass.com
Email: Michael@mironglassusa.com
> Suppliers of VioletGlass, the black amethyst glass bottles that alchemically protect and enhance anything in them. Bulk supplies only. Wholesale. Michael Sopkiw is Director of Sales.

Gabriel Mojay

The Institute of Traditional Herbal Medicine and Aromatherapy

3 Green Farm Barns,
Thursford Road,
Little Snoring,
Fakenham NR2 0JW England
Phone: (011 44) (0) 020 7193 7383
Email: info@aromatherapy-studies.com
Website: aromatherapy-studies.com

> Gabriel Mojay is the Founding Principal The Institute of Traditional Herbal Medicine and Aromatherapy (ITHMA Ltd), Founding Co-Chair of the International Federation of Professional Aromatherapists (IFPA), author of *Aromatherapy for Healing the Spirit*. Gabriel is an experienced Aromatherapy teacher, a leading authority on the application of Oriental Medicine to Aromatherapy, and teaches extensively in both the UK and abroad. The ITHMA offers courses and seminars, in the UK and US, on Aromatherapy and Energy Medicine.

National Association for Holistic Aromatherapy (NAHA)

Website: naha.org

> A US educational, nonprofit membership organization dedicated to the benefits of true aromatherapy. NAHA is actively involved with promoting and elevating academic standards in aromatherapy education and practice for the professional aromatherapist and with furthering the public perception and knowledge of true aromatherapy and its safe and effective application in everyday life.

Oshadhi Essential Oils

Dr. Malte Hozzel

AYUS GmbH

Oshadhi Essential Oils

As a naturalist, since 1971, internationally-recognized aromatherapy "nose," and creator of Oshadhi, Dr. Malte Hozzel has assembled a global network of farmers and distillers devoted to providing the purest, therapeutic quality, and vibrationally-conscious essential oils. AYUS GmbH with its Oshadhi collection was founded in Germany in 1990 and offers more than 450 essential oils and absolutes, as well as numerous skin care products, mostly derived from wild-grown plants or certified organic cultivation, many from rare subspecies and selected varieties of medicinal plants. www.oshadhi-essential-oils/distributors: Oshadhi's international distributors.

www.oshadhiusa.com: Oshadhi products are imported in North America (USA) by Lotus Light Enterprises, Inc. (since 1981). See separate listing.

www.oshadhiseminars.com: Oshadhi Aromatherapy Seminar Center is located at Orto de Prouvenço in Provence, France.

Pacific Institute of Aromatherapy

P.O. Box 6723
San Rafael, CA 94903 USA
Phone: 415.479.9120; Fax: 415.479.0614
Website: pacificinstituteofaromatherapy.com
Email: info@pacificinstituteofaromatherapy.com
> Founded by Kurt Schnaubelt, Ph.D. in 1983, joined by
> Monika Haas in 1988, and Julien Juillerat in 2012. A leader in
> educational and certification courses in aromatherapy since the
> 1980's.

Paperbark (Oils) Co.

Phone: +(8) 9385 1541
Website: paperbarkoils.com.au
Email: info@paperbarkoils.com.au
> Specializes in growing and distilling Western Australia
> Essential Oils since 1997. Focused on Fragonia™, Australian
> Sandalwood, Honey Myrtle Oils.

Perfumer's Apprentice

170 Technology Circle,
Scotts Valley, CA 95066
831-316-7137
Email: admin@perfumersapprentice.com
Website: https://shop.perfumersapprenctice.com/c-235-lifetree-
aromatix-by-john-steele.aspx
Website: perfumerapprentice.com
> Perfumer's Apprentice is a supplier of raw aromatic and flavor
> materials including pure and natural essential oils, absolutes,
> isolates, fragrance oils, aroma chemicals and specialty blends.
> Proud to offer the exquisite oils of John Steele.

Prima Fleur Botanicals, Inc.

84 Galli Dr.
Novato, California 94949
Phone: 415.455.0957
Fax: 415.455.0956
Website: primafleur.com
Email: sales@primafleur.com

> Founded by Marianne Griffith, over two decades ago. Provides essential oils, product development and manufacturing of personal care products. Wholesale.

Carol Corio

Quality of Life Associates (QLA)

Email: carolQLA@comcast.net

> Carol Corio started Quality of Life Associates in 1989 has represented Oshadhi essential oils and *Vibrational Aromatherapy by Ixchel*™ products and trainings, manufactured clay diffusers, publishes aromatherapy educational programs/booklets, and creates and teaches energy awareness courses. Carol Corio is Education Director for *Vibrational AromaTherapy by Ixchel*™. Contact Ixchel for information about education and training classes.

Kurt Schnaubelt, Ph.D

Original Swiss Aromatics

P.O. Box 6842
San Rafael, CA 94903 USA
Phone: 415.479.9120; Fax: 415.479.0614
Website: originalswissaromatics.com

> Founded by Kurt Schnaubelt, Ph.D., who is also an author of aromatherapy books and a contributing writer to aromatherapy journals. Original Swiss Aromatics offers a wide selection of organic and wild-crafted essential oils and other personal care products. Also see: Pacific Institute of Aromatherapy (Dr. Schnaubelt's educational programs).

John J. Steele

Lifetree Aromatix

3949 Longridge Avenue
Sherman Oaks, CA 91423
Phone: 818-986-0594

> John J. Steele is an aromatic consultant, archaeologist, author and thinker. His work, whether with aromas or philosophy, engages questions about the nature of memory, time, consciousness and being. As an aromatic consultant and skilled distiller of essential oils, John keeps a low profile. Steele's fragrance company, Lifetree Aromatix, is based in Sherman Oaks, California. and while Lifetree does not have its own website, the company's products are available from several online retailers, such as Perfumer's Apprentice.

Robert Tisserand

Tisserand Institute

Website: Tisserandinstitute.org
Email: hello@tisserandinstitute.org

> Founded by Robert Tisserand. Evidence-based essential oils education. The Institute offers online courses and workshops. Seeks experts in various aspects of aromatherapy to provide up to date and practical information. We aim to empower with knowledge, so that you can make your own informed decisions with confidence.

Vibrational AromaTherapy by Ixchel™

226 West Ojai Ave. 101-420 (post/mail only)
Ojai, CA 93023 USA
Websites: ArtisanParfums.com & IxchelLeigh.com
Email: fragrancealkemist@gmail.com
Instagram: @IxchelLeigh

Ixchel Leigh is the founder of Artisan Parfums and Creator-Founder of *Vibrational AromaTherapy by Ixchel™*. She is a purveyor of "ChakraSynergies," "ChakraSynergy Elixirs" and "Parfums with Purpose," available at select stores and on the above website.

For further information on educational possibilities for *Vibrational AromaTherapy* or *AlcheMystical Parfumerie*, please go to ArtisanParfums.com, click on: "Academie" listed on the very bottom of he pages (in small print). Carol Corio is Education Director for *Vibrational AromaTherapy by Ixchel™*. Contact Ixchel for information about education and training classes.

For inquiries to experience a bespoke *SoulParfum* by Ixchel, please contact Ixchel through the website. Find the heading "CustomScents" at the top of the page under the website name (ArtisanParfums).

Ixchel is available for guest speaking engagements, and educational inquiries. You can connect with her through website: ArtisanParfums.com.

Press Kit download available on IxchelLeigh.com.

White Lotus Aromatics

332 Carriage Dr.
Sequim, WA 98382 USA
Phone: 360.683.0137 - FAX:360.683.5550
Website: WhiteLotusAromatics.com
Email: chris@wlaromas.com

> Founded by Christopher McMahon. Suzanne and Christopher handle White Lotus Aromatics, a wholesaler of essential oils, absolutes, CO_2 extracts, ruhs, attars, and natural blends.

Uncommon Scents – Movie

Directors/Executive Producers: Kristina Bauer & Angela Ehmke
Phone: 208-304-6054
Email: info@uncommonscentsmovie.com
Website: uncommonscentsmovie.com

> An aromatherapy documentary, Uncommon Scents explores the breadth and depth of what aromatherapy is, what it offers, who is using it, how it works, who it's helping, and why it matters. It is an independent documentary informed by leaders in the field and grounded in defensible facts. Ixchel Leigh is one of the interviewees/participants of the film. Shortlink to our participants' page: http://bit.ly/USparticipants

Suggested Reading

Subtle & Esoteric Aromatherapy

Cunningham, Scott, *Magical Aromatherapy*. St. Paul, MN: Llewellyn Publications, 1989.

Damian, Peter and Kate, *Aromatherapy Scent and Psyche*. Rochester, VT: Healing Arts Press, 1995.

Davis, Patricia, *Subtle Aromatherapy*. Saffron Walden (Essex, England): C.W. Daniel Company Ltd., 1991.

Loughran, Joni Keim and Bull, Ruah, *Aromatherapy and Subtle Energy Techniques*. Berkeley, CA: Frog, Ltd., 2000.

Loughran, Joni Keim and Bull, Ruah, *Aromatherapy Anointing Oils*. Berkeley, CA: Frog, Ltd., 2001.

Aromatherapy, Essential Oils & the Plant Kingdom

Avery, Alexandra, *Aromatherapy and You, A Guide to Natural Skincare*. Birkenfeld, OR: Blue Heron Press, 1992.

Arvigo, Rosita, *Sastun*. San Francisco, CA: HarperCollins Publishers, 1994.

Buhner, Stephen Harrod, *Sacred Plant Medicine*. Boulder, CO: Roberts Rinehart Publishers, 1996.

Catty, Suzanne, *Hydrosols: The Next Aromatherapy*. Rochester, VT: Healing Arts Press, 2001.

Cowan, Eliot, *Plant Spirit Medicine*. Newberg, OR: Swan-Raven & Co, 1995.

Culpepper, Nicholas, *Culpepper's Complete Herbal*. England: 1652. Reprint, W. Foulsham & Co. Ltd.

Culpepper, Nicholas, *Culpepper's Herbal Remedies*. North Hollywood, CA: Melvin Powers Wilshire Book Co., 1971

Cunningham, Scott, *Encyclopedia of Magical Herbs*. St. Paul, MN: Llewellyn Publications, 1996.

Cunningham, Scott, *Magical Aromatherapy*. St. Paul, MN: Llewellyn Publications, 1989.

Damian, Peter and Kate, *Aromatherapy Scent and Psyche*. Rochester, VT: Healing Arts Press, 1995.

Davis, Patricia, *Aromatherapy an A–Z*. Saffron Walden (Essex, England): C.W. Daniel Co. Ltd., 1988.

Davis, Patricia, *Subtle Aromatherapy*. Saffron Walden (Essex, England): C.W. Daniel Company Ltd., 1991.

Doane, Nancy Locke, *Indian Doctor Book*. Privately published; Distributed by Aerial Photography Services, Inc., Charlotte, NC. (no date)

Greer, Mary K., *The Essence of Magic*. North Hollywood, CA: Newcastle Publishing, 1993.

Gurudas, *Flower Essences and Vibrational Healing*. Albuquerque, NM: Brotherhood of Life, 1983.

Heline, Corinne, *Magic Gardens*. Santa Monica, CA: New Age Bible & Philosophy Center, 1987.

Junemann, Monika, *Enchanting Scents*. Wilmot, WI: Lotus Light Pub., 1988.

Lavabre, Marcel, *The Handbook of Aromatherapy*. Culver City, CA: Privately published, 1986. (Revised edition now published as: *Aromatherapy Workbook*. Rochester, VT: Healing Arts Press, 1990.)

Lawless, Julia, *The Illustrated Encyclopedia of Essential Oils*. New York, NY: Element Books/Barnes & Noble, Inc., 1995.

Leigh, Ixchel, *Vibrational AromaTherapy Manual*. Dedham, MA: Quality of Life Associates, 1997.

Maury, Marguerite, *Marguerite Maury's Guide to Aromatherapy, The Secret of Life and Youth*. Saffron Walden (Essex, England): C.W. Daniel Co. Ltd, 1989.

Mojay, Gabriel, *Aromatherapy for Healing the Spirit*. New York, NY: Henry Holt and Co., Inc., 1996.

Prince, Menkit, *The Essential Oil Cookbook*. Carmichael, CA: Earth Love Enterprises, 1998.

Rain, Mary Summer, *Earthway*. New York, NY: Simon & Schuster Inc., 1990.

Reader's Digest, *Magic and Medicine of Plants*. Pleasantville, NY, 1986.

Rose, Jeanne, *The Aromatherapy Book*. Berkeley, CA: North Atlantic Books, 1992.

Rose, Jeanne, *Jeanne Rose's Modern Herbal*. New York, NY: Putnam Publishing Group, 1987.

Rose, Jeanne, *375 Essential Oils and Hydrosols*. Berkeley, CA: Frog Ltd/Vision, 1999.

Tisserand, Robert, *Aromatherapy for Everyone*. London, England: Penguin Books, 1988.

Tisserand, Robert, *The Art of Aromatherapy*. Saffron Walden (Essex, England): C.W. Daniel Co. Ltd., 1979.

Tisserand, Robert, *The Essential Oil Safety Data Manual*, Brighton, Sussex, England: Privately published, 1985.

Tisserand, Robert and Young, Rodney, *Essential Oil Safety, A Guide for Health Care Professional, 2nd Edition*, London, UK: Churchill Livingstone, 2014.

Tompkins, Peter, *The Secret Life of Plants*. New York, NY: Harper and Row, 1973.

Tompkins, Peter, *The Secret Life of Nature*. San Francisco, CA: HarperCollins, 1997.

The World of Aromatherapy, An Anthology of Aromatic History, Ideas, Concepts and Case Histories, by the NAHA Women of Aromatherapy. Berkeley, CA: Frog, Ltd, 1996.

Webb, Mark A., *Bush Sense; Australian Essential Oils and Aromatic Compounds*. Adelaide, Australia: Griffin Press, 2000.

Gems, Stones and Minerals

Cayce, Edgar, Edgar Cayce on the Power of Color, Stones, and Crystals. New York, NY: Warner Books, Inc., 1989.

Cunningham, Scott, Cunningham's Encyclopedia of Crystal, Gem & Metal Magic. St. Paul, MN: Llewellyn Pub., 1988.

Kunz, George Frederick, The Curious Lore Of Precious Stones. Philadelphia, PA: Lippincott Co., 1913.

Lorusso, Julia and Glick, Joel, *"Healing Stoned" The Therapeutic Use of Gems and Minerals*. Albuquerque, NM: Brotherhood of Life, 1976.

Melody, *Love is in the Earth, A Kaleidoscope of Crystals*. Wheat Ridge, CO: Earth-Love Publishing House, 1995.

Raphael, Katrina, *Crystal Enlightenment*. New York, NY: Aurora Press, 1985.

Richardson, Wally and Jenny and Huett, Lenora, *Spiritual Value of Gem Stones*. Marina del Rey, CA: DeVorss & Co., Publishers, 1980.

Stein, Diane, *Flower and Gemstone Essences*. Freedom, CA: The Crossing Press, 1996.

Gurudas, Gem Elixirs and Vibrational Healing, Vol. 1. Boulder, CO: Cassandra Press, 1985.

Color, Sound, Numbers & Energy Medicine

Anderson, Mary, *Colour Healing*. New York, NY: Samuel Weiser Inc., 1975.

Andrews, Ted, *How to Heal with Color*. St. Paul, MN: Llewellyn Publications, 1992.

Andrews, Ted, *The Healer's Manual*. St. Paul, MN: Llewellyn Publications, 1993.

Barrat, Rodford, *The Elements of Numerology*. Shaftesbury, Dorset (UK): Element Books Ltd, 1994.

Dinshah, Darius, *The Spectro-Chrome System*. Malaga, NJ: Dinshah Health Society, 1978.

Gerber, Richard, *Vibrational Medicine*. Santa Fe, NM: Bear & Co., 1998.

Hay, Louise, *Colors & Numbers 1996*. Carson, CA: Hay House, Inc., 1996 {Some information on Color and Foods was taken from a seminar given by Louise Hay in Santa Monica, CA in 1982 and attended by Ixchel Leigh.}

Heline, Corinne, *Color and Music in The New Age*. Marina del Rey, CA: DeVorss and Co., Publishers, 1964.

Irion, J. Everett, *Vibrations*. Virginia Beach, VA: A.R.E. Press, 1979.

Ouseley, S. G. J., *Colour Meditations*. London, England: L. N. Fowler & Co. Ltd., 1949.

Ouseley, S. G. J., *The Power of the Rays*. London, England: L. N. Fowler & Co. Ltd., 1951.

Stein, Diane, *The Women's Book of Healing*. St. Paul, MN: Llewellyn Publications, 1987.

You Are A Rainbow, Original insights into the work of Christopher Hills by researchers practicing his theory of Nuclear Evolution. Norah Hills, Editor. Boulder Creek, CA: University of the Trees Press, 1979.

Perfumery

Ackerman, Diane, *A Natural History of the Senses*. New York, NY: Random House, 1990

Ellena, Jean-Claude, *Perfume- The Alchemy of Scent*. New York, NY: Arcade Publishing 2016

Gilbert, Karen, *Perfume -The Art & Craft of Fragrance*. London, UK: CICO Books, 2017

Morris, Edwin T., *Fragrance-The Story of Perfume from Cleopatra to Chanel*. New Yoor, NY: E.T. Morris & Co., 1984

Nostradamus, Edited by Knut Boeser, *The Elixirs of Nostradamus*. London, UK: Moyer Bell, 1996

St. John Foster, *The Secret Language of Perfume*. London, UK: Aquarian, An Imprint of Harper Collins, 1994.

Worwood, Valerie Ann, *Aromantics*. London, UK: Pan Books Ltd., 1987.

Alchemy, Chakras, Auras, Inspirational, Indigenous, Myth, Goddess, and Philosophy

Albertus, Frater, *Alchemist's Handbook*. York Beach, ME: Samuel Weiser, Inc., 1974.

Arrien, Angeles, *Signs of Life: The Five Universal Shapes and How to Use Them*. New York, NY: Jeremy P. Tarcher/ Putnam, 1998.

Austen, Hallie Iglehart, *The Heart of the Goddess*. Berkeley, CA: Wingbow Press, 1990.

Beasley Ph.D., Victor, *Intuition by Design*. Livermore, CA: Oughten House Publications, 1995.

Barks, Coleman, *RUMI, We Are Three*. Coleman Barks, 1987.

Bulfinch, Thomas, *Bulfinch's Mythology*. New York, NY: The Modern Library, 1796-1867.

Bradley, Marion Zimmer, *The Mists of Avalon*. New York, NY: Ballantine Books, 1982.

Bruyere, Rosalyn L., *Wheels of Light*. New York, NY: Simon & Schuster Inc, 1989.

Campbell, Joseph, *Oriental Mythology, The Masks of God*. New York, NY: Penguin Group, 1962.

Cheney, Margaret, *Tesla: Man Out of Time*. New York, NY: Dell Publishing/Bantam Double Day, 1981.

Choquette Ph.D., Sonia, The Wise Child; A Spiritual Guide to Nurturing Your Child's Intuition. New York, NY: Three Rivers Press, 1999.

Conway, D. J., *Celtic Magic*. St. Paul, MN: Llewellyn Publications, 1997.

Cotterell, Arthur, *A Dictionary of World Mythology*. Oxford, UK: Oxford University Press, 1986.

Cunningham, Scott, *Earth, Air, Fire & Water*. St. Paul, MN: Llewellyn Publications, 1991.

Davidson, H R Ellis, *Scandinavian Mythology*. London, UK: Paul Famlyn, 1969.

Eliot, Alexander, *Myths*. Maidenhead, England: McGraw-Hill Book, 1976.

Garland, Linda and Roger and Suckling, Nigel, *SHE, The Book of the Goddess*. Cornwall, UK: Lakeside Gallery, 1998.

Gibran, Kahil, *Broken Wings*. New York, NY: Citadel Press, 1957.

Gilchrist, Cherry, *The Elements of Alchemy*. Shaftesbury, Dorset, UK: Element Books Limited, 1991.

Gyatso, Tenzin, The Fourteenth Dalai Lama, *Kindness, Clarity, and Insight*. Ithaca, NY: Snow Lion Publications, 1984.

Gendler, J. Ruth, *The Book of Qualities*. Berkeley, CA: Turquoise Mountain Publications, 1984.

Hamilton, Edith, *Mythology*. Boston, MA: Little, Brown & Co., 1942.

Ions, Veronica, *Indian Mythology*. New York, NY: Peter Bedrick Books, 1983.

Ives, Steve, *I Am, The Power of Words and Suggestion*. San Anselmo, CA: Publishing to Encourage, 1998. (This is a wonderful "divination book" that can be used daily for meditations.)

Krishnamurti, J., *Life in Freedom*. Eerde, Ommen, Holland: The Star Publishing Trust, 1928.

Lee, Scout Cloud, *The Circle is Sacred, A Medicine Book for Women*. Tulsa, OK: Council Oak Books, 1995.

Meadows, Kenneth, *Earth Medicine*. Shaftesbury, Dorset, UK: Element Books, 1989.

Glossary

Absolute: Divine, Divine Source, Great Spirit, God, Allah, Infinite Source.

Absolute(s): In Perfumery, absolutes are an essence that is solvent extracted and diluted with alcohol to make it easier to use in composing fragrances.

Accord: In perfumery composition, two or more scented ingredients, expertly blended together so that the composition of the two (or more) smells is different than each individual scent.

AlkemicalElements: A concept created by Ixchel, the Elements that are contained in each of us and hold the promise of transformation towards personal evolution. The Body is as the Earth; the Heart is as the Water; the Mind is as the Air; the Spirit is as Fire; and the Soul is as Aether.

alchemy: The study of related and unrelated materials and how they interact and connect together with the intention of bringing about changes that creates a more perfected form and with aspirations of seeking knowledge of creation and universal order.

alchemystical and AlcheMystical: The combination of the principles of alchemy and mysticism. The philosophy of the human desire to blend the physical and spiritual worlds together for the overall growth, transformation, and wellbeing of humanity.

AlcheMystical Parfum and AlcheMystical Parfumerie: To compose a fragrance that is focused on raising overall vibrations in our world, through raising the energetic and vibrational aspects of the individual.

AlkemicalFragrance: (aka Soul Parfum, *SoulParfum*). A signature fragrance for a moment in time (created by Ixchel Leigh, for an individual(s) or a group, and referenced in the original (2001) Aromatic Alchemy book.) In this New Edition (2020) of Aromatic Alchemy, "AlkemicalFragrance" has changed its name to: "Soul Parfum" and is described at length in PART SIX: *AlcheMystical Aromatics*. Employs the principles and blending techniques for *AlcheMystical Parfumerie*.

animalic: Having a scent that is slightly like Pan, the god of the forests, who was part man and part goat. Collins English Dictionary: "a harmonious fusion of rich and resinous aromas, the cumulative effect of which is warm, sensuous and animalic."

archetype: The repetition throughout different cultures of apparent similar symbols, myths, or types, which create a prototype, thus creating what can be termed an ideal example of a type (as in a feminine or masculine archetype).

aromatherapy: The art and science of using pure essential oils (not synthetics) to promote well-being of the body, mind and spirit.

Aromatic Alchemy: Awakening your deepest inner dreams through your inner voice with assistance from Nature's Gifts. (Ixchel Leigh used this term for the first edition of her book, *Aromatic Alchemy – Recipes for Transformation*, in 2001.)

Astral Body: Considered the second layer of the four primary auric fields of energy, it is known as the 9th ChakraAura, relates to our emotional body and the subconscious, and is the "home" to your Soul.

at home self-healing: Allows the client, or yourself, to take personal responsibility for self-healing by continuing some form of meditation and healing at home.

attars: a perfume made from a botanical (like roses) that usually contains some residue of solvents.

aura: The energy fields that surround the body and act as a filter and guide to the physical.

auric field: The numerous fields of energy that surround the body.

Aumakua: A word that comes to us from the Hawaiian kahunas, or shamans. The "Soul Self."

balance: Physical, mental or emotional steadiness or equilibrium and return to the ideal state of well-being.

Base Note: See: Soul Note.

beauty space: A special place where you place objects of symbolic importance that are reminiscent of the pleasurable aspects of all life. Also referred to as an altar.

Bodhisattva: One who is the essence of enlightenment and compassionately chooses to be in physical form to assist others.

Causal Body: Considered the fourth layer of the four primary auric fields of energy (not included in ChakraAuras). Is about the integration of intuition and inspiration and their relationship to the superconscious, where the energy of the Soul exists.

chakra: A Sanskrit word meaning Wheel of Light and Time. The name given to the seven major energy centers in the human body.

ChakraAura: A concept created by Ixchel Leigh for use in Vibrational AromaTherapy, it refers to all of the energy centers within the human body or surrounding it.

ChakraSpritz: A concept created by Ixchel Leigh for use in *Vibrational AromaTherapy,* a vibrationally effective aromatherapy mist in an atomizer spray bottle that is created with distilled water, fractionated coconut oil, and the appropriate vibrational dosage of ChakraSynergy Elixirs or pure essential oil. Recommended for balancing ChakraAuras and clearing and preparing your healing space.

ChakraSynergy: Created by Ixchel Leigh for *Vibrational AromaTherapy.* A composition of several true, vibrationally-conscious essential oils, the alchemical combinations of energetic and vibrational properties create a synergy suitable for transformational use. All created personally by Ixchel with "conscious intent." Alchemically promotes wellbeing and balance for the ChakraAuras (chakras and auras) and entire wellbeing.

ChakraSynergy Elixirs: The same pure therapeutic-grade essential oils used in the ChakraSynergies (as above), blended into organic jojoba and sunflower oil, and ready to be used by anyone (even without previous essential oil training or knowledge) to benefit their wellbeing.

chemotype: Plants from the same species and genus – they look alike, however the chemical constituents of the essential oil change due to fluctuating growing conditions.

CO₂ Extract: Botanical essences extracted using carbon gas under pressure (no petrochemicals used).

cohobation: In alchemy (or pre-modern chemistry), the process of repeated distillation of the same botanical raw material. The liquid is drawn from it, then poured over the material again, and again, and finally collecting the scented essence from the raw material.

cold pressed: The process used to collect the scented essence from the peel of citrus fruits, by pressing the skins to collect the essential oil.

concretes: In perfumery, a semi-solid substance obtained by solvent extraction from the fresh plant material, used as a scented raw material.

Creation Myths: Different cultures have their individual stories about how the world was created and how humanity was created.

Creative Intellect: To create something using a group of skills that first utilize the power to generate the idea, then analyze, imagine, and employ deductive reasoning to finally assume the final product.

Creatrix: A female who brings forth or produces, ie: creator, author, founder.

Creative Renewal JourneyQuest Retreats: Retreats are offered in the US and UK. In the US, the retreat is held on ancient Indian lands in Southwestern Colorado near Mesa Verde. Guided by Ixchel, it is an opportunity to work directly with her to learn to develop your intuitive capabilities on a deeper level. The 7-Day JourneyQuest focuses on learning to create VibrationalSynergies, for those who are seeking certification and registration as a Vibrational AromaTherapy Teachers. The 4-Day JourneyQuest is for anyone and focuses on personal transformation, developing intuition, and enhancing creativity. Also called 7-Day JourneyQuest and 4-Day JourneyQuest.

conscious intent: A focused method of thinking used for transformational goals. Often used in creating aromatherapy blends, products, or preparations that truly have alchemical properties. Alchemical products have enhanced positive, therapeutic, and wellness qualities created by the "intent" combined with the ingredients.

conscious: The identified and intentional awareness of your existence and its purpose and reason for being. Cognizant.

consciousness: The state of having the awareness of your existence and purpose for being.

chromotherapy: Color healing science.

Destiny Number: Your Destiny Number, in this lifetime, refers to the energy around how you, the individual, express yourself in the world overall with insights into who you are becoming. Your Destiny Number is also your current life path or what fate has brought your way. Based on the numerology of your birth date.

Directions, The: Referred to as cosmic intelligences that affect all living creatures including the environment and the atmosphere of the Earth Mother. Includes east, south, west, north, above, below, center.

Divine aka Divine Source, Divine Spiritual Source: God, Infinite Source, Creator, Great Spirit, Allah, etc.

Divine Creative Essence: The feminine archetype essence of God.

Divine Life Essence: The masculine archetype essence of God.

Divine Light: The Soul of God or Great Spirit, symbolized by white light.

Divine Will: The will of God.

dowsing: The process of using a pendulum or other similar divining rod to determine answers to questions.

dry down: In perfumery (or describing the scent in aromatherapy), the aroma that is left after a few days when it has dried and only the odor remains.

dry distillation: A process used primarily in India to extract the scent from raw materials like seashells and amber resin.

egret: a water bird like a heron, usually with all white plumage.

Earth Mother: The planet we inhabit, a sentient being, holding the energy of the creative feminine force; same as: earth.

Elements, The: Considered the energies of the Earth and associated with the creative energies of the universe. Includes the Western – Earth, Water, Air, Fire, and Aether; the Oriental – Earth, Water, Wood, Fire, and Metal.

energy centers: The chakras and auras, or driving forces for activity and thought. They hold vital life forces and act to transmit and assimilate energy and information for the human body and spirit.

energy work: Any number of modalities of healing which focuses on helping to restore an individual's inner balance and total well-being. Energy work is subtle and non-invasive.

energy healing: Uses your focused intention for healing and transformational growth, and can incorporate vibrational medicines as healing tools.

Enlightened Being: One who has achieved the final blessed state of awareness, free from desire and suffering.

Essence of Life Realms: In *Vibrational Aroma Therapy*, one word that describes each ChakraSynergy (as its name) and also the area of an individual's life that is affected by any of Nature's Vibrational Medicines (ie: essential oils, colors, shapes, etc.)

Essence Self: In *Vibrational Aroma Therapy* a term used to describe the individual who has "married" their masculine and feminine archetypes within themselves, in order to create a new expression of themselves; their optimum self, their perfected form, the valuable gold.

essential oils: The extracted essence from botanicals, consisting of transformed solar energy. Perceived as scent from the plant matter. The botanicals are usually collected early in the morning, just before sunrise.

Etheric Body: Considered the first layer of the four primary auric fields of energy, it is known as the 8th ChakraAura, relates to the sensations of the physical body, is the densest of all the auras, and helps to generate the electromagnetic energy and vitality for the physical body.

Evil-eye: Believed to be a curse generated by jealousy, from someone who wants something you have, usually directed towards you when you are unaware. In many cultures, it is believed to cause misfortune or injury. Some cultures have an object created to protect against the "evil-eye," which often looks like a blue eye, with a black pupil, in a white eye socket.

focus: Specifically directed attention.

focused intention: Specifically directed attention for a desired goal.

focused session: Specifically directed attention to bring about healing and well-being.

fractionated coconut oil: coconut oil that has been processed or "fractioned" so to create a shelf-stable oil; great as a carrier for essential oils.

Gaia: Another name for the Earth Mother.

God: Supreme Being; Divine Source; Great Spirit; Divine.

god: A male diety or dieties.

Goddess: A female deity

Head Note aka Top Note: The first odors you smell in a fragrance, usually lighter scents like citruses that disappear quickly.

healing: Bringing the quality of health and well-being to Body,

Heart, Mind, Spirit, and Soul.

healing arts practitioners: someone who practices any form of alternative or complementary modalities used for the benefit and wellbeing of an individual.

healing tools: Any of Nature's Gifts – essential oils, stones, shapes, color, sound, etc., that are used to facilitate healing and transformational growth.

Heart Note aka Middle Note: Quite often the odors from heart note (middle note) flowers appear after the head notes (top notes) and form the central basis of the composition of a fragrance.

Herstory: History from the perspective of the feminine, the Goddess.

homeostasis: A relatively stable state of equilibrium created by the different combined elements in a preparation or treatment.

humanity: Hu is derived from a Sufi word meaning Spirit; manity refers to mankind, the beings which inhabit the Earth Mother. (The spiritual beings that inhabit the Earth Mother.)

hundredth monkey theory: As one or more are gathered with the same thought, that thought is expanded to others, eventually influencing all.

hydrodistillation: A variant of steam distillation normally used to collect essential oils from plant materials, in which the material is soaked first before the heated water/steam passes through the raw material, to ultimately collect the scented essence.

individuation: Recognizing and acknowledging you as an individual, and then integrating that You into the whole of society and finding your place and contribution.

intuition: A method of perceiving information independent of any reasoning process and often described as an inner knowing or gut feeling.

jojoba: From a botanical indigenous to the American Southwest, used for a carrier. It is actually a wax when in warm weather is liquid.

Kala Chakra: Wheel of Light and Time in Sanskrit, refers to the energy centers called chakras.

kinesiology: A method of accessing information through the human body anatomy. Also referred to as muscle testing.

Life's Work Number: This number is the combination of your Soul's Path Number and your Destiny Number and gives you insights into how you might express yourself in your work in the world.

Light Body: The human Spirit.

mass consciousness: As one or more are gathered with the same thought, that thought is expanded to others, eventually influencing all.

medicine: A stimulus, or remedy, found in Nature that directly influences the activity of a living organism or part of that organism. It has a positive effect on wellbeing.

Medicine Wheel: A teaching and healing tool used by Native American cultures that incorporates the Directions. It can hold within it messages of balance, information for self-awareness, and deeper connections and attunement with the natural world.

meditation: A passive act or ritual performed to clear the mind of chatter.

Melange: A blend of several different odors to create a fragrance.

Melody: Ixchel Leigh's terminology for combining several different types of the same aroma, but from different countries and/or different growing practices. (Like: A Melody of Frankincense.)

Mental Body: Considered the third layer of the four primary auric fields of energy (not referred to in *Vibrational Aroma Therapy*). Guides our mind and intellect, our mental abilities, thoughts, and the conscious mind in action.

metaphysics: From the Greek, meaning *after the things of nature*. Recognizes that there is a world beyond what can be perceived on the physical plane, that all is composed of energy, and that every individual has both a physical and a non-physical body. Acknowledges the unseen realities of our universe.

metaphysician: A person who honors the principles of metaphysics, seeks to explore and discover ways of perceiving unseen realities, and uses these principles in their life and/or work.

metempsychosis: Patterns that reoccur in our universe.

Middle Note: See: Heart Note.

Moon Phases: There are eight different 3 ½ day phases of the Moon in a 28-day period and 13 sets of complete phases in a single year, with each phase representing a different type of energy.

mysticism: Refers to the attainment of insight in ultimate or hidden truths and to human transformation supported by various practices and experiences. Also, the belief that direct knowledge of the Creator (Divine Source, God) or of spiritual truth and ultimate reality can be attained through subjective experience, via intuition or insight.

myths: Traditional or legendary stories that involve gods, goddesses, heroines, and heroes, to explain a cultural practice, natural object, or phenomenon.

nature: The creative force in the universe. Also refers to that which can be found or grows on the Earth Mother and was not created in a laboratory.

Nature's Gifts: Refers to Nature's Vibrational Medicines, see definition below.

Nature Herself: The expressly feminine aspect of the creative force in the universe and the aspect that gives birth to what is found in nature.

Nature's Vibrational Medicines: A concept created by Ixchel Leigh, refers to various stimuli found indigenously in nature. Through their individual essence and energy, they have the ability to effect change. Some of Nature's Vibrational Medicines are essential oils, gemstones, color, shapes, the elements, numbers, the directions, sound and myths.

Net of Light: As explained by Ixchel, an energetic net of light consciously created by humans holding a common goal to seek enlightenment. This Net of Light energetically supports our Earth Mother.

new self: After the "marriage" of your masculine and feminine energies, that occurs during the transmuting process of becoming your optimum self (the child of the Sacred Marriage), you grow to becomes the Essence Self.

numerology: The mystical and mathematical significance of numbers.

Original Creation: The first thought by God who set into motion the creation of all things.

Original Source, Original Divine Source: God, the Divine Creator in the universe.

Ouroboros: From old alchemical texts, dating back to ancient Egypt, a symbol (in the form of a circle) of a snake consuming its tail. It represents the ability for an individual to perfect itself through physical transmutation and spiritual transcendence, with a focus towards eternal unity.

Parfumerie: French for perfumery, the art of making scents; a store or place where scents/fragrances are sold.

Parfumeur: French for perfumer, a person who composes scents.

pendulum: Used in dowsing to determine the yes or no answers to questions. It is a string or chain with a weighted object on it that swings back and forth, or in circular motions, from a rested position.

PEO: Pure Essential Oil.

physics: The study of related and unrelated materials, matter and energy, and how they interact and *are* connected together, with a purpose to discover the true laws of nature in order to create a more perfected form and with aspirations of seeking knowledge of natural phenomena.

prayer: An active act or ritual performed to effect change.

Primordial Mother Goddess(es): A diety thought to be responsible for creation.

prima materia: From alchemy, the original substance; also the individual.

pueblo: A stone or earthen home, traditionally a Native American dwelling of the Southwestern United States.

quinta essentia: The element Aether holds the essence of the Soul. In medieval alchemy, aether was so highly regarded that it became known as quinta essentia. Essential oils are also known as quinta essentia. Refers to life force and the essence of all.

quintessential: Ideal or essential.

reddening: In alchemy, Rebedo. The final stage in the alchemical process that takes you to the final goal. Both gold (and the Philosopher's Stone) are considered the goal. Also, the perfected self, the Essence Self.

Reflexology: An alternative or complementary modality involving pressure to the feet and hands with specific thumb, finger, or hand techniques. No oil or lotions are used, however essential oils can be used for further benefits. Each organ of the body and areas of the body are represented in the hands and feet.

RejuveTreat: Created by Ixchel Leigh for use in a *Vibrational AromaTherapy* Session, this treatment includes a combination of some foot reflexology for balancing the body and some classical Oriental facial acupressure for rejuvenating the facial tissues for use with ChakraSynergies.

ruh: A type of scented essences used in making perfumes.

ritual: A customarily repeated often formal act or series of acts.

Sacred Marriage: A pre-Christian term. A marriage between god and goddess, king and queen, symbolizing the unity of opposites, yet honoring both.

sacred ritual: An often-repeated act, performed with reverence. A focused act that brings beauty and a sense of peacefulness into your life, honoring life's sacredness. A prayer or meditation is an example of sacred ritual.

sage bundle: Dried sage herb tied together with string, and when lit on fire produces a smoke for purifying.

sensing: Perceiving something instinctually, often a vague awareness or impression. One method for receiving intuitive information.

seventh generation principle: From the Native Americans, no decision is made for the tribe without first taking into consideration how the effects of that decision will affect their children's children for seven generations.

Shiatsu: Similar to reflexology, a Japanese bodywork modality, to improve wellbeing and health.

smudge; smudging: The act of using smoke or scent to purify and cleanse the environment or an individual; used in many spiritual rituals.

Soul: An energy body of light that is the vehicle for the Spirit. It is the force of life-energy that enables the Spirit within to gain experience and to express itself. "The Soul retains what the individuated Spirit has accomplished with the Life-force." (Kenneth Meadows, *Where Eagles Fly*)

Soul Note aka Base Note: The heaviest of the scented odors, are usually resins or more resinous essential oils, in a fragrance their scent lasts for days.

***Soul Parfum*:** Ixchel Leigh's name for perfumes that are created with the intention to assist or facilitate personal growth, transmutation, and transformation. Uses the principles in *AlcheMystical Parfumerie. SoulParfum:* spelled as one word, the perfumes that Ixchel herself creates for others. (Formerly: AlkemicalFragrance) (SoulParfum.com goes to Ixchel Leigh's website.)

Soul's Path Number: The Soul's Path Number is what your Soul came here to experience and do in this lifetime; it is the intrinsic expression of who you are. Your Soul's Path is what your Soul is comprised of or your character. Based on the numerology of your name.

Soul Self: The intelligence or spirit of the Soul. The knowledge and wisdom of the Soul Self is gained from an accumulation of lifetimes.

Spirit: The intelligent essence that animates the life form and is aware of its own being. It is usually sensed, felt, or experienced rather than actually seen.

spiritual path: Consciously choosing to become a more enlightened person with no judgments on spiritual expression.

steam distillation: The process of collecting essential oils from raw materials of botanical origins, by passing steam through the material and collecting the scented essence from the condensed water.

Supreme Creator: God, Divine, etc.

synergy: A blend of pure essential oils without any carrier oil added which combines the individual action of each essential oil.

subconscious: Information possibly stored away from your immediate awareness that relates to existence on a more physical rather than spiritual level.

superconscious: Information and awareness possibly originating in the higher realms of universal truth which acts as a guide to elevate your consciousness on a spiritual level. Offers possibilities and potentialities.

Thousand-Petalled Lotus: Referred to in Hinduism and Buddhism as the Crown Chakra or the 7th ChakraAura.

Time Machines: The Tibetans refer to the chakras as Time Machines. They conceive that through lifetimes individuals grow, change and transform. Therefore, the major energy centers (chakras) are producing Enlightened Beings as a result of the effort of change.

Tiwa: Native American pueblo peoples of the United States.

Tools for Transformation: The many tools created by Ixchel, or recommended by her, that can be used to help assist personal growth and transformation, either in a healing session or during personal meditations. (See also Vibrational Tools for Transformation.)

traditional aromatherapy: The art and science of using essential oils to affect the well-being of the physical body, mind and emotions.

transcend: To go beyond any limitation.

transform: To change form from one thing to another on a deep cellular level.

transformation: The act of having been changed to something very different than its original form.

transformation process: a method, or something that occurs, which takes you to being changed in someway.

transformed solar energy: A botanical plant breathes in solar active energy during the day and at night it exhales lunar passive energy.

transmute: To change or alter form or appearance, especially to a higher form.

transmutation process: a method, or something that happens or occurs, which alters or changes the form or appearance of the original substance (or person).

Universal Creation or Universal Creator: The originator of all things.

Universal Love: The response from the heart, to the feelings and the existence of all life. You are touched and moved by people (and all of Nature) for not only their joy and sweetness, but also their suffering.

Universal Mother: See: Universal Creation.

vibration and vibrational: Of energy. An emanation, aura, spirit or energy which is infused or vitalized, and can instinctively be sensed or experienced.

***Vibrational Aroma Therapy by Ixchel*™**: A concept, terminology and system of energetic healing created by Ixchel Leigh through years of study, research, divine guidance, and intuition. This multi-faceted modality combines energetic, alchemical, and transformative use of true, vibrationally-conscious essential oils and Nature's Vibrational Medicines such as color, shape, sound, stones, the elements, the directions and myths from goddess and ancient cultures, to transform and enliven the ChakraAuras and to create well-being of Body, Heart, Spirit, Mind, and Soul. (Acronym: VbAT)

vibrational aromatherapy: A term accepted within the field of aromatherapy. The energetic and transformative use of pure essential oils.

Vibrational Aroma Therapy Session: A concept created by Ixchel Leigh for use in *Vibrational Aroma Therapy*, it can be as simple as a focused meditation or as expansive as a bodywork-oriented (using a massage table) session. It can be administered with a client or self-directed for your own personal growth. It uses as many Vibrational Tools for Transformation as is appropriate and intuitively guided. It often includes the RejuveTreat and it always includes determining which ChakraAura(s) are not in balance.

Vibrational Aroma Therapy Practitioner: A Certified & Registered Vibrational Aroma Therapy Practioner has completed a Vibrational Aroma Therapy Practitioner Training and is qualified to administer consultations and Vibrational Aroma Therapy Sessions with clients. (Acronym: VbATP) (See "Resources" for more information.)

Vibrational Aroma Therapy Teacher: A Certified & Registered Vibrational Aroma Therapy Teacher is qualified to teach introductory and Level I courses. The prerequisite is Vibrational Aroma Therapy Practitioner certification and registration. (Acronym: VbATT) (See "Resources" for more information.)

Vibrational Aroma Therapy Instructor: A Certified & Registered Vibrational Aroma Therapy Instructor is qualified to teach introductory and Level I and II courses, and is a candidate to be a mentor and supervise HomeStudy. The prerequisite is Vibrational AromaTherapy Practitioner and Teacher certification and registration. (Acronym: VbATI) (See "Resources" for more information.)

vibrational medicines: The many gifts from nature which assist in healing and transformational growth.

vibrational monograph: The description of the esoteric, spiritual, subtle qualities of essential oils and perfume materials, for assisting healing, wellbeing, and transmutation and transformation.

vibrationally-conscious essential oils: A vibrationally-conscious essential oil would be one in which, as a consumer of the finished product, you have the highest degree of confidence that you trust your knowledge of the quality and energy that has been exchanged at every step of the creative cycle: planting (*seed*); growing, harvesting, distilling, bottling (*bottle*); shipping, and finally the actual use of the essential oil on an individual basis (*inhalation*).

VibrationalSynergy: Pure therapeutic-grade essential oil compositions, used by people trained in vibrational aromatherapy, who understand how to create compositions safely and with empowerment for specific goals.

VioletGlass: Imported from Europe, VioletGlass is a product of the Miron Glass Company (developed in Germany) and used to hold essential oils, healing remedies, herbal tinctures, teas, or any other product. Made from finely ground, dark amethyst, the glass has been tested and proven to enhance the potency and length of freshness of anything within the container.

Uttati: Originated in Egypt, it means seeing with both eyes, to see things in a balanced way, or seeing both sides of something. Such as the feminine archetype of intuition and mysticism and the masculine archetype of intellect and vitality.

Addendum

I have been composing bespoke (custom) parfums for decades. I absolutely love doing this. It feels intimately like what I am here to do. These *SoulParfums* have supported me as a good friend throughout my past forty years. Offering them to others, gives me profound joy and sweet satisfaction to see the positive changes and growth in their lives.

I use only the highest vibrationally-conscious, therapeutic-grade essential oils, sourced throughout the world from organic, wild-crafted, and bio-dynamic (when available) botanicals. I gradually have also incorporated precious absolutes and other natural raw materials when I am guided to do so.

Each bespoke fragrance comes in a rare imported VioletGlass bottle to preserve the fragrance. Scientific research demonstrates that the dark amethyst glass (created using actual ground amethyst stones) also enhances the efficacy of any product within. The *SoulParfum* is presented in an elegant golden pouch with talisman gemstones and your personal guidance intuited by me.

I feel like a visionary-parfumeur-alkemist as I compose and listen to the information for each individual. One person called me, "The Fragrance Alkemist." Deeply intuitive, I use my visions to concoct a fragrance that triggers a process of transformation, ignites a new way of thinking, and rejuvenates the zest of your dreams, often leading to life changing revelations.

Testimonials for *SoulParfums*

aka Alkemical Fragrances, Parfum Alkemie, Fragrance for a Moment-in-time

Aromas, fragrance, scent and the Alchemy of good taste is so very important in the world of fine food. Having Ixchel create and blend my very own personal 'AlkemicalFragrance' has enriched my life and proven irresistible to the people who count.

– Alex von Bidder, Managing Partner, The Four Seasons Restaurant, NYC, NY, USA

Thank you (Ixchel) so much. Amazing, unexpected, potent!

– Amanda McBroom, Songwriter, Singer, California, USA

I received it today. It is phenomenal. The combination of fragrances is so complex and fascinating. Everyone says it smells like me. The fragrance is one of the only things helping me. It keeps me centered in all of this chaos. Thank you again for everything.

– Hayes Hamilton. New York, New York, USA

… utterly wonderful and miraculous. I've been using the vibrational aromatherapy oil – which I love – every day, and am finding it much easier to stay centred, focused and TIDY. Wow.

– Jo Fairley, Beauty Editor, YOU Magazine, London, England

Well first of all thank you – I have had some lovely journeys with the oils and stone. It was lovely to meet you and I thank you for all you did.

– Sarah Stacey, London, England

Hi Ixchel, you could not have been more right about my life changing. I have really enjoyed working with the oils.

— **Carolyn Maggard**, Atlanta, Georgia, USA

THANK YOU for your wonderful gift of my Vibrational Fragrance (AlkemicalFragrance). It really has made a marked improvement ... I'm sure you've given me a Karmic boost – I've been much more focused and positive since the session and I've spent much more time with my family – despite being so busy!

— **Joanne Sawicki**, Channel Health,
London, England

I was Ixchelled on Saturday eve – how gracious the process was, and so affirmative. I strongly feel the effect.

— **Stewart Pearce**, Master of Voice,
Shakespeare's Globe Theatre, Sound Healer,
London, England

Ixchel's session with me was expanding and clarifying. In her gentle way, she led me into focusing on my short term intentions. This was challenging for me, as I tend to see the big picture and have trouble with the little steps in between my huge leaps. I was easily able to see clearly four objectives or goals that my heart was seeking to apply in my life. Ixchel then lead me to the feeling that the completion of these steps would bring into my life. The immediate feeling came as if by magic – contentment. By the end of our time together, I received my special essence created by Ixchel to open the energetics within my emotional field and to manifest my next steps. Through her intuitive council, she was able to zero in on my next steps. To me, it was a grounding experience funneling my vast energies and resources into focus that clarified the simple basics I was over- looking on my journey. I am enjoying my special essence, contentment, and the sacred experience of holding that space we achieved together in our session. Thank you Ixchel

— **Nancy Joy Hefron**, Mount Vernon,
Iowa, USA

… With your help I was able to finally focus on the important issues and create a working order of my own, instead of being in a constant panic. The perfume was wonderful because it always helped me to come back and focus when circumstances seemed to spin out of control. I actually still carry the little pouch with me … even though the little bottle is now empty.

– Ingrid, New York, USA

Shelley von Strunckel, Internationally Published Astrologer and Consultant, London and New York, received a succession of *SoulParfums* (aka AlkemicalFragrances) from Ixchel over the course of a year. As she became more familiar with them, her viewpoint changed. Read her comments:

… this particular fragrance worked like a tonic. Suddenly everything seems so simple! Talk about a transformation of viewpoint! Using my fragrance removed all the heaviness from my mind, attitude, and aura – shifting, no lifting – the energy immediately. (8/2000)

… Received my scent today. I am beginning to discover that the introduction to a new blend is a mind-bending experience. It's an olfactory glimpse into the future – a 'sense' of where one's going, what I will be like when I get there. The scents smell somewhat strange at first – foreign – yet familiar. This is as it should be, since each time I am just encountering a part of me … the part I have yet to meet. (12/2000)

… Your amazing fragrance has just arrived – I sensed, smelled the power of it even before I opened the bottle. Where as before the first sensation was one of entering a slightly foreign – no, UNEXPLORED – territory, this scent makes me feel as if I am coming home. But coming home in power and glory, striding with strength. I am almost reeling from its impact. I feel giddy, light. Perhaps it's that I'm becoming more adept at sensing their potential impact, yet I am already feeling as if it's enabling me to shake off useless restrictions. (4/2001)

Ixchel Leigh

I have been luxuriating in and loving essential oils for over four decades. In the 1980's I finally pursued my dream: to compose fragrances that can produce transformation. I've had products in several magazines, notable stores, and renowned Spas. I've been a published writer since the early 1980's. I'm now on my fifth re-incarnation and re-invention of myself!

This is the Second Edition of *Aromatic Alchemy – Recipes for Transformation*. I edited out seventy pages, re-wrote every paragraph, updated new essential oil information, and I newly present my secrets for composing *AlcheMystical Parfumerie*. Essentially, this is a brand new book!

What You May Not Know About Me

I'm a Sensitive Intuitive ...

I feel deeply and receive information in many forms: Clairvoyant (pictures), Clairaudient (thoughts), Clairsentient (feelings), Clairgustance (taste and smell), and Claircognizance (sense of knowing). These gifts allow me to perceive what is possible.

Secretly, I'm a Hermit ...

Because the world can be overwhelming. However, I unapologetically embrace all that is beautiful on this Earth, including tears. What motivates me? I give myself permission to blossom.

I Love Life's Sensuous Pleasures ...

Taste: the salty, sweet, spiciness of foods.
Sight: the intense grandness of the oceans and mountains; flowers and birds and the outrageous brilliance of Nature inspire me.
Touch: to know the ecstasy of the body.
Sound: music encourages my body to move.

Scent: takes me on a journey into taste, sight, touch, and sound. I feel scent and it changes my Life.

Below is an overview of my scented path in this world ....

A Journey Through Scent

2020 – Second Edition, Revised and Updated – *Aromatic Alchemy*.

2018 – Launch of *Artisan Parfums* and *Parfums with Purpose*.

2010 – Opened apothecary and gallery in Carmel, CA: Ixchel Ecoluxe.

2009 – Five months in Mumbai, India with *Shivaz Spa*, creating *SoulParfums* for individuals.

2007 – *Ixchel Leigh Parfumerie & Escentials*, products created.

2001-Present: *The Fragrance Alkemist*-Raw materials perfumer to inspire Transformation.

2001 – *Aromatic Alchemy – Recipes for Transformation*. Book, first edition.

1990-Present: Conceived and teach healing modality: *Vibrational AromaTherapy by Ixchel*™

1989-Present: Create signature scents for businesses: The Golden Door, The Peaks Telluride, The Phoenician Spa, CordeValle Resort & Golf, Skin Spa/CA, Tara Spa Therapy, and others.

1989-1995: *Essence AromaTherapy-Crystal CandleEssence*-candles and massage oils found in leading department stores, boutiques, and spas (Bergdorf Goodman, Nordstrom, Barneys New York, Henri Bendel, Ventana Spa, etc.).

1988-1989: Marketing Director for *Aroma Vera*. Established and taught U.S.A.'s first aromatherapy certification seminars along Marcel Lavabre.

1985-Present: Published writer and author. Published articles on wellness in journals, magazines, and newspapers; *Vibrational*

AromaTherapy – *Manual for Training Health Professionals* published.

1971-1972/Present: Explorations with essential oils launched with a year in Provence, France, modeling in Paris, and traveling Europe. Further self-study discoveries in aromatherapy and natural botanical perfumery, will continue until my last breath.

My heart and my life
are committed to Love and Transformation
and to guiding myself and others
to make the many changes which enrich all Life.

Index

Lightning Source UK Ltd.
Milton Keynes UK
UKHW021930160320
360448UK00009B/135